Land Grants in Anne Arundel County Maryland

1650–1704

South River Hundred

Robert W. Hall

HERITAGE BOOKS
2012

HERITAGE BOOKS
AN IMPRINT OF HERITAGE BOOKS, INC.

Books, CDs, and more—Worldwide

For our listing of thousands of titles see our website
at
www.HeritageBooks.com

Published 2012 by
HERITAGE BOOKS, INC.
Publishing Division
100 Railroad Ave. #104
Westminster, Maryland 21157

Copyright © 2002 Robert W. Hall

Other Heritage Books by the author:
Land Grants of the Middle Neck Hundred of Anne Arundel County, Maryland, 1650–1704

All rights reserved. No part of this book may be reproduced or transmitted in any form or by any means, electronic or mechanical, including photocopying, recording or by any information storage and retrieval system without written permission from the author, except for the inclusion of brief quotations in a review.

International Standard Book Numbers
Paperbound: 978-1-58549-779-9
Clothbound: 978-0-7884-3412-9

Foreward

This book is a compilation of patent documents, in synopsis form, and tract diagrams drawn from the original boundary courses specified in patent documents. I obtained the information used to prepare each synopsis and drawing from land records held in the Maryland Hall of Records. The original land records and drawings were burned in courthouse fire on October 17, 1704. The patents were re-recorded over a period of years following the fire but the drawings were never replaced. It is my hope that these drawings will be helpful to anyone interested in the settlers and their land in the South River Hundred from 1650-1704.

Surveying in 17th Century Maryland was far from an exact science. In many cases tract size (acreage) does not match the amount certified. Boundaries overlap and often do not "close." There are records of numerous complaints by owners that their acreage was significantly less than the amount certified. It became a common practice for tract owners to request a Special Wart (Warrant) of Resurvey to identify "surplus" land within, or "vacant" land contiguous to, a tract's boundaries and to regrant the tract, including any surplus or vacant land found, to the owner. There are instances of tracts being reduced in acreage because of a conflict with a boundary of a "more ancient" tract. I also found one tract that was certified, surveyed, and granted within the boundaries of an existing tract. Further confusion results from sale of tracts among individuals outside of the patent system. In some instances such tracts were regranted by the Lord Proprietor to the new owner. In other instances the property simply passed from one person to another by indenture or contract. The identification, drawing, and placement of Middle Neck Hundred tracts is like attempting a jig saw puzzle with an unspecified number of pieces and no pattern to follow. There are missing pieces, surplus pieces, pieces that do not fit and all of the pieces come in a box mixed with unpatterned pieces from other puzzles.

Some understanding of the Conditions of Plantation is necessary to appreciate and understand the complexities of land ownership in Maryland during this period and to appreciate the variations found in patent documents. The first conditions were written in 1633, before the settlers arrived. Amendments adjusting the ratio of acreage granted to persons transported were issued in 1636, twice in 1648, and in 1649. Charles, the third Lord Baltimore, abolished the "land rights" system on April 5, 1684. Thereafter land ownership was based on purchase, inheritance, etc. A more complete description of the Conditions of Plantation can be found in <u>Flowering of the Maryland Palatinate</u>, by Henry Wright Newman, 1984, Genealogy Publishing Co., Baltimore, MD.

Basically, the Conditions of Plantation codified the conditions and terms of the land patent process and served as a contract between the Lord Proprietor and the grantee. Ownership, as we know it today, remained with the Lord Proprietor although the grantee enjoyed all rights of ownership in fee simple including the unrestricted sale, transfer, or bequeathal to others, even before a tract had been patented. In 1648, the Assembly enacted a bill authorizing a 50-acre grant for each indentured servant at the time of service completion. Property granted to persons dying without heirs, failing to pay rents, or abandoning their tracts reverted to the Lord Proprietor through a process called "Escheat." Following Escheat, the property was available to be regranted. Until 1684, land rights were based on either favor with the Lord Proprietor or immigration to and settlement in Maryland. The number, age, social status, and sex of the settlers transported to Maryland by the grantee determined the number of acres granted. Individuals were free to claim land rights based on transporting themselves, family members, servants, and strangers. The Conditions also address alienation fees, quick rents and the payment schedule, which was tied to specific religious feast days. In addition to quit rents and alienation fees, grantees were also required to pay recording fees for all official documents including land certifications, surveys, and patents. A fee schedule can be found in the Acts of Assembly, 1650 (L7/33-35 SR7343).

Governor Calvert adopted the "hundred system" in Maryland shortly after the establishment of St.Maries. Hundreds, in Maryland, are usually described as geographical subdivisions that served as voting districts until about 1671. The earliest reference found to a specific hundred (St. Maries) is 1637. According to Newman, "...if there was an official decree or proclamation, it was recorded in one of the early lost libers." The Assembly of February/March 1638/9 established that each hundred be under the management of a commander who was empowered to appoint a high constable and a sergeant to train all men able to bear arms.

As was the case with my earlier book on the Middle Neck Hundred, I found nothing specific concerning either the establishment date or the precise boundaries of the South River Hundred. It is generally accepted that the southern and central regions were bounded on the north and east by the South River and on the west by the Patuxent. Based on the location of tracts shown in the rent rolls as South River Hundred tracts, it extended northward to about present day Laurel (and occasionally westward into present day Prince George's County) running between the Little Patuxent and Patuxent Rivers and southward from the river's mouth a short distance down the Chesapeake Bay to a point roughly due east of the Rhode River and then westward to the Patuxent.

Patent/survey/certification documents exclude mention of "hundreds." Because there is often little else to go on, the use of rent rolls to identify (and geographically place) tracts is a necessary step in approximating boundaries of the hundreds. Since not all tracts found in the land records are included in the rent rolls, linking these "excluded" tracts to adjoining or nearby "included" tracts, is also necessary in determining a hundred's boundaries. Like many historical records, rent rolls are both useful and valuable but there are occasional inconsistencies. I have found tracts clearly identified to a particular hundred that are not included in Anne Arundel County Land Records. I have seen several instances of tracts listed in more than one hundred and there are instances of tracts listed in one hundred that are surrounded by tracts listed as being in another hundred. For example, Sharpe Pointe and The Diligent Search are listed as being in the Rhode River area of the South River Hundred. Yet both are surrounded by West River Hundred tracts and both are located on (or near) the boundary between the West River and Herring Creek Hundreds, well to the south of other South River Hundred tracts. The point is that that there are few absolutes and that occasionally rent rolls cannot be taken at face value. I have included a small number of tracts that were also included in my earlier book, <u>Landgrants of the Middle Neck Hundred, 1650-1704.</u> The evidence suggests that they were in the South River Hundred but there is the possibility that they were not.

I have attempted to retain the special flavor of the patent documents by using the quaint phrasing, misspelled words and grammar as it was found. All names and references of historical or genealogical interest are presented in bold type and are indexed in the "People"Index.

I am indebted to a number of persons for their help and encouragement in preparing this book and would like to give special thanks to Chris Allen and Jennifer Hafner at the Maryland Hall of Records and to my wife Sandy. Without their special help this would not have been possible.

Landgrants in the South River Hundred of Ann Arundell County

1650-1704

Table of Contents

	Pages
Foreword	I
Table of Contents	III
Drawing of South River Hundred area showing old Cr./ Br/ Names	V
Text and Tract Drawings	1-91
Appendices Cover Sheet and Explanation	93

- Appendix A. Northern Patuxent River Area 95
- Appendix B. South River at mouths of No/So Runns 97
- Appendix C. West side of South Runn (South River) 99
- Appendix D. East side of North Branch of The Patxent River 101
- Appendix E. The Flatt Creek near The South River 103
- Appendix F. The Flatt Creek near The Patuxent River 105
- Appendix G. Area between Flatt & Beard's/Jacob's Creeks 107
- Appendix H. Central Area near The Patuxent River 109
- Appendix I. Area between Beard's/Jacobs & Burges Creeks 111
- Appendix J. Mouth of South River southward down the Chesapeake 113
- Appendix K. Area north and west of The Rhode River 115
- Appendix L. The Rhode River eastward to Chesapeake Bay 117
  Appendix L does not exist

Bibilography	119
Index of Tracts	121-125
List of Tract Owners	127-133
Index of People Mentioned in Patent Documents	135-140

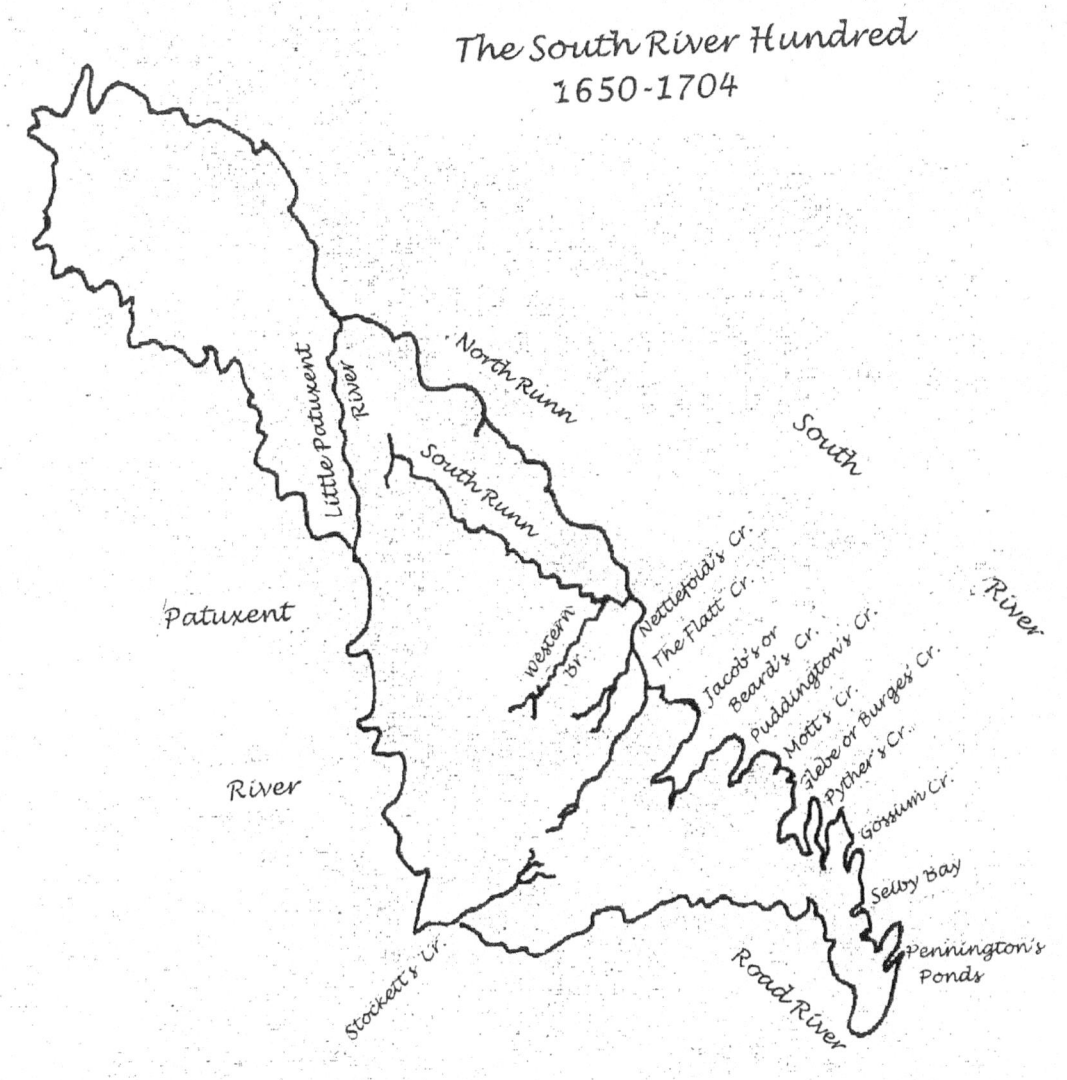

South River Hundred

Abingdon (Robert Proctor & John Gather) 9/20/1664 - 875/876 acres. L7/387 SR7349

Know Yee that Wee for and in consideration that Robert Proctor and John Gather of this Province, Planters, hath due unto them two hundred and seventy five acres of land by afsignment of **John Mears** and two hundred and fifty acres by afsignment of **Samuel Withers** and three hundred and fifty acres more upon warrant of the s'd Proctor as appears upon record. Upon such considerations and termes as are exprefsed in our Conditions of Plantation of our Province of Maryland, doe hereby grant unto the s'd Robert Proctor and John Gather a parcell of land lying in Ann Arundel County at the head of the South River about three miles into the woods, adjoining Freeman's Fancy. Begins at a marked Oak standing near the main branch of the South Run of the South River. *Adjoins Freeman's Fancy.*

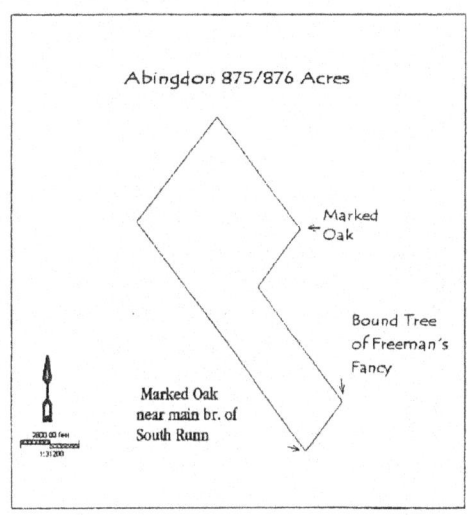

Abingdon, Part Of (John Gaither) 8/27/1699 – 364/364 acres. DD5i/44 SR7378

By virtue of a Speciall Warrant granted unto John Gaither and **Jerome Finley** of this County bearing date 5/27/1698, for the resurvey of a certaine tract of land called Abingdon lying in the s'd County above the head of South River granted unto the s'd Gaither and **Robert Proctor** in 1664, for 875 acres. The s'd Gaither and Proctor sold and conveyed six hundred acres to **James Finley** of the County. In order to rectify some errors found in the former course differences and to afford to them the s'd Gaither and Finley the surplus, if any appears, according to his LOP's late instructions in such cases provided, I have laid out for the s'd Gaither his part of the former grant being what

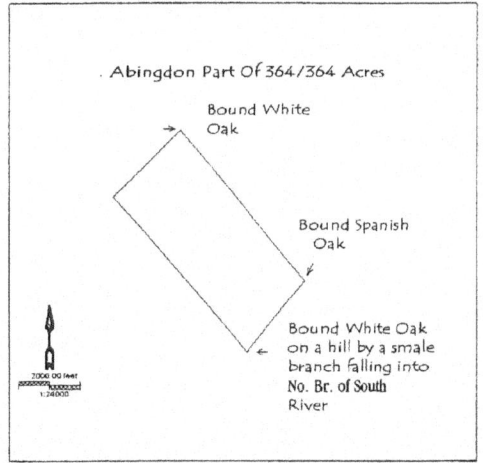

remains after the s'd Finley's six hundred acres were conveyed, beginning at a bounded White Oak standing on a hill on the South side of a small branch falling into the North Branch of the South River. Then issued pattent to the above John for the above land. *Note 1: Although not mentioned in the patent, it is assumed that this special warrant of resurvey was issued to John Gaither Jr. Note 2: Although this document clearly states that, "..then issued patent to the s'd John for the s'd land," John Gaither again had this tract resurveyed and regranted (see Abingdon resurveyed). No explanation for this has been found.*

Abingdon Resurveyed (John Gaither Jr.) 5/10/1701 – 364/364 acres. LWD/375 SR7372
Know yee that for and in consideration that John Gaither *(Jr.)* of Ann Arundell County in our Province of Maryland to our Deputy did sett forth that he is seized in fee simple of two hundred seventy five acres of land being what remains of a tract called Abingdon originally granted **Robert Proctor** and the deceased **John Gaither** in 1664 for eight hundred seventy five acres but supplicating that there might be surplus therein he humbly prayed *(that he)* might have our Speciall Warrant for Resurvey thereof and that upon return of such Resurvey our Letters Pattent might to him be issued. By virtue thereof it is certified into our Land Office that there is the quantity of eighty nine acres over and above the afsigned quantity. Our instructions to **Coll Henry Darnall** our agent in our s'd Province dated 12/13/1697 *(are that)* 217 pounds of tobacco are to be paid to us being

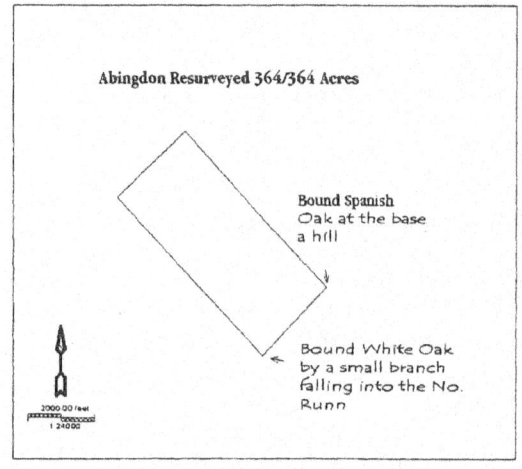

for the Rights of the s'd surplus and also the sum of one pound, sixteen shillings, eight pence, *(and one)* half-penny sterling being for the rent of the s'd surplus from the time of original survey. Wee doe in consideration thereof give, grant, confirm unto him the s'd John Gaither all that remaining part of a tract of land called Abingdon beginning at a bounded White Oak standing on a hillside and on the South side of a smaller branch falling in the North Runn of the South River.

Anthony's Purchase (Anthony Smith) 6/16/1699 – 325/325 acres. LCC4i/132 SR7325

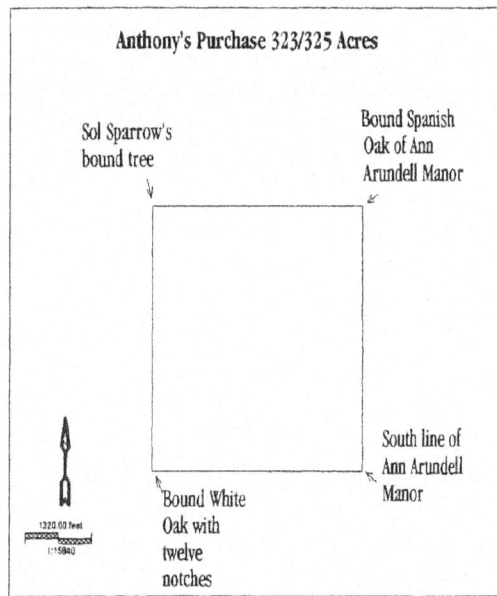

By Virtue of a wart to me directed from **Coll Henry Darnall** for the laying out of his LOP's Mannor for Anthony Smith of Ann Arundell County three hundred twenty five acres of land on 8/1/1699, I have laid out for the s'd Smith the s'd land called Anthony's Purchase beginning at a marked White Oak with twelve notches standing at the head of a branch of the Road River it being a bounded tree of **Soloman Sparrow**. Pursuant to his LOP's orders Coll Henry Darnall directed patt to the above Cert 6/16/1699. *This tract bounds the south line of Ann Arundell Manor.*

Arnold Gray (Richard Arnold & John Gray) 8/3/1688 – 300/303 acres. L12/121 SR7354

Grant for three hundred acres of land issued to Richard Arnold and Robert Gray bearing the date 8/3/1688, in consideration that Richard Arnold of the County of Ann Arundell in our s'd Province of Maryland, Planter, hath due unto him fifty acres of land for completion of services within our s'd Province. Also, one hundred acres more by afsignment from John Gray of the s'd County part of a warrant for four hundred fifty acres formerly granted to the s'd Gray and also for and in consideration that the s'd John Gray hath due unto him one hundred fifty acres formerly granted the s'd Gray part of the aforesaid warrant for four hundred fifty acres to him granted. *Note: The patent document does not include either a land description (location) or boundary courses. There is a reference to the "Cert" to be found in Liber GG Folio 6. However, it is not there. This tract was drawn using dimensions and angles found in surrounding tracts.*

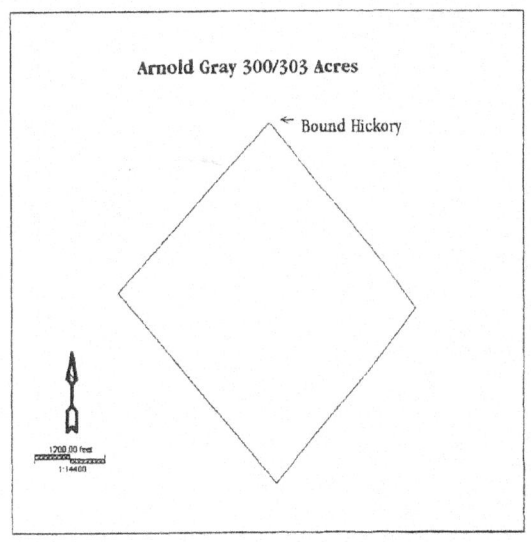

Arnold Gray Res. (Silvester & John Welsh) 10/20/1703 – 605/634 acres. LCD/61 SR7376

Know yee that whereas Silvester and John Welsh of Ann Arundell County in our s'd Province of Maryland have by their humble petition to us heretofore presented sett forth that granted to **Richard Arnold** and **John Gray** during their lifetimes a tract of three hundred acres called Arnold Gray. And, that the s'd John Gray and his wife **Rachell** did on 5/10/1671, sett down and afsign all rights, title, and interest in the s'd tract to the s'd Arnold. Whereby the s'd Arnold became seized of an estate in fee simple of same. **John Welsh** (*the elder*), of the same County, Gent, deceased, the father of the s'd Silvester and John Welsh, was in his lifetime seized of an estate of fee simple of and in the premises by virtue of some mean conveyance made of the s'd land and did by his Last Will and Testament devise same to his sons to be farely, indifferently, and equally divided between them. By virtue of which devise the s'd Silvester and John Welsh became seized of an estate in fee simple in the s'd tract and being desirous as well to discover the surplus land they suppose to be thereof contained

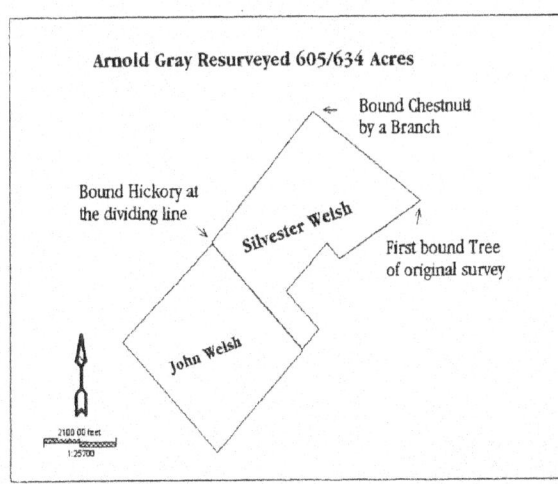

as to make equal indifferent division thereof to them. They prayed for our Speciall Warrant for resurvey to include any surplus found and to make the equal division thereof in a separate grant to each. Accordingly, our Speciall Warrant certified that there is in the quantity of three hundred five acres above the quantity originally granted. Pursuant to a clause of our s'd instructions the s'd Silvester and John Welsh have served to our agent **Col Henry Darnall** the sum of seven hundred thirty four pounds of tobacco for the rights as well as ten pounds, twelve shillings and 18 pence for the rent in arrears since the time of the original survey. Wee doe therefore hereby grant and confirm unto them the s'd Silvester and John Welsh the s'd land together with the surplus called Arnold Gray. *Adjoins Roper Gray and Godwell. Note 1: This patent resurveys the tract to include surplus land and to divide the total equally between the sons and heirs of John Welsh, the elder. The drawing shows the adjoining portions conveyed to each heir. Actually, there were two separate patent documents (identical except for the names and boundary courses specified) which I have combined. Note 2 (from MSA Tract Index 73): Sold by Silvester to John 1708. John sold to **Gerald Hopkins** in 1789/90.*

Ayne (Henry Hanslap) 8/2/1683 – 400/401 acres. LSDA/408 SR7369

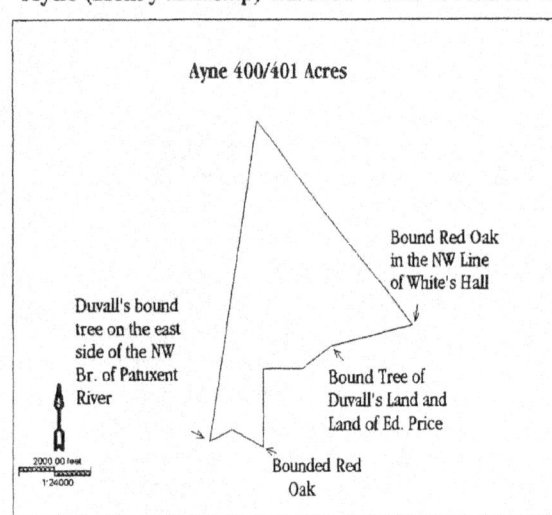

Know yee that for and in consideration that Henry Hanslap of Ann Arundell County in our Province of Maryland hath due unto him four hundred acres of land within our s'd Province out of a warrant for one thousand acres granted to him 9/15/1682, as appears on record. Upon such conditions and terms as are exprefsed in our Conditions of Plantation of our late father **Cecilius**, of noble memory, wee doe hereby grant unto the s'd Henry Hanslap all that tract or parcell of land called Ayne lying in the s'd County on the Eastern side of the North Branch of the Patuxent River beginning at a bounded Red Oake it being a bounded tree of the land of **Marin Duvall** called Duvall's Range. *Also adjoins Bright Seate (**Edwin Price**) and White's Hall (**Jerome White**). Note: The name of the tract could be Ayno rather than Ayne.*

Batchellor's Hope (James Sanders) 8/8/1670 – 200 acres. L13/49 SR7355
Know yee that for and in consideration that James Sanders of the County of Ann Arundell hath due unto him two hundred acres of land within our s'd Province by afsignment of **George Yate** the afsignee of **David Poole** for his the s'd Pooles transporting of severall persons here to inhabit as appears on record. Upon such conditions and terms as are exprefsed in our Conditions of Plantation of this our Province of Maryland, wee doe hereby grant unto the s'd James Sanders all that parcell of land called Batchellor's Hope lying in the s'd County on the North side of South River beginning at a bounded Hickory in the north line of land laid out for **Robert Franklin**, it being a bounded tree of **Neale Clark** of the s'd County. *Also adjoins the land of **John Dearing**.*

Note: This tract cannot be drawn because the third course lacks direction and the fourth (and final) course lacks distance and direction.

Beard's Habitation (Richard Beard) 9/22/1663 - 1,260/1,247 acres. L5/590 SR7347

Know yee that wee for and in consideration that Richard Beard of this Province, Planter, hath due unto him three hundred ten acres of land being part of an old warrant granted him and six hundred acres by afsignment from **Richard Preston,** Gent, and also one hundred acres for transporting **Richard Orchard** into this Province Anno 1650, more, one hundred fifty acres for transporting **William Jones and Richard Foster** Anno 1667. Upon such conditions and terms as are exprefsed in our Conditions of Plantation of this our Province of Maryland, wee doe grant unto the s'd Richard Beard all that parcell of land called Beard's Habitation lying in Ann Arundell County on the South side of the South River next adjoining the land of

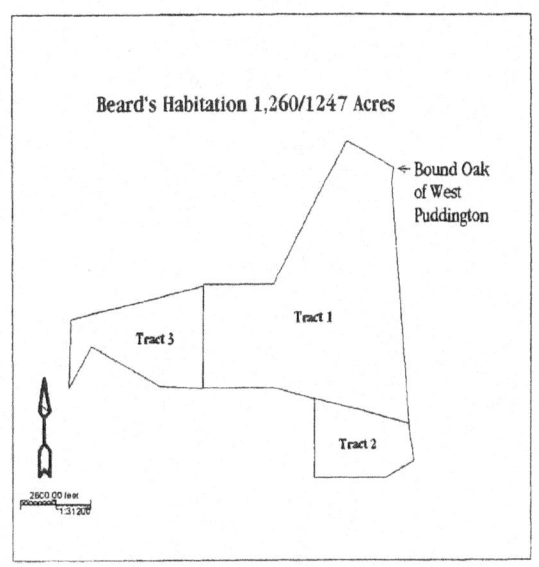

George Puddington beginning at a bound tree on the northmost line of the s'd land. *Note: This patent conveys three adjoining tracts beginning at the northmost line of West Puddington.*

Beaver Dam Neck (John Gray) 6/10/1671 -100/100 acres. L14/225 SR7356

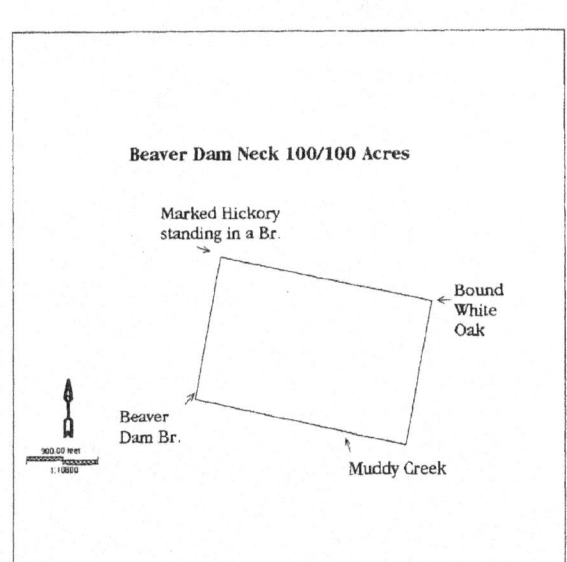

Know yee that wee for and in consideration that John Gray of Ann Arundell County in our s'd Province of Maryland hath due unto him one hundred acres of land within our s'd Province part of a warrant for one hundred fifty five acres granted unto him 5/24/1669, as appears on record. Upon such conditions and terms as are exprefsed in our Conditions of Plantation of our Province of Maryland, do hereby grant unto the s'd John Gray all that parcell of land called Beaver Dam Neck lying in the west side of Chesapeake Bay and on the west side of the Road River in a creek called Muddy Creek beginning at a bound White Oak.

Beaver Dam Neck (Dennis Macconnough) 12/7/1662 – 100/100 acres. L5/624 SR7347

Laid out for Dennis Macconnough of this Province, Planter, a parcel of land called Beaver Dam Neck lying on the west side at the head of the Road River on the south side of Muddy Branch in Ann Arundell County beginning at a marked Pokehikary on the south side of the s'd branch. *Bound on the north by the Beaver Dam and Beaver Dam Br. Note: Patent not found.*

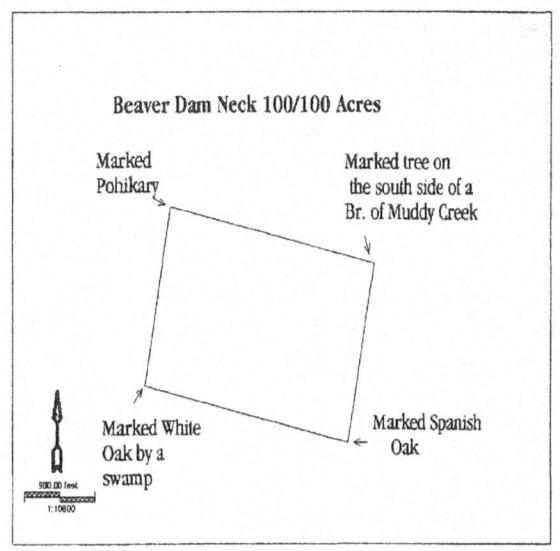

Besson's Den (Thomas Besson) 2/11/1650 - 450/330 acres. L4/405 SR7375

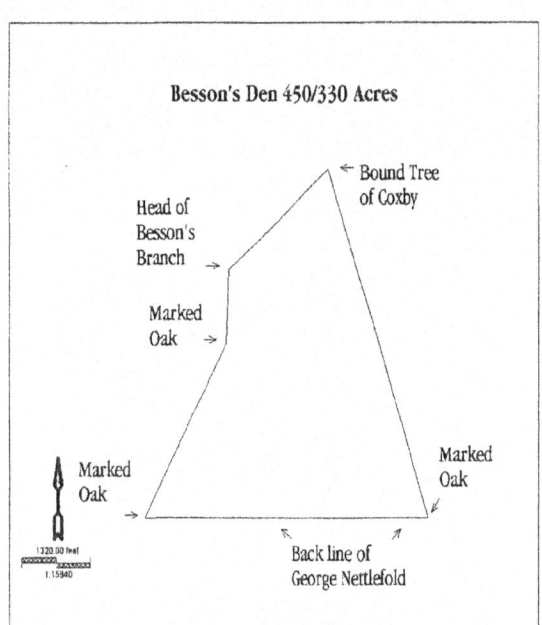

Know yee that wee for and in consideration that Thomas Besson hath transported himself, **Ann** his wife, **Thomas** and **Ann** his children and **Edward Cox,** his servant, into this Province here to inhabit. Upon such conditions and terms as are exprefsed in our Conditions of Plantation of this our Province, wee doe hereby grant unto the s'd Besson all that tract or parcel of land called Besson's Den lying on the West side of the Chesapeake Bay and on the south side of the South River and on the south side of Besson's Branch next adjoining to the land lately laid out for the s'd Cox of the s'd County, Planter. Begins at a bound Hickory of Cox's land. *Note: It is interesting that Cox, who was brought into Maryland as Besson's servant, owned adjoining land and that this land was obtained by a patent that predated Besson's patent by seven days. See Coxby.*

Bessonton (Thomas Besson, Capt.) 2/10/1650 – 350/350 acres. L4/504 SR7346

Know yee that wee for and in consideration that Captain Thomas Besson of this Province hath due unto him three hundred fifty acres of land. Upon such consideration and terms as are exprefsed in our Conditions of Plantation of this our Province of Maryland, doe hereby grant unto the s'd Besson a parcell of land on the west side of Chesapeake Bay and on the west side of a river called the Road River and on the north side of a branch called Muddy Branch, beginning at a bound Pohikary tree it being a bound tree of land formerly laid out for **Thomas Sparrow** and **George Nettlefold**.

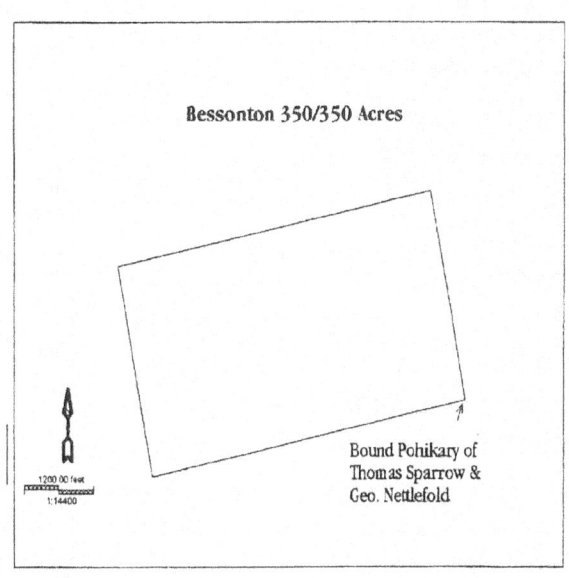

Brewer's Chance (John Brewer) 9/1/1687- 152/154 acres. LNS2i/402 SR7371

Know yee that for and in consideration that John Brewer of Ann Arundell County in our s'd Province of Maryland hath due unto him one hundred fifty two acres of land within our s'd Province by afsignment of **Richard Beard** of Ann Arundell County, parte of a warrant for one thousand acres granted unto the s'd Beard 4/21/1684, as appears on record. Upon such conditions and terms as are exprefsed in our Conditions of Plantation of our s'd Province of Maryland, doe hereby grant unto the s'd John Brewer a parcell of land called Brewer's Chance lying on the south side of the South River and on the north side of Pitcher's (*Pyther's*) Creek beginning at a bound White Oak by the side of the s'd Cr. *Also adjoins Burges' Cr.*

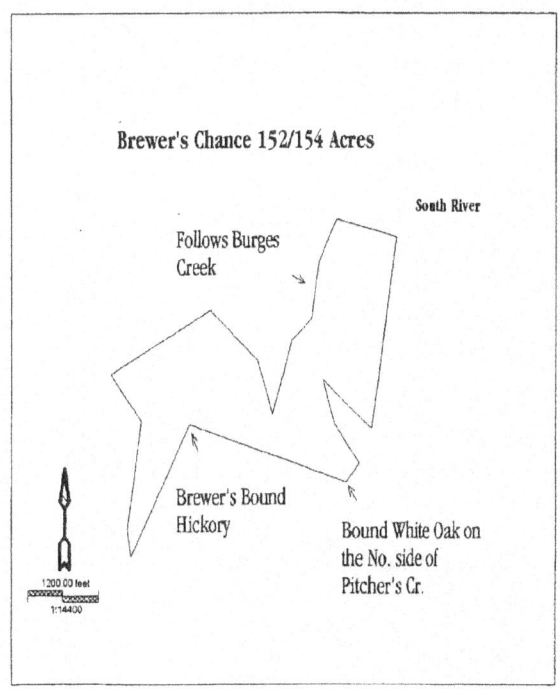

Brewerston (John Brewer)
2/16/1659 – 400/396 acres. L4/505 SR7346
Know yee that wee for and in consideration that John Brewer of this Province, Planter, hath due unto him four hundred acres of land. Upon such considerations and terms as are exprefsed in our Conditions of Plantation of our s'd Province of Maryland, wee doe hereby grant unto the s'd John Brewer a parcell of land called Brewerston lying on the west side of Chesapeake Bay and on the west side of the Road River adjoining the land of **Thomas Besson** *(the elder)* beginning at Besson's westernmost bound tree, it being a Pohikary tree.

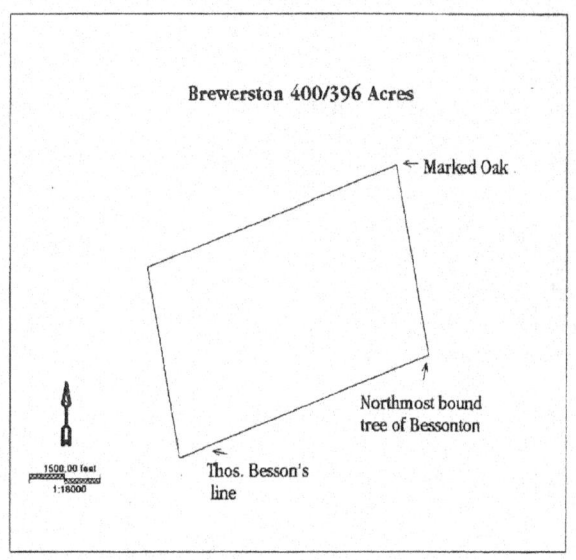

Bridge Hill **(Henry Stocket)** 7/9/1671 – 663 acres. L16/287 SR7357
Know yee that wee for and in consideration that Henry Stocket of the County of Ann Arundell in our s'd Province of Maryland hath due unto him six hundred sixty three acres of land within our s'd Province part of a warrant for two thousand acres granted to the s'd Henry Stocket, **Francis Stocket,** and **Thomas Stocket** 4/26/1669, as appears on record. Upon such conditions and terms as are exprefsed in our Conditions of Plantation of our Province of Maryland, doe hereby grant unto the s'd Henry Stocket all that parcell of land called Bridge Hill lying in Ann Arundall County to the north of Ann Arundall Manor in the woods, beginning at the northwest bounded tree of a parcel of land called Taylor's Choice. *Also adjoins Dodon. Note: This tract cannot be drawn because none of the courses specify distance and/or direction.*

Bright Seate (Edward Price) 4/10/1673 - 400/443 acres. L17/111 SR7358
Know yee that for and in consideration that Edward Price of Ann Arundell County, Planter, hath due unto him four hundred acres of land within our s'd Province by afsignment from **George Yate,** part of a warrant for eleven hundred fifty acres to the s'd Yate granted 6/11/1672, as appears on record. Upon such conditions and terms as are exprefsed in our Conditions of Plantation of this our s'd Province of Maryland, wee doe hereby grant unto the s'd Edward Price all that parcell of land called Bright Seate lying in the s'd County on the

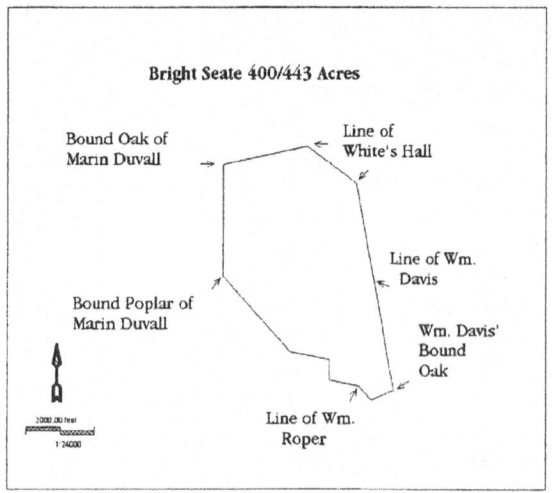

South side of the South River in the woods beginning at a marked Oak in the line of *White's Hall* and running with the line of **Evan Davis**.

Burges (William Burges) 1/31/1651 – 200 acres. LAB&H/263 SR7344
Laid out for William Burges of the County of Ann Arundell, Planter, a parcel of land lying on the south side of the South River beginning at a marked Oak near a swamp. *Note 1: The following note was found in the Rent Rolls, AA County, South River Hundred, SR 4376, "I doe not find that Coll Burgess ever pattented this land nor do I find he ever pay rent for it nor left it to any person by name in his will nor has anyone claimed it." Note 2: This tract cannot be drawn because of incomplete boundary course information in the certification document.*

Burges' Choice (William Burges) 12/9/1666 – 400/436 acres. L10/421 SR7352

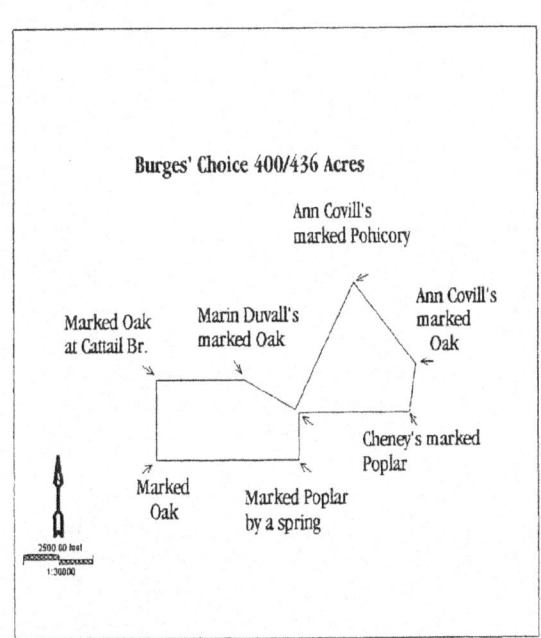

Know yee that for and in consideration that Capt. William Burges of our Province of Maryland, Gent, hath due four hundred acres of land within our s'd Province by afsignment of **Robert Franklin**, afsignee of **John Shaw** being a warrant of five hundred and ninety acres afsigned to Shaw by **George Puddington**, as appears on record. Doe hereby grant unto the s'd Burges a parcel of land called Burges' Choice lying in Ann Arundell County in the woods on the south side of the South River beginning at a marked Oak in the line of **Ann Covill**. *Also adjoins tracts belonging to Richard Cheney and Marin Duvall. Note: This tract was initially patented by John Covill (the elder) as Covill's Lott (4 May 1664). However, the same 400 acre tract was surveyed for John Shaw in November 1665. On 23 August 1666, Shaw sold the certification to Robert Franklin and on the same day Franklin assigned the tract to Capt. William Burges. By this time, John Covill the elder had died and Burges claimed that ownership of the tract had not passed properly to his son and heir John Covill Jr. Covell Jr and his mother and guardian Ann Covill failed to show up at Provincial Court hearing in October 1666, and the tract was awarded to Burges (L10/419). The tract was resurveyed again (4/13/1708) by Benjamin Burges (son and heir of William Burges) and found to be 747 acres.*

Burges His Right (Edward Burges) 2/18/1688 – 153/153 acres. LNS#B/627 SR7370
Know yee that for and in consideration that Edward Burges of Ann Arundell County in our s'd Province of Maryland hath due unto him one hundred fifty three acres of land within our s'd Province by virtue of an afsignment for the same quantity to him made by **Thomas Richardson** of Baltimore County part of a warrant for two thousand eight hundred eighty two acres granted to the s'd Richardson 2/27/1687, as appears on record. Upon such conditions and terms as are exprefsed in our Conditions of Plantation of our s'd Province of Maryland, we doe therefore grant unto the s'd Edward Burges all that tract or parcel of land called Burges His Right lying in Ann Arundell County on the south side of the South River and on the east side of Jacob's Creek beginning at a point on the creek mouth. *Adjoins Puddington's Creek and Puddington's Long Point.*

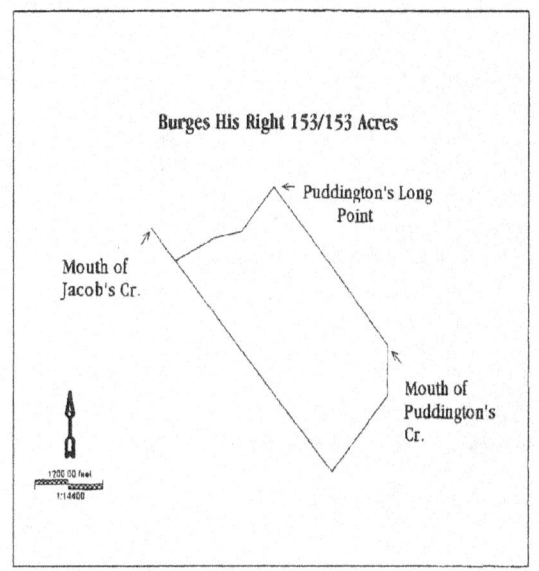

Champe's Adventure (John Champe) 8/8/1670 – 300/300 acres. L13/44 SR7355

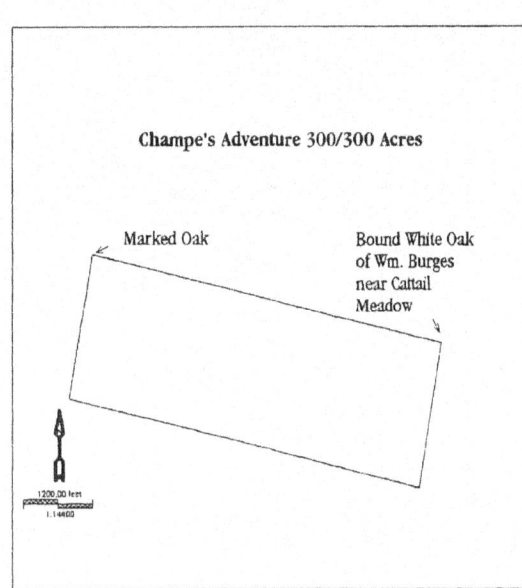

Know yee that for and in Consideration that John Champe of the County of Ann Arundell, Planter, hath due unto him three hundred acres of land within our s'd Province by afsignment of **George Yate** out of a warrant of a greater number of rights afsigned the s'd Yate by **David Poole** of Ann Arundell County as appears on record. Upon such conditions and terms as are exprefsed in our Conditions of Plantation of this our Province of Maryland, wee doe hereby grant unto the s'd John Champe all that tract or parcel of land called Champe's Adventure lying on the West side of South River in the s'd County about four miles in the woods beginning at a bound White Oak of **Capt. William Burges** at the lower end of Cattail Meadow.

Cheney's Hazard (Richard Cheney) 5/30/1663 – 100 acres. L5/299 SR7347
Know yee that wee for and in consideration that Richard Cheney of this Province, Planter, hath due unto him one hundred acres of land within this Province as appears on record. Upon such conditions and terms as are exprefsed in our Conditions of Plantation of our Province of Maryland, wee doe hereby grant unto the s'd Cheney a parcell of land called Cheney's Hazard near to the plantation he now liveth upon being about a mile from the s'd plantation beginning at a marked Oak in the woods. *Note: This tract cannot be drawn because the first and fourth courses lack distance.*

Cheney Hill (Richard Cheney) 1/20/1659 – 100/83 acres. L4/439 SR7346

Know yee that wee for and in consideration that Richard Cheney hath transported himself and his wife **Charity** to this Province to inhabit. Upon such conditions and terms as are exprefsed in our Conditions of Plantation of our Province of Maryland, wee doe hereby grant unto the s'd Richard Cheney a parcell of land called Cheney Hill on the west side of Chesapeake Bay and on the south side of the South River and on the south side of a creek in the s'd River called The Flatt Creek. *Adjoins Cheney's Purchase.*

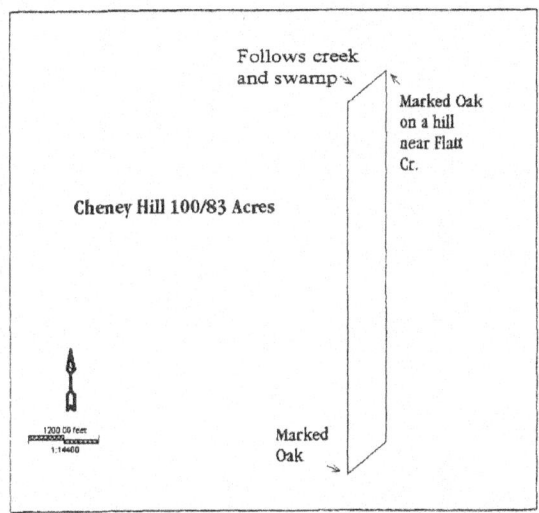

Cheney's Neck (Richard Cheney) 5/29/1663 – 110/109 acres. L5/294 SR7347

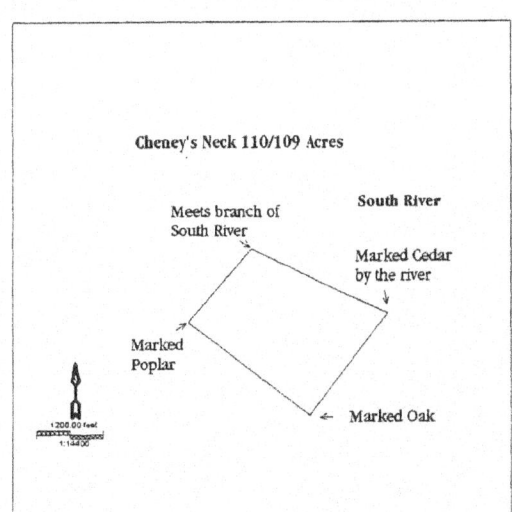

Know yee that wee for and in consideration that Richard Cheney of this Province, Planter, hath due unto him one hundred ten acres of land within this Province as appears on record. Upon such conditions and terms as are exprefsed in our Conditions of Plantation of our Province of Maryland, wee doe hereby grant unto the s'd Richard Cheney a parcell of land called Cheney's Neck lying on the South River beginning at a marked Cedar tree upon a point by the River. *Adjoins Cheney's Cr. and the South River.*

Cheney's Purchase (Richard Cheney) 5/30/1663 – **100/65 acres.** L5/298 SR7347

Know yee that wee for and in consideration that Richard Cheney of this Province, Planter, hath due unto him one hundred acres of land within our s'd Province as appears on record. Upon such conditions and terms as are exprefsed in our Conditions of Plantation of our Province of Maryland, wee doe hereby grant unto the s'd Richard Cheney a parcell of land called Cheney's Purchase lying on the south side of the South River in Ann Arundall County and on the East side of Flatt Creek near to *Cheney Hill* beginning at a marked Oak on the south side of Cheney Hill.

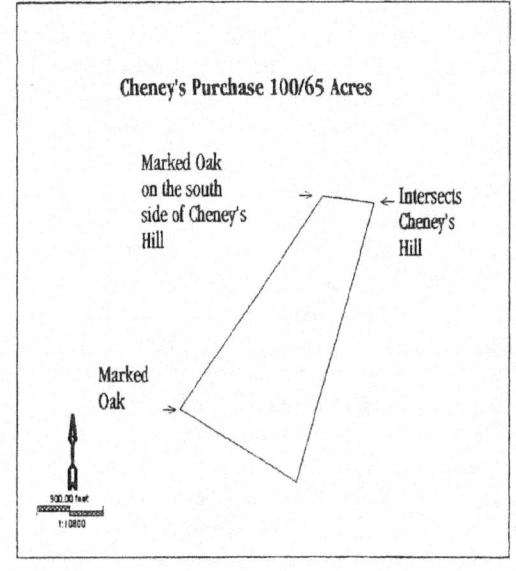

Cheney's Resolution (Richard Cheney) 5/29/1663 – **400/507 acres.** L5/287 SR7347

Know yee that for and in consideration that Richard Cheney of this Province, Planter, hath due unto him four hundred acres of land within our s'd Province as appears on record. Upon such Conditions and terms as are exprefsed in our Conditions of Plantation of our Province of Maryland, wee doe hereby grant unto the s'd Richard Cheney a parcell of land called Cheney's Resolution on the South River beginning at a marked Oak in the southeast line of the three hundred acres last surveyed (*Cheney's Rest*).

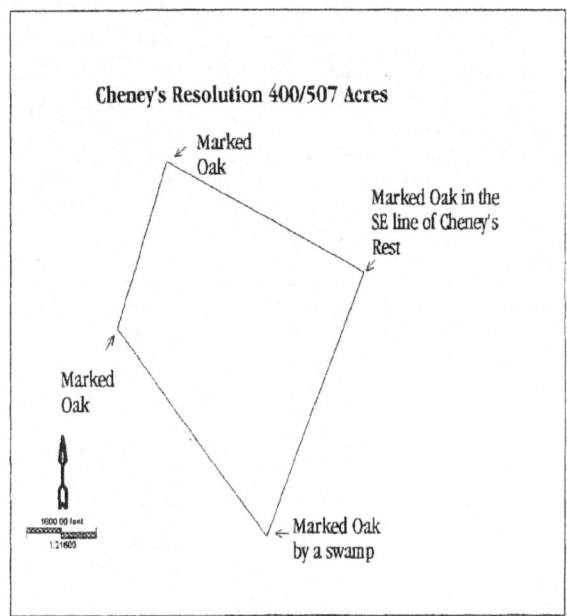

Cheney's Rest (Richard Cheney 300/300 acres. L5/295 SR7347
Know yee that wee for and in consideration that Richard Cheney of this Province, Planter, hath due unto him three hundred acres of land within our s'd Province for transporting severall persons into this Province here to inhabit as appears on record. Upon such conditions and termes as are exprefsed in our Conditions of Plantation of our Province of Maryland, doe hereby grant unto the s'd Richard Cheney a parcell of land called Cheney's Rest on the South River in Ann Arundell County beginning in a swamp of a creek called The Flatt Creek about a mile from the water.

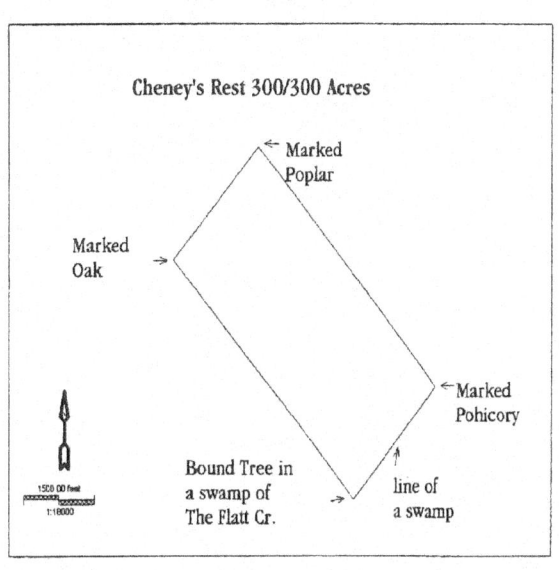

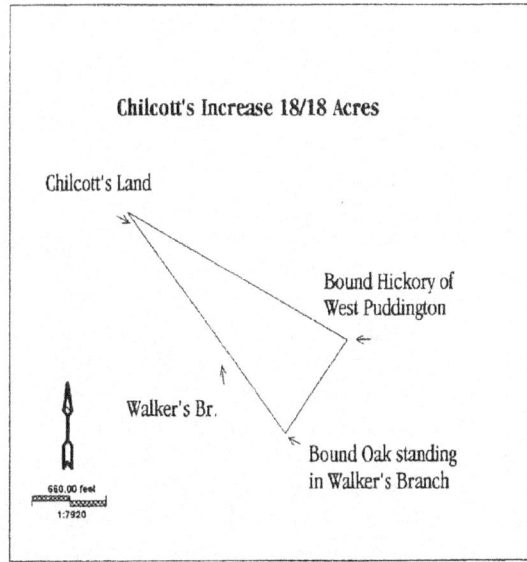

Chilcott's Increase (John Chilcott) 5/1/1672 – 18/18 acres. L16/575 SR735
Know ye that wee for and in consideration that John Chilcott of Ann Arundell County in our s'd Province of Maryland hath due unto him eighteen acres of land within our s'd Province by afsignment of **George Yate** part of a warrant for one hundred ten acres granted to the s'd Yate 6/20/1671, as appears on record. Upon such conditions and terms as are exprefsed in our Conditions of Plantation of our s'd Province of Maryland, doe hereby grant unto the s'd John Chilcott all that parcel of land called Chilcott's Increase lying in the s'd County near the head of the South River beginning at a bound Hickory of *West Puddington. Also adjoins Walker's Branch.*

Clarken Well **(John Clark)** 8/20/1665 – 100 acres. L8/144 SR7350
Know yee that wee for and in consideration that John Clark of this Province, Planter, hath due unto him one hundred acres of land within our s'd Province for transporting **Elizabeth Wattson** into this Province here to inhabit as appears on record. Upon such conditions and terms as are exprefsed in our Conditions of Plantation of our Province of Maryland do hereby grant unto the s'd

John Clark a parcell of land called Clarken Well lying in Ann Arundell County and on the south side of the South River adjoining to the west upon land laid out for **Richard Cheney**, being a marked Poplar standing by the river. *Also adjoins Chandler's Creek. Note: Tract cannot be drawn because of incomplete boundary course data.*

Clarkes Inheritance (Neale Clarke)
8/8/1670 – 400/394 acres. L14/33 SR7356

Know yee that for and in consideration that Neale Clark of Ann Arundell County, Planter, hath due unto him four hundred acres of land within our s'd Province of a warrant for the same quantity formerly granted to him as appears on record. Upon such conditions and terms as are exprefsed in our Conditions of Plantation of this our s'd Province of Maryland, wee doe hereby grant unto the s'd Clark all that parcell of land called Clarke's Inheritance lying in the s'd County on the West side of South River about three miles from the s'd river beginning at a

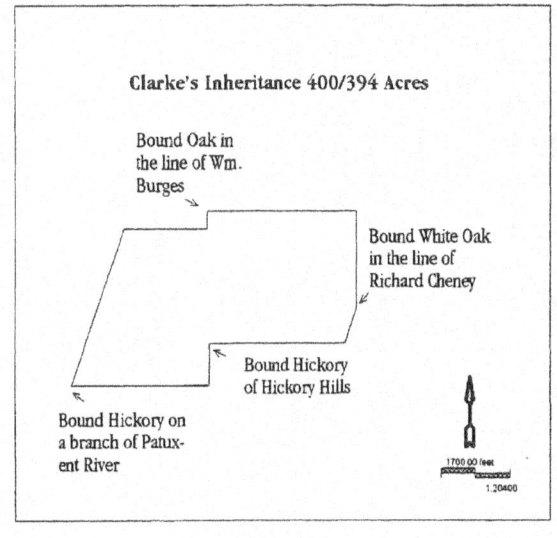

bound White Oak in the head of a line of **Richard Cheney** being the Westernmost bound tree of land called *Indian Range. Adjoins Hickory Hills, the land of Wm. Burges, and the Patuxent River.*

Clark of the Councill (Richard Clark) 11/10/1701 – 191/191 acres. LDD5i/219 SR7378

By virtue of a warrant for five hundred acres granted unto Richard Clark of Ann Arundell County bearing the date 10/8/1701, these are therefore to certifie that I have laid out for the s'd Clark a parcell of land called Clark of the Councill lying in the s'd County on the North side of the North Branch of Patuxent River beginning at a bounded Red Oake at the end of the east by south line of *Champ's Adventure.* Note: (Same reference) "Know all Men that I Richard Clark have made over unto **Daniel Richardson** and his heirs the above Certificate" (11/10/1701).
"Know all men by these prefents that I Daniel Richardson have made over to **Henry Hall** the above Cert" (10/29/1706). Hall's patent not found. Land probably absorbed in other patent or patents.

14

Coape's Hill (George Coape) 8/10/1683 – 40/26 acres. LSDA/95 SR7369

Know yee that for and in consideration that George Coape of Ann Arundell County in our s'd Province of Maryland hath due unto him forty acres of land within our s'd Province by afsignment from **Henry Hanslap** the afsignee of **Coll Thomas Taylor,** part of a warrant for one thousand acres granted to the s'd Taylor 4/13/1681, as appears on record. Upon such conditions and terms as are exprefsed in our Conditions of Plantation of this our s'd Province of Maryland, wee doe hereby grant unto the s'd George Coape all that parcell of land called Coape's Hill lying in the s'd County in the woods beginning at a bound White Oak of the land of **Evan Davis** *(Evan's Rest)* and the land of **Edward Price** *(Bright Seate).*

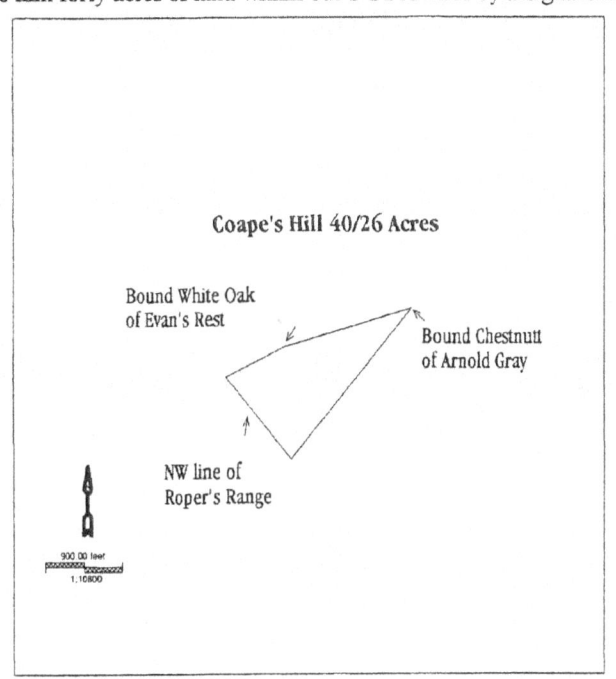

Collierby (John Brewer) 4/13/1678 – 150 acres. L20/68 SR7361

Know yee that whereas our Late Father **Cecilius**, of noble memory, did by his Lettters Pattent grant unto **John Collier** a parcel of land of one hundred fifty acres called Collierby lying on the west side of Chesapeake Bay and on the south side of the South River. The s'd John Collier did, for a valuable consideration afsigne, sell, and make over same to **John Brewer (the elder)** of Ann Arundell County, deceased, as appears on record. Upon such conditions and terms as are exprefsed in our Conditions of Plantation of our Late Father Cecilius, of noble memory, doe hereby grant unto the s'd John Brewer, son and heir of the s'd John Brewer, deceased, all that parcell of land called Collierby next adjoining land lately laid out for **Ellis Brown** beginning at Brown's bound Pohikary tree by the Riverside. *Also adjoins the land of **Edw. Selby**. Note: Cannot be drawn because three of the four boundary courses specified lack the necessary combination of distance and direction.*

Covell's Folly (Ann Covell) 5/29/1663 - 500/386 acres. L5/293 SR7347

Know yee that for and in consideration that Ann Covell, widow, the relict of **John Covell** late of this place, deceased, hath due unto her five hundred acres of land within this Province as appears on record. Upon such conditions and terms as are exprefsed in our Conditions of Plantation of our Province of Maryland, wee doe hereby grant unto her the s'd Ann Covell a parcell of land called Covell's Folly lying on the south side of the South River and on the west side of Flat Creek next adjoining the land of **Archer Arbuckle**, Planter, beginning at Arbuckle's bound Oak next to the Creek.

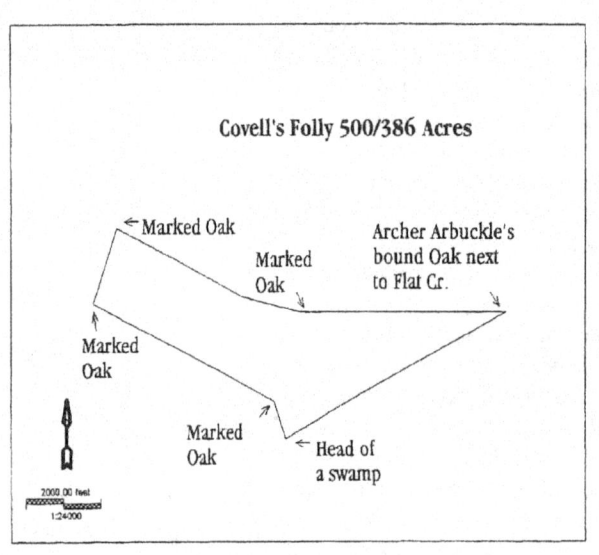

Coxby (Edward Cox) 2/18/1650 – 100/104 acres. LQ/397 SR7345

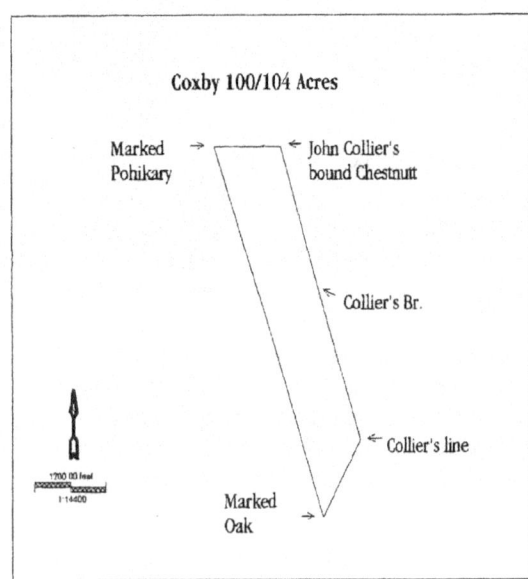

Know yee that for and in consideration that Edward Cox hath transported himself and **Joan,** his wife into this Province here to inhabit and, upon such conditions and terms as are exprefsed in our Conditions of Plantation of our s'd Province of Maryland, doe hereby grant unto the s'd Edward Cox a parcell of land called Coxby lying on the west side of Chesapeake Bay and on the south side of the South River next adjoining to the land lately laid out for **John Collier** *(Collierby)* of this Province, Planter, beginning at the s'd Collier's bounded Chestnutt tree. *Also adjoins Besson's Den and Collier's Branch.*

Davis His Rest (Evan Davis) 9/10/1672 – 200/112 acres. L17/288 SR7359

Know yee that for and in consideration that Evan Davis of Ann Arundell County in our s'd Province of Maryland hath due unto him two hundred acres of land within our s'd Province by afsignment from **Robert Wilson** part of a warrant for two thousand acres to the s'd Wilson granted 4/9/1671, as appears on record. Upon such considerations and terms as are exprefsed in our Conditions of Plantation of this our s'd Province of Maryland, wee doe hereby grant unto the s'd Davis all that parcell of land called Davis His Rest lying in Ann Arundell County on the South side of the Severn River in the woods beginning at a bounded White Oake of the land of **John Gray**.

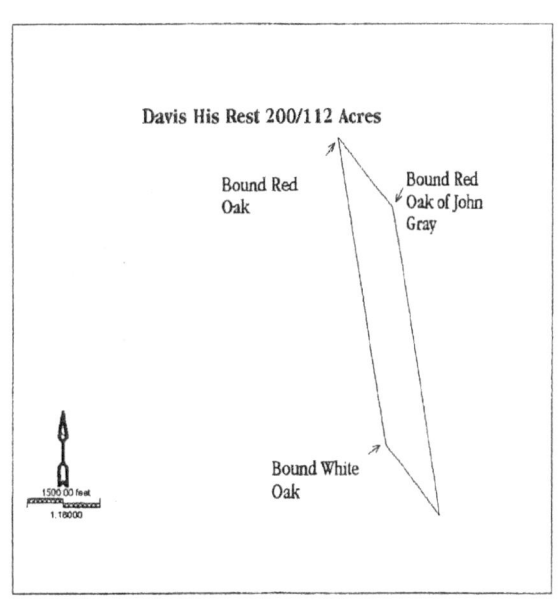

Dodderidge's Forrest (John Dodderidge) 3/26/1696 – 200/223 acres. LC3i/365 SR7377

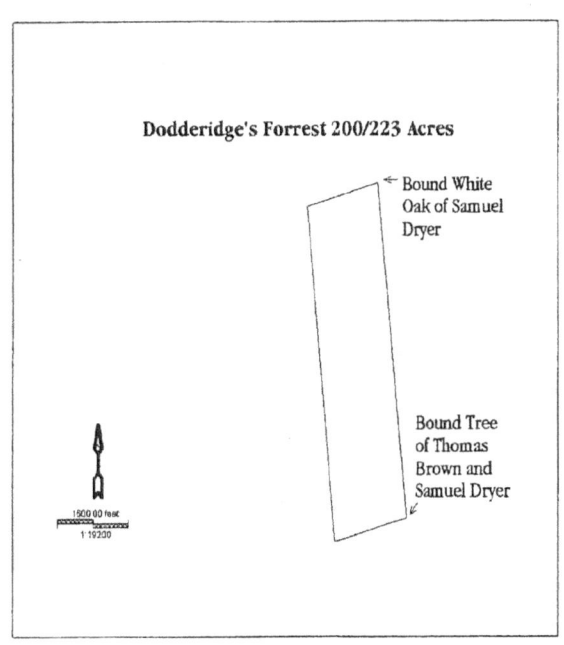

Know yee that for and in consideration that John Dodderidge of Ann Arundell County in our s'd Province of Maryland hath due unto him two hundred acres of land within our s'd Province being due unto him by virtue of a warrant of three hundred acres granted unto him 2/7/1695, as appears on record in our land office. Upon such conditions and terms as are exprefsed in our Conditions of Plantation of this our Province, wee doe therefore hereby grant unto the s'd John all that tract or parcell of land lying on the West side of the North Branch of Patuxent River beginning at a bounded Red Oak it being a bound tree of **Thomas Brown** and **Samuel Dryer**. *Note: The certification is for 100 acres more than the amount granted. No explanation found.*

Dodon (Francis Stocket) 7/20/1671 – 664 acres. L14/329 SR7376
Know yee that wee for and in consideration that Francis Stocket of the County of Ann Arundall in our s'd Province of Maryland hath due unto him six hundred sixty four acres of land within our s'd Province part of a warrant for two thousand acres granted to the s'd Francis Stockett, **Henry Stocket,** and **Thomas Stocket** 4/26/1669, as appears on record. Upon such conditions and terms as are exprefsed in our Conditions of Plantation of our s'd Province of Maryland, doe hereby grant unto the s'd Francis Stocket all that parcell of land called Dodon, lying in Ann Arundall County to the north of Ann Arundall Manor. *Adjoins Obligation, Stocketts Runn, Taylor's Chance, and Bridge Hill. Note: This tract cannot be drawn because all of the boundary courses are incomplete.*

Duvall's Addition (Marin Duvall) 8/8/1670 – 165/169 acres. L14/22 SR7356

Know yee that for and in consideration that Marin Duvall of the County of Ann Arundell in our s'd Province hath due unto him one hundred and sixty five acres within our s'd Province by afsignment from **George Yate** the afsignee of **David Poole** being due the s'd Poole for transporting severall persons to this Province here to inhabit as appears on record. Upon such conditions and terms as are exprefsed in our Conditions of Plantation of this our Province of Maryland, wee doe hereby grant unto the s'd Marin Duvall all that parcell of land called Duvall's Addition lying in the s'd County on the West side of South River about three miles from the s'd river beginning at a bound White Oak of *Middle Plantation. Adjoins Arnold Gray and Puddington's Enlargement.*

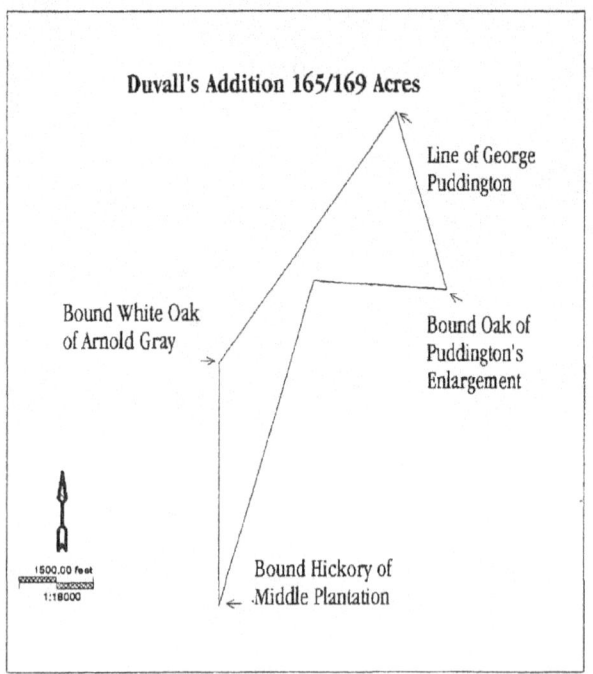

Duvall's Delight (John Duvall) 12/10/1695 – 1,000/1,374 acres. LWD/132 SR7372-2

Know yee that for and in consideration that John Duvall of Ann Arundell County in our Province of Maryland hath due unto him one thousand acres of land within our s'd Province being due unto him by virtue of a warrant for that quantity granted unto him 6/19/1694, as appears on record in our Land Office. Upon such conditions and terms as are exprefsed in our Conditions of Plantation of this our Province, wee doe therefore grant unto him the s'd John Duvall all that tract or parcel of land called Duvall's Delight lying on the northeast side of Patuxent River beginning at a bounded Red Oak. *Note: Another patent for Duvall's Delight was found in LC3i/323 SR7377.*

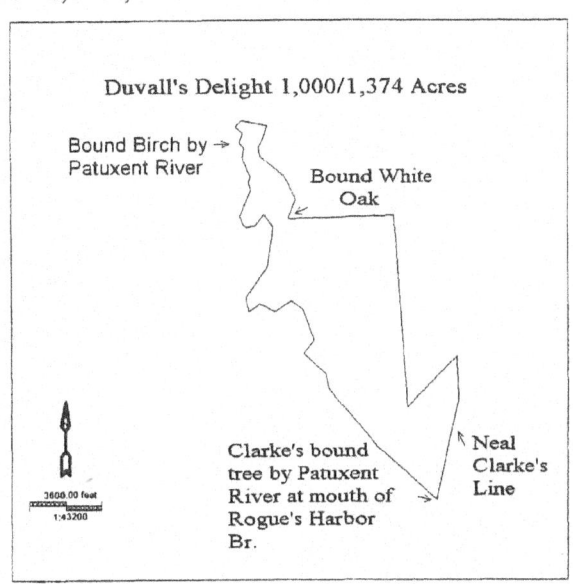

Duvall's Pasture (Lewis Duvall) 5/10/1705 – 62/64 acres. LD5i/208 SR7378

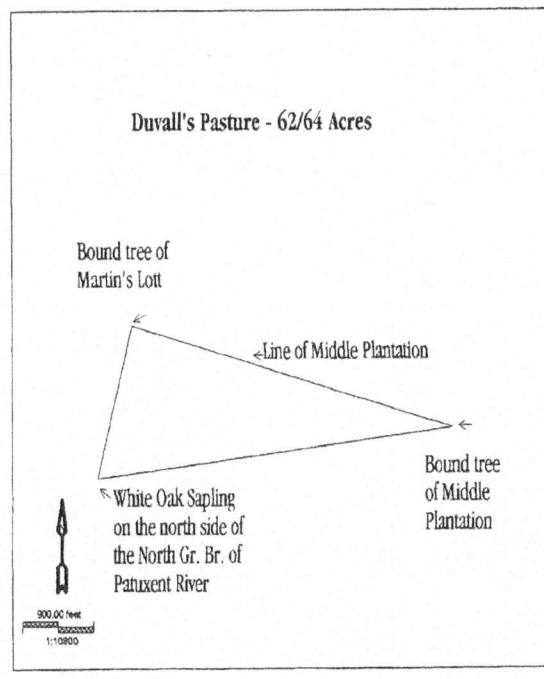

By virtue of a warrant granted unto Lewis Duvall for one hundred forty three acres of land dated 1/6/1704, these prefents are therefore to certifie that I **Thomas Larkin**, Deputy Surveyor, have laid out for the s'd Duvall a parcell of land lying in the s'd County called Duvall's Pasture beginning at a White Oake saplin it being a bound tree of *Burges' Choice* lying on north side of the North Great Branch of Patuxent River in the woods and upon a meadow called Cattail Meadow. *Note: According to the Cert, the warrant was for 143 acres. However, the survey notes state that the tract was laid out for 62 acres. No explanation found.*

Duvall's Range (Maryne Duvall) 9/10/1672 – 200/198 acres. L17/291 SR7358

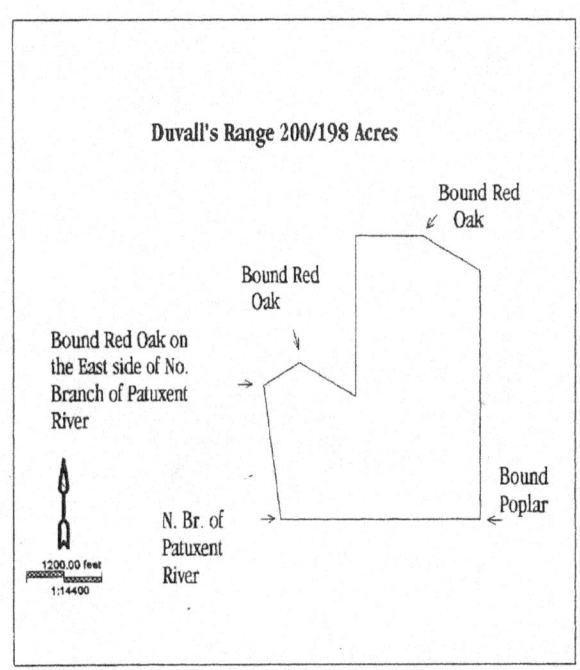

Know yee that wee for and in consideration that Maryne Duvall of Ann Arundell County in our s'd Province of Maryland hath due unto him two hundred acres of land within our s'd Province by afsignment of **George Yate** the afsignee of **Thomas Taylor** the attorney for **Jerome White Esq,** part of a warrant for eleven hundred acres to the s'd White granted 4/9/1672, as appears on record. Upon such conditions and terms as are exprefsed in our Conditions of Plantation of our s'd Province of Maryland, wee doe hereby grant unto the s'd Duvall all that parcell of land called Duvall's Range lying in the s'd County on the east side of the North Branch of Patuxent River beginning at a bound Red Oak standing by the s'd branch.

Duvall's Range Resurveyed (John Duvall) 11/10/1695 – 708/615 acres. L23Ii/293 SR7365

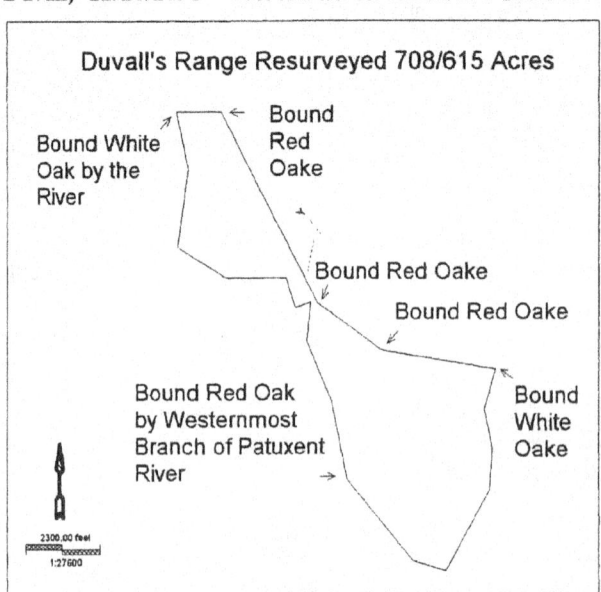

Know yee that wee for and in consideration that John Duvall of Ann Arundell County in our Province of Maryland hath due unto him seven hundred eight acres of land within our Province by virtue of a warrant granted unto him on 6/9/1694, as appears on record. Upon such conditions and terms as are exprefsed in our Conditions of Plantation of our Province of Maryland, wee doe therefore grant unto the s'd John Duvall all that tract or parcell of land called Duvall's Range lying in Ann Arundell County in the forke of the Patuxent River. Begins at a bounded Red Oake by the westernmost Branch of the s'd

River.

Duvall's Range Resurveyed (Hezikiah Lynthicum) 11/25/1703 – 1,527/1,493 acres. LDD5i/469 SR7378

By virtue of a Special Warrant granted unto Hezikiah Lynthicum of Ann Arundell County dated 4/3/1703, to resurvey a tract called Duvall's Range and to take up such surplus land as found within the ancient metes and bounds. These are therefore to certifie that I have resurveyed and laid out for the s'd Hezikiah that parcel of land now called Duvall's Range Resurveyed beginning at the end of the (*north*) end of the south eighty three degrees east line of a tract called *Owen Wood's Thickett*.

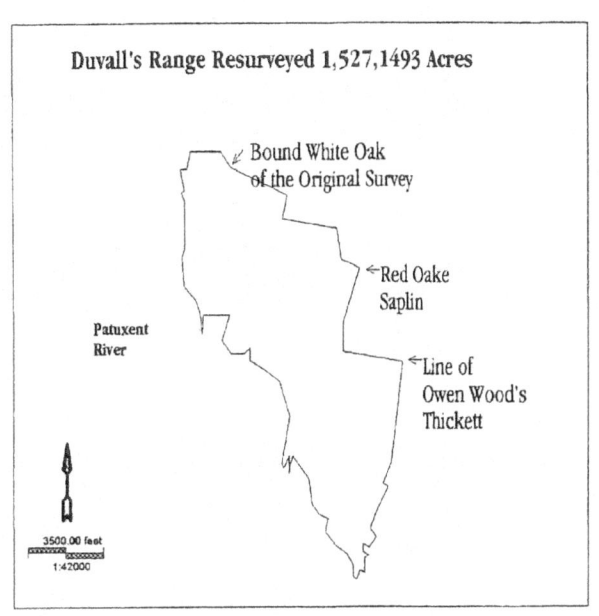

Efford's Delight (Will Efford) 10/10/1704 – 180/191 acres. LCD/180 SR7376

Know yee that for and in consideration that Will Efford of Ann Arundell County hath due unto him one hundred eighty acres of land within our s'd Province being due unto him by virtue of an afsignment of **Richard Snowden Jr**, afsigned unto him out of a warrant of three thousand five hundred acres granted unto **James Carroll** of the s'd County 2/1/1702, as appears on record. Upon such conditions and terms as are exprefsed in our Conditions of Plantation, wee doe therefore hereby grant unto the s'd Will Efford all that tract or parcell of land called Efford's Delight lying in the forke of Patuxent River to the north of *Robin Hood's Forrest* beginning at a bounded Pine standing at the head of Cobbler's Branch. *Note: Now in Prince George's County.*

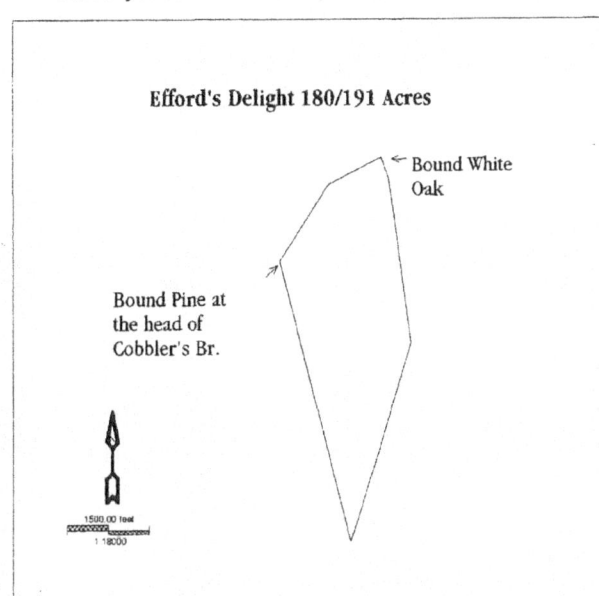

Elizabeth's Fancy (Richard Clarke) 6/4/1702 – 225/211 acres. LCD/106 SR7376

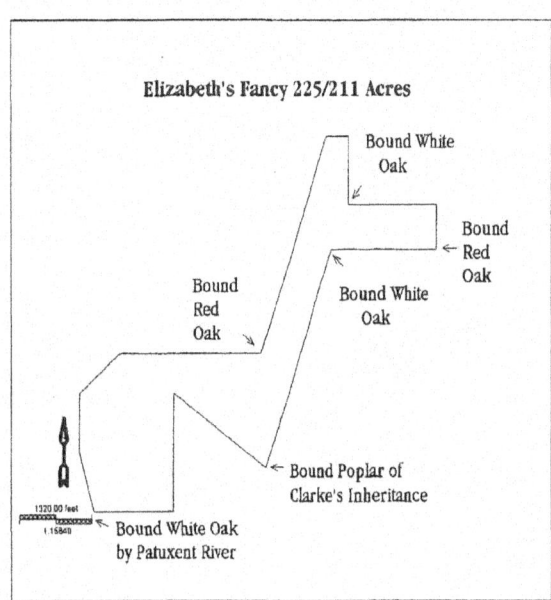

For and in consideration that Richard Clarke of Ann Arundell County in our s'd Province of Maryland hath due unto him two hundred twenty five acres of land within our s'd Province being due unto him by virtue of a warrant for one thousand acres granted him 4/19/1701, as appears on record in our land office. Upon such considerations and terms as are exprefsed in our Conditions of Plantation of our s'd Province of Maryland, wee doe therefore grant unto the s'd Richard Clarke all that tract or parcel of land called Elizabeth's Fancy lying on the south side of the South River beginning at a bound Poplar of the land called *Clarke's Inheritance*.

Elk Thickett (Archibald Arbuckle) 1/20/1659 - 150/149 acres. L4/438 SR7346

Know yee that for and in consideration that Archibald Arbuckle and **Dyna** his wife hath performed their time of service in this our Province of Maryland and there is due to him eighty acres more by afsignment of **John Clark** due to the s'd Clark for his time of service. Upon such considerations and terms as are exprefsed in our Conditions of Plantation of our s'd Province of Maryland, do hereby grant unto the s'd Archibald Arbuckle a Parcell of land lying on the West side of Chesapeake Bay and on the West side of a river in the s'd Bay called the South River. Begins at a marked Oak standing by a valley upon a branch called Arbuckle's

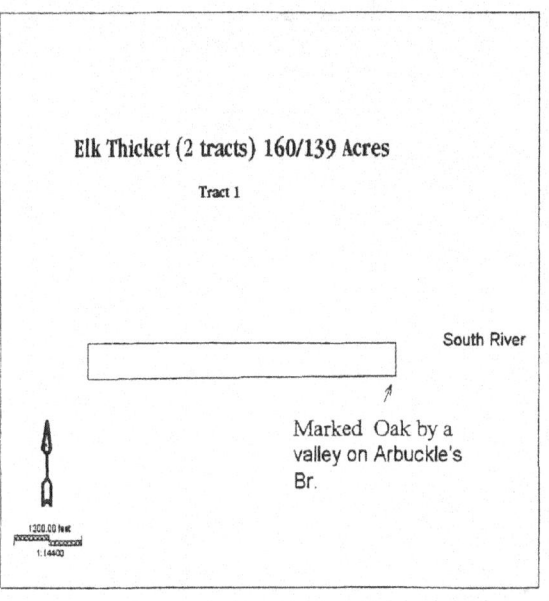

Branch and runs north down the River. And also, that neck of land lying near unto the former called Elk Thickett. *Note: The grant is for two tracts; an unnamed tract of 50 acres and Elk*

Thickett, which is described above. The second tract cannot be drawn due to incomplete boundary course data.

Elk Thickett Resurveyed (Walter Phelps) 4/13/1701– 35/35 acres. LDD5i/16 SR7378

Whereas **Robert Davis** of Ann Arundell County did obtain out of his LOP's Land Office a speciall warrant dated 5/18/1700, to resurvey the bounds of a certaine tract of land in the s'd County called Elk Thickett, these are to certifie that I have resurveyed for the s'd Davis a tract of land lying at the head of South River in the s'd County, beginning at a bounded White Oak stump standing on a path called Hugging's Path. *Adjoins Covell's Folly. Note: On the same date (same reference) the tract was assigned to, and patented by, Walter Phelps.*

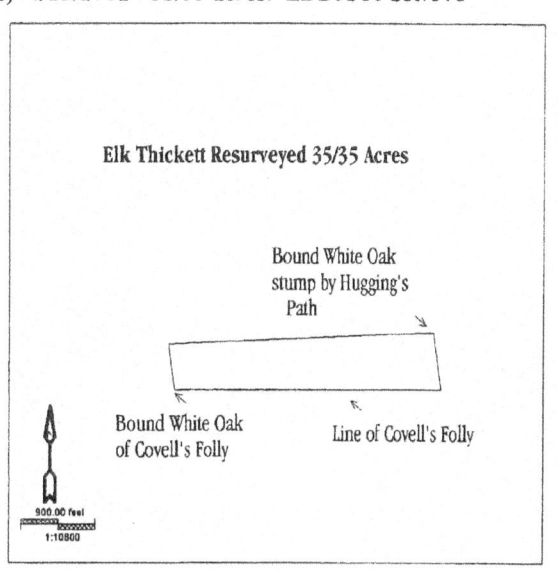

Eversail (Lewis Duvall) 5/10/1709 – 200/211 acres. LDD5i/576 SR7378

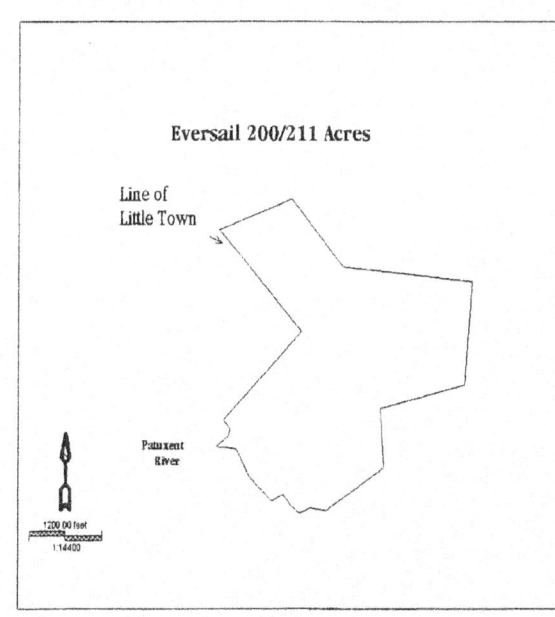

By virtue of a warrant for two hundred acres of land within this Province granted unto Lewis Duvall of Ann Arundell County dated 2/3/1706, these are to certifie that I have laid out for the s'd Duvall all that tract or parcell of land called Eversail lying in the s'd County in the Forke of Patuxent River next below a tract called *Littleton*. Begins at a bounded Gumm just by and below the mouth of a small gutt near the s'd riverside and bounds on the river. Then issued pattent for the above land to the above named Lewis Duvall pursuant to the above.

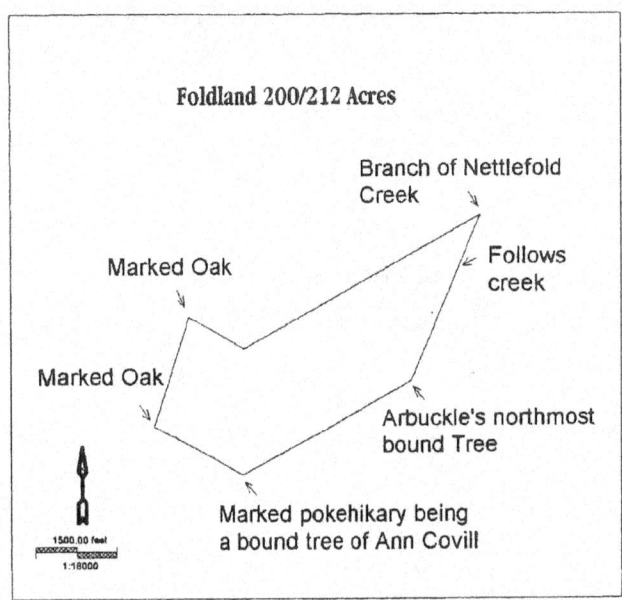

Foldland (George Nettlefold) 2/26/1661 - 200/212 acres. L5/290 SR 7347

Know yee that for and in consideration that George Nettlefold of this Province, Planter, hath due unto him two hundred acres of land within our s'd Province as appears on record. Upon such conditions and terms as are exprefsed in our Conditions of Plantation wee doe therefore grant unto the s'd George Nettlefold a parcell of land called Foldland lying on the West side of the South River adjoining the land of **Archibald Arbuckle** beginning at Arbuckle's northmost bound tree in the woods. *Note 1 (from MSA Tract Index 73): Assigned by Nettlefold and wife Ruth Nettlefold to Richard Tydings 8/1663. Sold by Tydings to Elizabeth Burns, widow (no date shown).*

Fortune (John Gresham) 4/16/1687 – 54/61 acres. L22/316 SR7363

By virtue of a warrant granted unto **Richard Beard** of this County for four thousand acres of land dated 2/27/1686, fifty six acres thereof was afsigned by the s'd Beard to John Gresham of the same County as appears on record. These are to certifie that I have laid out for the s'd Gresham a parcell of land called Fortune lying on the northeast side of the Road River beginning at a bound White Oak of **Edward Selby's** land. *Note: MSA Land Index 54 shows that this tract was not patented until 1750.*

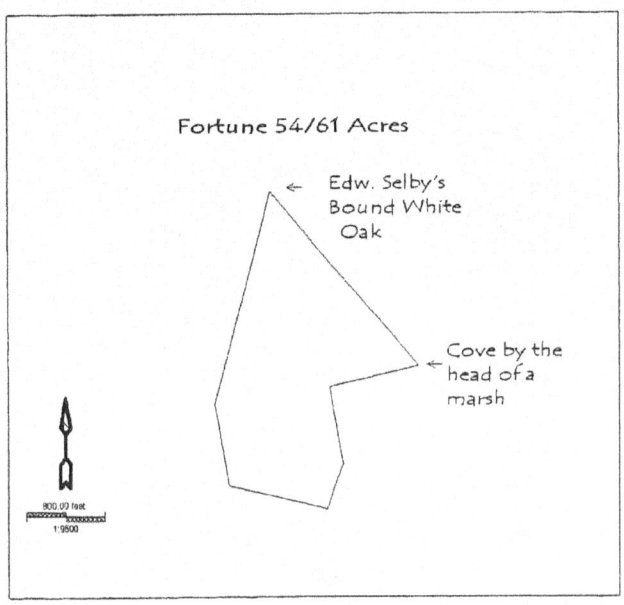

Foster & Lewis (Richard Foster & John Lewis) 9/10/1666 – 100/102 acres. L10/165 SR7352

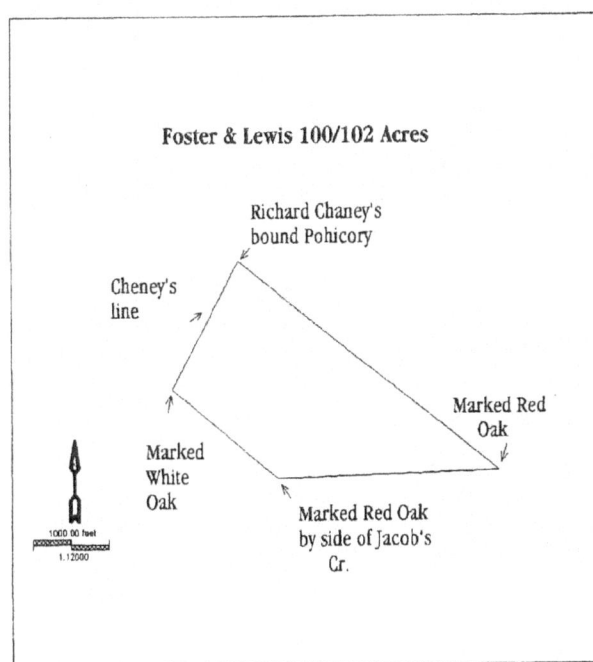

Know yee that wee for and in consideration that Richard Foster and John Lewis, Planters, hath due unto them one hundred acres of land within our s'd Province by afsignment from **George Yate**, Gent, part of a warrant for two hundred fifty acres as appears on record. Upon such conditions and terms as are exprefsed in our Conditions of Plantation of our s'd Province of Maryland, doe hereby grant unto the s'd Foster & Lewis a parcell of land lying on the south side of the South River and on the west side of Jacob's Creek beginning at a marked Red Oak by a valley. *Adjoins the land of Richard Cheney.*

Foster's Point (John Foster) 5/1/1672 – 50/45 acres. L16/575 SR 7357

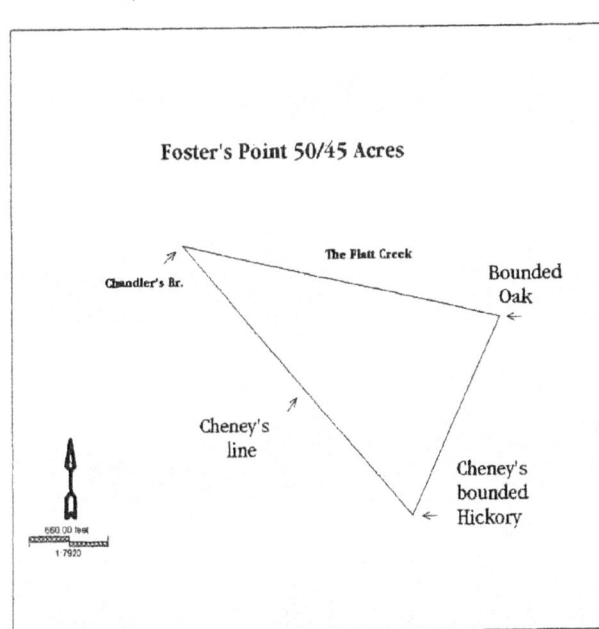

Know yee that wee for and in consideration that John Foster of Ann Arundell County, Planter, hath due unto him fifty acres of land for **Mary**, his wife's time of service in this Province as appears on record. Upon such conditions and terms as are exprefsed in our Conditions of Plantation of our Province of Maryland, doe hereby grant unto the s'd John Foster all that parcel of land called Foster's Point lying in the s'd County on the south side of the South River at the head of Flatt Creek beginning at a bound Hickory being a bound tree of **Richard Cheney**.

Francis His Addition (Thomas Francis) 9/10/1674 – 42/42 acres. L15/267 SR4327

Know yee that wee for and in consideration that Thomas Francis of the County of Ann Arundall, Gent, hath due unto him forty two acres of land in this Province by afsignment of **George Yate** part of a warrant for twelve hundred acres to him formerly afsigned as appears on record. And, upon such considerations and terms as are exprefsed in our Conditions of Plantation of our Province of Maryland, doe hereby grant unto the s'd Thomas Francis a parcell of land called Francis His Addition lying in the County aforesaid near

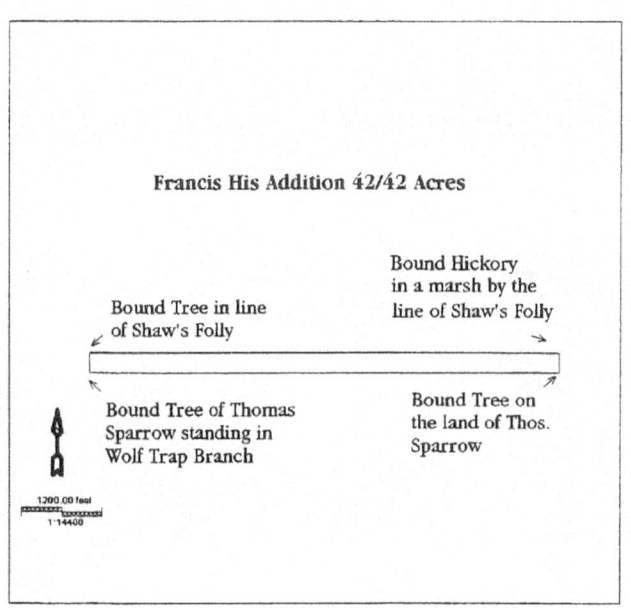

a branch called Nettlefold's Branch. Begins at a bound Hickory standing in a marsh by the line of land of **John Shaw** (*Shaw's Folly*).

Franklin's Enlargement (Robert Franklin) 8/8/1670 – 240/374 acres. L14/9 SR7356

Know yee that for and in consideration that Robert Franklin, Gent, of the County of Ann Arundel in our s'd Province of Maryland hath due unto him two hundred forty acres of land by afsignment of **George Yate** the afsignee of **David Poole** for his the s'd Poole's, transporting of severall persons here to inhabit as appears on record. Upon such conditions and terms as are exprefsed in our Conditions of Plantation of this our Province of Maryland, wee doe hereby grant unto the s'd Franklin a parcell of land called Franklin's Enlargement lying about two and one half miles in the woods in South River adjoining to a parcell called *Indian Range* laid out for the s'd Franklin and **Richard Beard** beginning at a bound Red Oak at the end

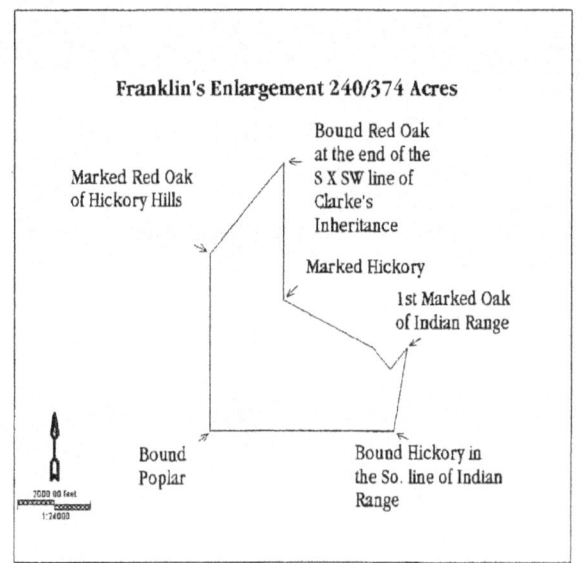

of the south by southwest line of a parcell laid out for **Neale Clark** called *Clark's Inheritance*. *Also adjoins Hickory Hills.*

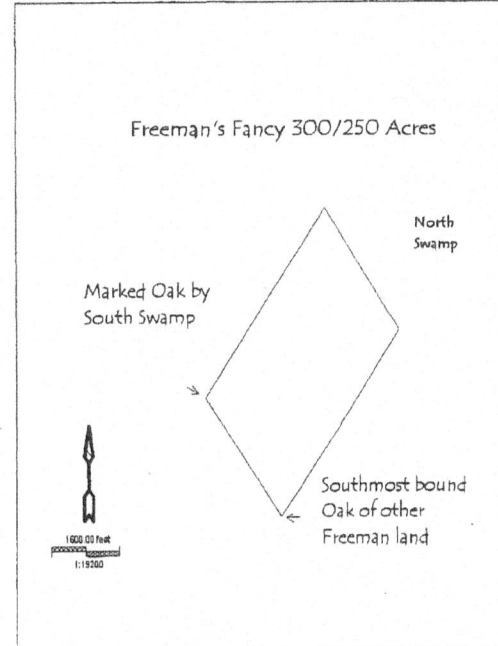

Freeman's Fancy (John Freeman)
5/27/1663 - 300 /250 acres. L5/289 SR 7347

Know yee that we for and in consideration that John Freeman of this Province hath due unto him three hundred acres of land in this Province for the Transportation of Severall Persons in to this Province here to inhabit, as appears upon record. Upon such considerations and terms as are exprefsed in our Conditions of Plantation of our Province of Maryland, do grant unto him the s'd John Freeman a parcell of land called Freeman's Fancy lying a mile and half from the head of the South River in the County of Anne Arundel at the end of land formerly conveyed to him. Begins at his Southmost bounded Oak in the woods. *Note (from MSA Tract Index 73): Devised to wife **Elizabeth Freeman** who later became the wife of **Robert Proctor**. Sold in 1673 by the Proctors to **George Puddington** who, in 1674, sold it to **Edward Burges**.*

Free Manston (John Freeman)
2/15/1659 - 150/131 acres. L5/127 SR 7347

Know yee that we for and in consideration that John Freeman of this Province, Planter, hath due unto him one hundred and fifty acres of land in this Province. Upon such considerations and terms as are exprefsed in our Conditions of Plantation of our s'd Province of Maryland, do hereby grant unto the s'd John Freeman a parcell of Land called Freeman's Neck or Freemanston lying on the West side of Chesapeake Bay in a river of the s'd Bay called the South River near to the head of the said river between the two main branches. Begins at a marked Oak on the East side of the West branch. *Note 1: A note in the margin of this grant refers to the tract as Freeman's Neck. The Index of Tracts (Index 55) at the Maryland Hall of Records shows both names. However, the text of the grant is clear that the tract being granted was called Free Manston. Note 2 (from MSA Tract Index 73): Devised to wife **Elizabeth Freeman** who later became the wife of **Robert Proctor**. Sold in 1673 by the Proctors to **George Puddington** who, in 1674, sold it to **Edward Burges**.*

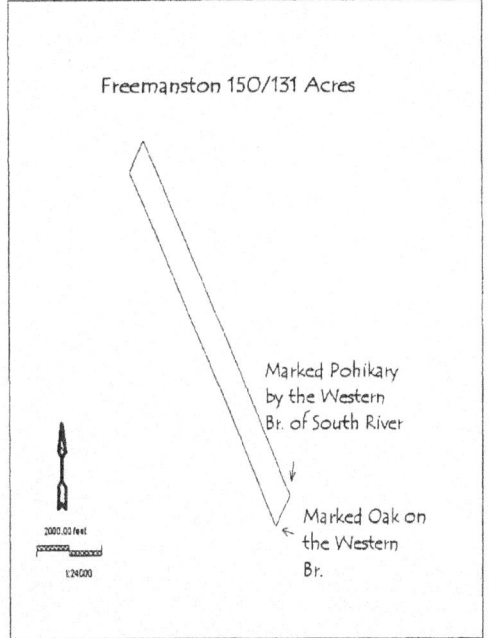

Gater's Range (John Gater)
9/10/1675 - 200/*147* acres.
L17/293 SR 7358

Know yee that we for and in consideration that John Gater of Ann Arundell County in our s'd Province of Maryland, Planter, hath due unto him two hundred acres of land within our s'd Province by afsignment from **George Yate** the afsignee of **Thomas Taylor**, attorney for **Jerome White Esq**, part of a warrant for eleven hundred fifty acres to the s'd White granted 4/9/1672, as appears on record. Upon such considerations and terms as are exprefsed in our Conditions of Plantation of this our Province of Maryland we doe hereby grant unto

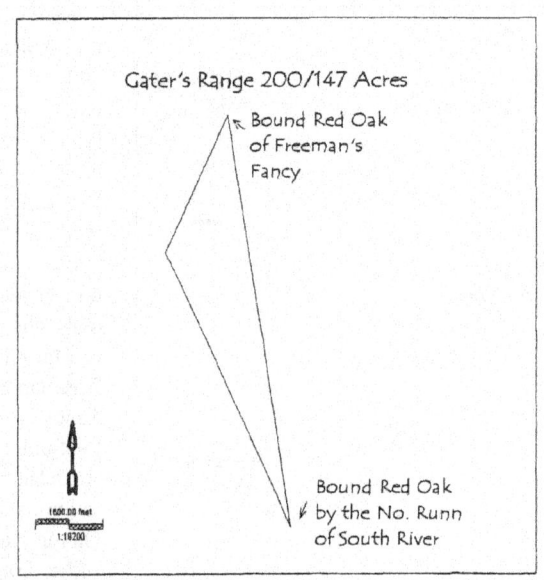

the s'd Gater a parcel of land called Gater's Range lying in the said county at the head of the South River. Begins at a bounded Red Oak standing on the west side of the North Runn of the South River. *Adjoins Freeman's Fancy.*

Godwell Resurveyed (William Parker) 10/13/1679 - 805/774 acres. LC/21 SR7362

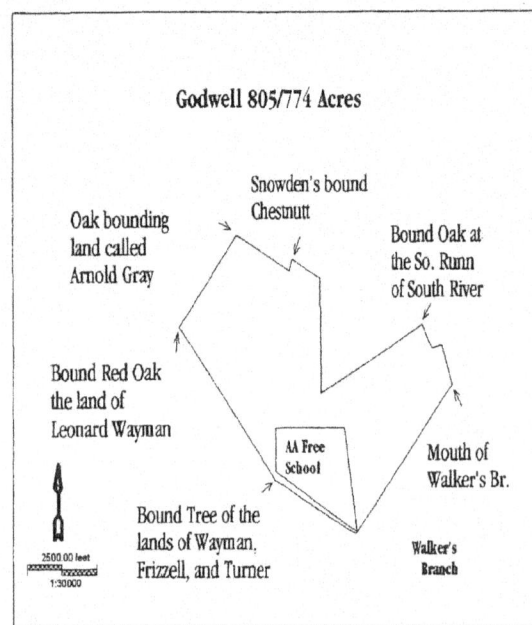

Know yee that whereas our late father Cecilius, of noble memory, did pattent a parcell of land of two hundred acres to **George Nettlefold** called *Nettle Land* lying in Ann Arundell County on the West side of the South River and also did pattent unto **Marin Duvall** a parcell of land for one hundred acres called *Lavall* and, also did pattent unto **John Chilcotte** a parcell of land of one hundred ninety acres called *The Addition*. And whereas **George Parker** of Calvert County has informed us that these tracts are adjoining to each other and are now in his pofsefsion and that there are severall mistakes in the surveys. And, also that within the intended boundaries there is a greater quantity of acreage than is mentioned in the aforesaid grants through the negligence or ignorance of the surveyor. The s'd Parker humbly requests a resurvey of these parcells into one tract according to the ancient bounds rectifying any errors in the former surveys and, upon making good rights for the surplus found (if any found), he might benefit of a Patent of Confirmation for the whole. The s'd Parker has bargained and sold his rights and interest to **William Parker** of Calvert County as appears on record. Upon such conditions and terms as are exprefsed in our Conditions of Plantation of our late father Cecilius, of noble memory, wee doe hereby grant unto the s'd William Parker all that parcell of land resurveyed called Godwell lying in Ann Arundel County near the head of the South River and at the mouth of a Branch called Walker's Branch. *Adjoins the South Runn of South River, Walker's Branch and the lands of **John Gray**, **Richard Snowden**, **John Welch**, **Leonard Wayman**, and **William Frizzell**. Note: Although the patent document calls this a "resurvey," it is the initial patent of Godwell (rather than a resurvey of Godwell).*

Gray's Chance (John Gray) 1/15/1684 Cert – 64/65 acres. L22/230 SR7363
By virtue of a warrant granted unto **John Dorsey** of this County for two hundred forty two acres of land dated 1/30/1689, sixty four acres thereof was afsigned by the s'd Dorsey to John Gray of this County as appears on record. These are therefore to certifie that I have laid out for the s'd John Gray a parcel of land called Gray's Chance lying on the south side of the South River and on the north side of Jacob's Creek beginning at a bound Red Oake of **Richard Cheney's** tract called *Cheney Hills*. *Also adjoins the WNW line of Beard's Habitation.*

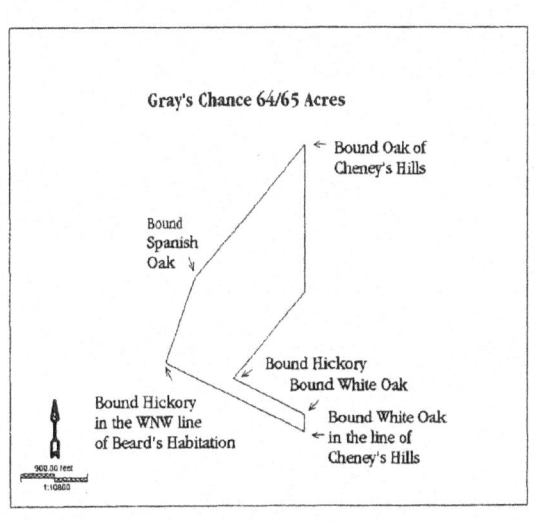

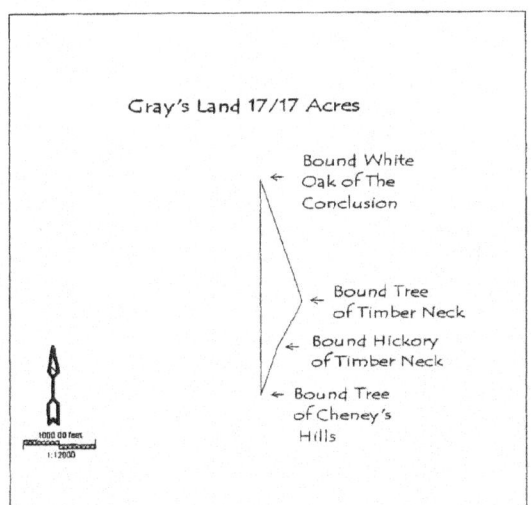

Gray's Land (John Gray) 2/15/1684/5 – 17/17 acres. L22/220 SR7363
By virtue of a warrant granted unto **John Dorsey** for two hundred forty two acres of land bearing date 2/30/1685, seventeen acres thereof was afsigned by the s'd Dorsey unto John Gray of this County, as appears on record. These are therefor to certifie that I have laid out for the s'd Gray a parcell of land called Gray's Land *(lying)* on the south side of the South River and on the north side of a creek in the s'd River called Jacob's Creek beginning at a bound White Oak it being a corner tree of a parcel of land formerly laid out for **Richard Foster** of this County called *The Conclusion* and running with the s'd land. *Also adjoins Cheney Hill.*

Green's Beginning **(John Green)** 10/5/1683 – 70 acres. LCB3i/513 SR7367
Know yee that for and in consideration that John Green of Ann Arrundell County in our s'd Province of Maryland hath due unto him seventy acres of land within our s'd Province by afsignment of **Henry Hanslap**, parte of a warrant for twelve hundred fifty acres granted to the s'd Hanslap 8/30/1683, as appears on record. Upon such conditions and termes as are exprefsed in our Conditions of Plantation of this our s'd Province of Maryland, we doe hereby grant unto the s'd John Green a parcel of land called Green's Beginning lying in the s'd County on the south side of the South River in the forke of a creek called Nettlefold's Creek beginning at the northmost bound tree of land laid out for **Archer Arbuckle** (*Elke Thickett*) and running with the line of land of **William Brewer** called *Foldland. Also adjoins a tract laid out for George Walker now in the possession of Gabriel Parrott. Note: The tract cannot be drawn because of incomplete boundary course information in the patent document.*

Greene's Town (George Green) 6/29/1673 – 50/50 acres. L17/507 SR7358

By virtue of a warrant granted unto **William Wheatly** of London, Mariner, for twenty three hundred acres of land bearing date of 5/11/1673, which s'd warrant was afsigned unto **Robert Wilson** of this County of Ann Arundell, Gent, fifty acres warrant thereof was afsigned by the s'd Wilson unto George Green, as appears on record. These are to humbly certifie that I **George Yate**, Deputy Surveyor under **Baker Brooke Esq.**, Surveyor General, hath laid out for the s'd George Green a parcel of land called Greene's Town lying in the s'd County on the south side of the South River beginning at a bound Red Oak standing on the south side of the main branch of Flatt Creek. *Adjoins Richard Cheney.*

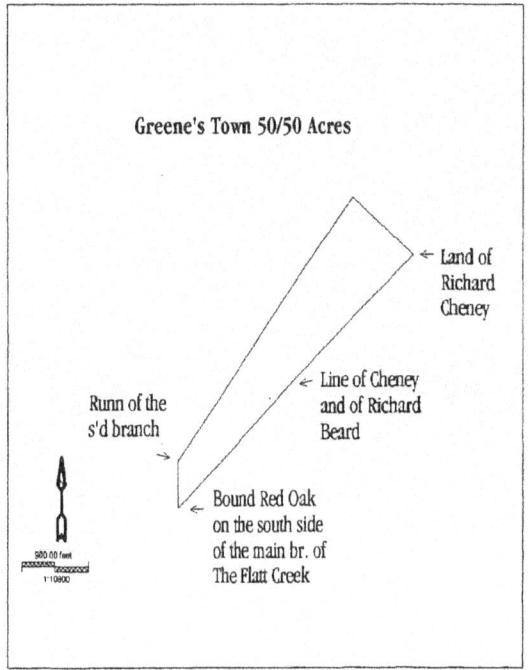

Hall's Inheritance (Christopher Hall) 8/8/1670 – 180/184 acres. L14/43 SR7356

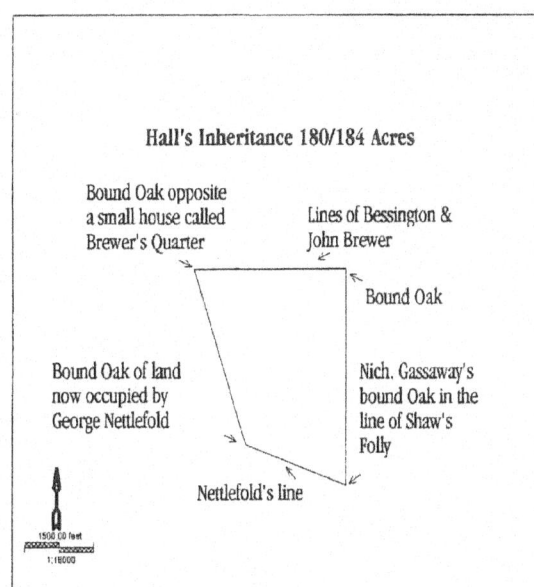

Know yee that wee for and in consideration that Christopher Hall of our s'd Province, Planter, hath due unto him one hundred eighty acres of land within our s'd Province parte of a warrant for the same quantity to him formerly granted as appears on record. Upon such considerations and terms as are exprefsed in our Conditions of Plantation of our s'd Province of Maryland, do hereby grant unto him the s'd Christopher Hall a parcel of land called Hall's Inheritance lying on the north side of the Road River in the County of Ann Arundell beginning at a bound Oak of the land of **Nicholas Gassaway** in the line of land called *Shaw's Folly. Also adjoins Bessington, Brewer's Quarter and land owned by George Nettlefold.*

Harness' Range (Isaac Harness) 9/6/1670 250/263 acres. L14/104 SR7356

Know yee that for and in consideration that Isaac Harness of the County of Ann Arundell hath due unto him two hundred fifty acres of land within our s'd Province by afsignment of **Robert Wilson** the afsignee of **Jerome White Esq.**, part of a warrant granted unto him for two thousand one hundred and fifty acres of land on 2/20/1669, thereof afsigned over to Robert Wilson of the County of Ann Arundell and two hundred and fifty acres thereof afsigned by the s'd Wilson unto Isaac Harness as appears on record. Upon such conditions and terms as are exprefsed in our Conditions of Plantation of our s'd Province of Maryland, wee doe therefore grant unto the s'd Isaac Harness a parcel of land lying in Ann Arundell County called Harness' Range beginning at a bound Red Oake in the line of a parcel laid out for Jerome White Esq. called *White's Hall* near unto the south Runn of South River.

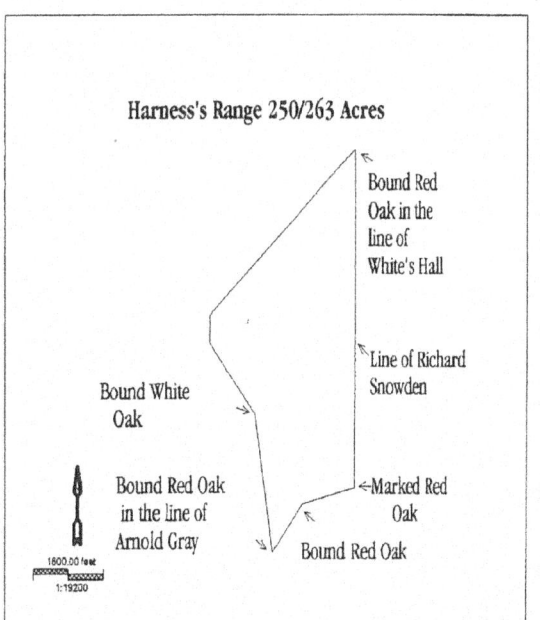

Haslenut Ridge (John Gray) 9/20/1665 – 200/196 acres. L8/392 SR7350

Know yee that for and in consideration that John Gray of this Province hath due unto him two hundred acres of land within our s'd Province parte of a warrant for two hundred acres afsigned him out of a warrant for six hundred acres from **Richard Ewen** as appears on record. Under such considerations and terms as are exprefsed in our Conditions of Plantation of our Province of Maryland, doe hereby grant unto the s'd John Gray a parcel of land called Haslenut Ridge lying in Ann Arundall County at the head of the Road River at a marked Oak being the southern most bound tree of **Nicholas Gassaway**.

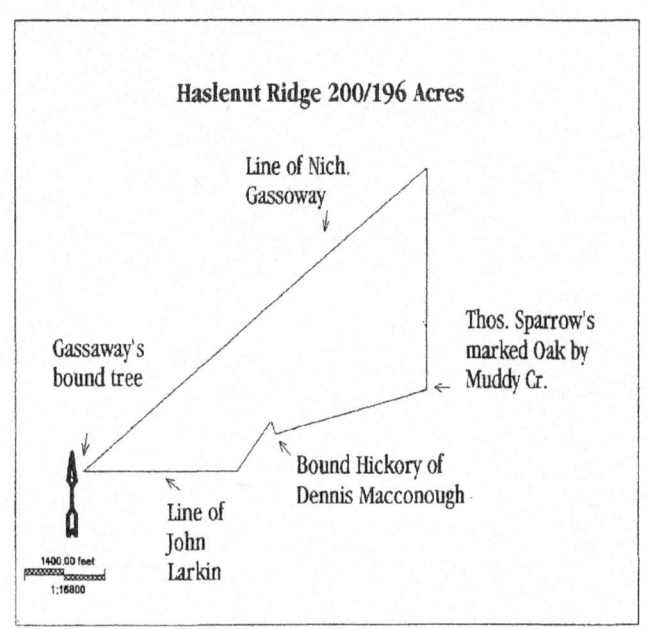

Hasslin (Jerome Hasslin) 8/4/1658 – 200/200 acres. LQ/87 SR7345

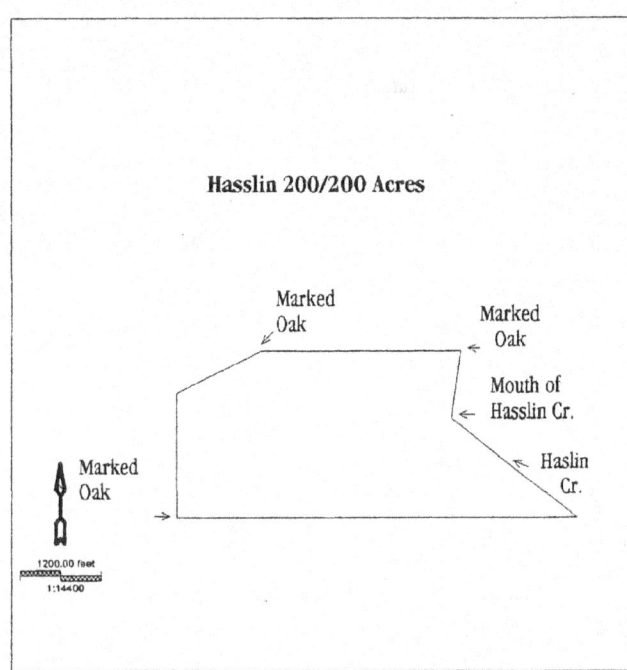

Know yee that wee for and in consideration that Jerome Hasslin hath transported himself and one servant into this Province here to inhabit. Upon such considerations and terms as are exprefsed in our Conditions of Plantation of our s'd Province of Maryland, doe hereby grant unto the s'd Jerome Hasslin all that tract or parcell of land lying in the County of Ann Arundell within this Province of Maryland, lying on the west side of Chesapeake Bay and on the south side of the South River beginning at a marked Oak near the mouth of Hasslin Cr.

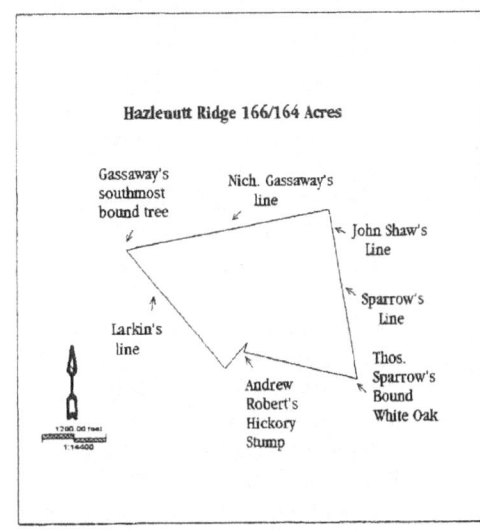

Hazlenutt Ridge Resurveyed (Richard Tideings) 7/13/1680 – 166/164 acres. LCB2i/14 SR7366

Know ye that whereas **John Gray** of Ann Arundell County in our s'd Province of Maryland both by Letters Pattents dated 9/28/1665, had granted unto him a parcell of land within the aforesaid County called Hazlenutt Ridge then laid out for two hundred acres whereof Richard Tideings of the same County who purchased and had posfesfion of the same for severall years. Alleging that through the mistakes of the surveyors in returning the Cert thereof to the clerk of his LOP's office and entering the same upon record, the bounds of the s'd tract as certified in the Letters Pattents were not according to the survey thereof. He hath humbly supplicated a Speciall Warrant to resurvey the same according to the true intent of the first survey and laying out thereof which was accordingly granted unto the s'd Richard Tydings having accordingly thereupon caused the parcell of land to be resurveyed up to the original grant to John Gray into our Office for Lands to be vacated upon record. We do therefore grant and confirm unto the s'd Richard Tydings all that parcel of land now resurveyed called Hazlenutt Ridge lying in Ann Arundell County near the head of the Road River beginning at the southmost bound tree of **Nicholas Gassaway** now in the posfesfion of **Thomas Smithrick**. *Also adjoins The Triangle (Thomas Taylor) and land owned by Thomas Sparrow. Note: The patent document spells the name both ways, i.e., Tideings and Tydings.*

Hedge Park (Thomas Hedge) 5/29/1675 – 94/76 acres. L8/381 SR7359

Know yee that for and in consideration that Thomas Hedge of Ann Arundell County in our s'd Province of Maryland hath due unto him ninety four acres of land within our s'd Province parte of a warrant for nine hundred thirty acres granted him 3/7/1673, as appears on record. Upon such considerations and terms as are exprefsed in our Conditions of Plantation of our s'd Province of Maryland, doe hereby grant unto the s'd Hedge a parcell of land called Hedge Park lying in Ann Arundell County on a creek of the Road River called Harwood's Cr. beginning at a bounded Red Oak being a bound tree of land now in the possession of the s'd Hedge, called *Margaret's Field* near the head of a creek called Hasslin Creek and running with the head lines of lands owned by **Adam DeLapp** and **Thomas Lynecomb**. *Also adjoins Harwood's Br.*

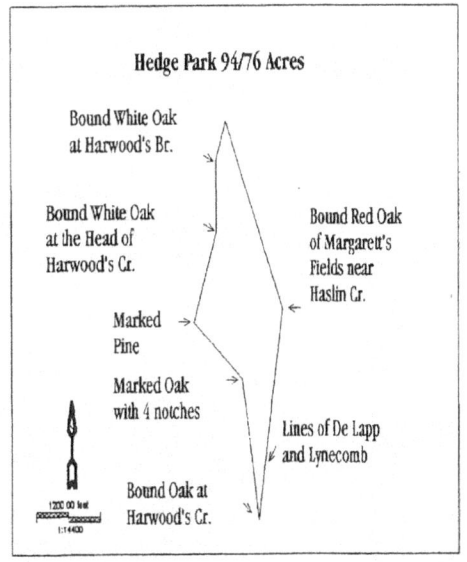

Herring's Purchase (John Herring) 1/26/1684 – 205/209 acres. L22/194 SR7363

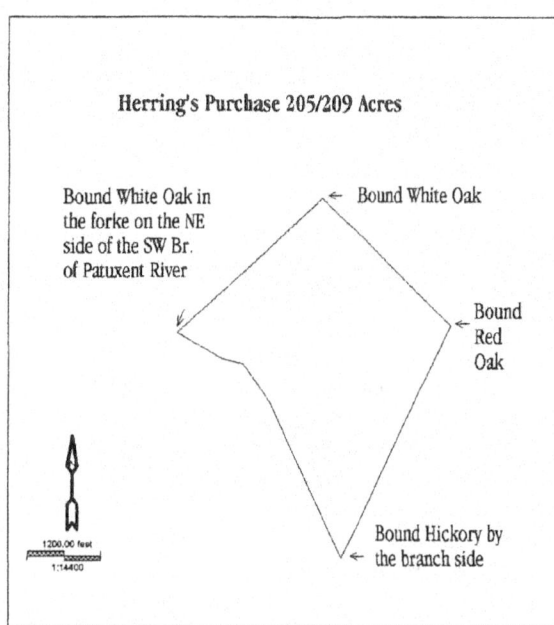

By virtue of a warrant granted unto **John Dorsey** of this County for two hundred forty acres of land dated 1/30/1683/4, one hundred sixty acres thereof were afsigned unto John Herring, Carpenter, of this County. Also, forty five acres of land, it being a parte of a warrant granted unto the s'd Dorsey for two hundred acres of land dated 10/4/1684, was also afsigned unto the s'd Herring as appears on record. These are therefore to certifie that I hath laid out for the s'd Herring a parcell of land called Herring's Purchase lying in the forke of the Patuxant River and on the Northeast side of the Southwest Branch. Begins at a bounded White Oak. *Note: Patent not found.*

Hester's Habitation (Hester Beard) 6/24/1679 - 118/124 acres. L20/187 SR7361

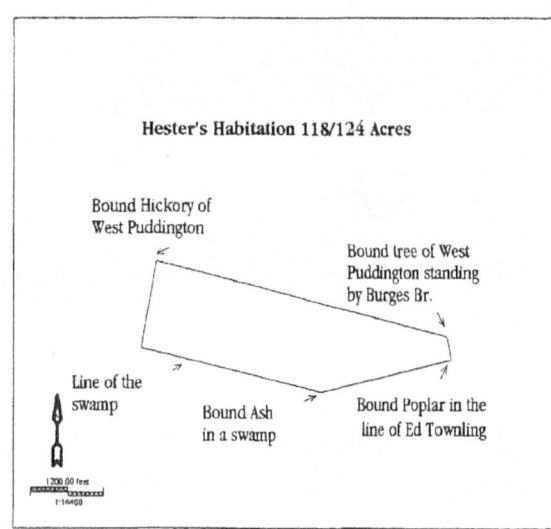

Know yee that for and in consideration that Hester Beard of Ann Arundell County in our s'd Province of Maryland hath due unto her one hundred eighteen acres of land within our s'd Province by afsignment from **George Yate** part of a warrant for two thousand and ninety one acres granted to the s'd Yate 3/7/1678, as appears on record. Upon such considerations and terms as are exprefsed in our Conditions of Plantation of our Province of Maryland, doe grant unto the s'd Hester Beard a parcell of land called Hester's Habitation lying in the s'd County on the south side of the South River in the woods beginning at a bound Oak standing on the north side of a branch called Burges His Branch, it being a bound tree of *West Puddington. Also adjoins the land of Edward Townling (probably Edward Townhill).*

Hickory Hills (Robert Franklin) 1667 – 550/530 acres. L11/213 SR7353

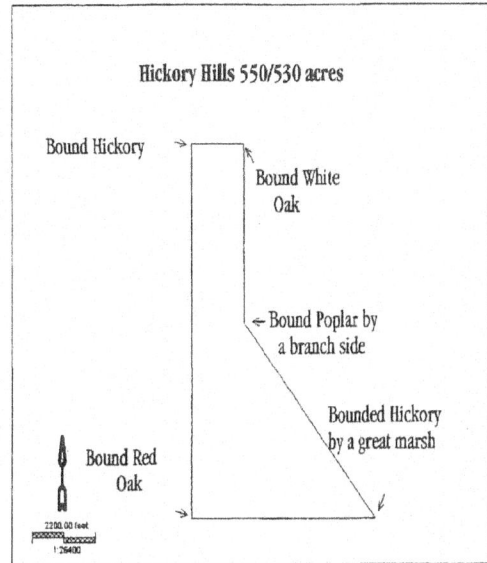

Know yee that for and in consideration that Robert Franklin, Merchant, of Anne Arundall County hath due two hundred acres of land by asfignment from **Capt. William Burgess** the afsignee of **George Nettlefold** for his, the s'd Nettlefold's, having transported himself and his wife into our Province to inhabit. Also, one hundred fifty acres more by afsignment of **George Yate**, Gent, the afsignee of **Thomas Cole**, part of a warrant for 300 acres formerly granted to him the s'd Cole and **Robert Simkin**. And also, two hundred acres more for the s'd Franklin for transporting himself, **William Stimson, Ann Hatt**, and **Augustine Skinner** into our Province here to inhabit. Within the considerations and termes of our Conditions of Plantation doe grant unto the said Franklin a parcell of land in Anne Arundall County called Hickory Hills lying about four miles from the South River beginning at a bound Hickory tree on a hill near a great marsh. *Adjoins The Friend's Choice (Jones & Gray).*

Honest Man's Lott (John Duvall) 7/23/1704 –110/119 acres. LCD/220 SR7376

Know yee that for and in consideration that John Duvall of Ann Arundell County in our Province of Maryland hath due unto him one hundred ten and one half acres of land within our s'd Province being due unto him by virtue of a warrant for two hundred ten acres granted him 6/24/1704, as appears on record. Upon such considerations and terms as are exprefsed in our Conditions of Plantation of our Province of Maryland, wee doe therefore hereby grant unto the s'd Duvall all that tract or parcel of land called Honest Man's Lott lying in the s'd County on the North Branch of the head of the South River beginning at a bound Poplar standing by a gate post which stands by a roadside which leads from the house of **Richard Warfield** to **Mrs. Ruth Howard's** door. *Adjoins The Good Mother's Endeavor and Howard and Porter's Range (both tracts are in the Middle Neck Hundred).*

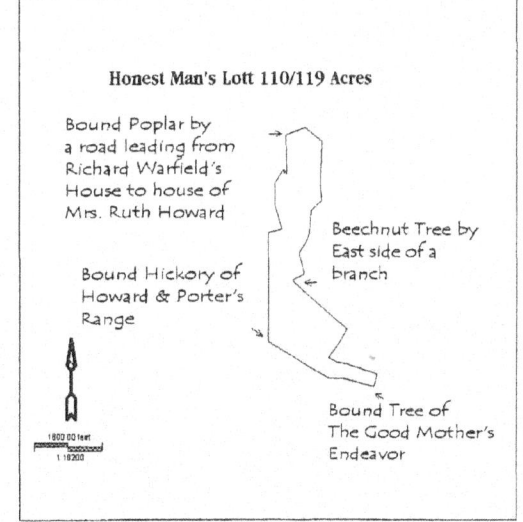

Hugging's Advantage (Richard Huggings) 8/5/1664 – 50/50 acres. L7/294 SR7349

Know yee that wee for and in consideration that Richard Huggings of Ann Arundell County hath due unto him fifty acres of land within our s'd Province by afsignment of **John Version** who hath transported **John Hutton** into this Province to inhabit Anno 1657, as appears on record. Upon such considerations and terms as are exprefsed in our Conditions of Plantation of our s'd Province of Maryland, wee doe hereby grant unto the s'd Richard Huggings a parcel of land called Hugging's Advantage lying in Ann Arundell County adjoining the plantation he now liveth upon beginning at a marked Oak on the south side of the South River. *Adjoins the land of Archibald Arbuckle and Ann Covell (Covell's Folly).*

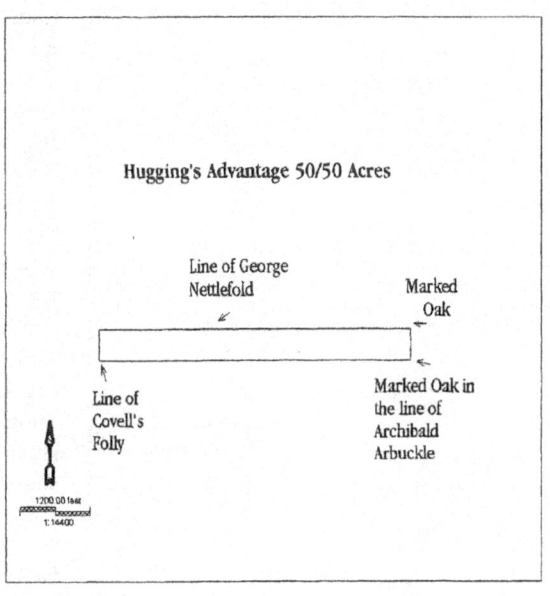

Jacob's Point (James Smith) undated -21/19 acres. L21/280 SR 7362

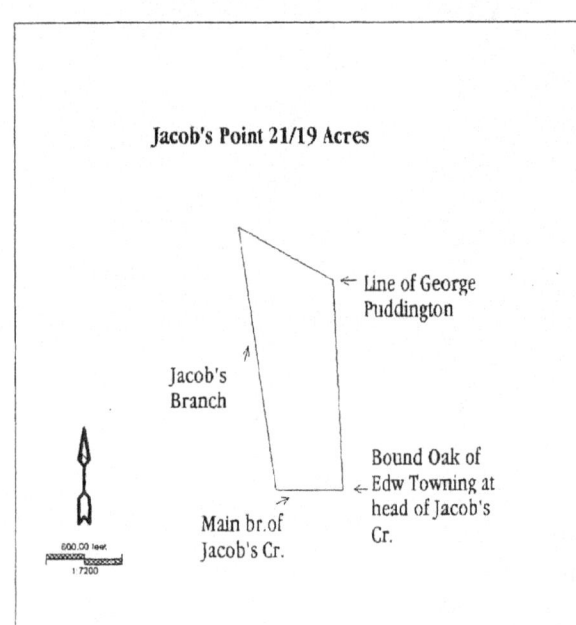

By virtue of a warrant granted unto **George Holland** of Ann Arundell County for three hundred thirty acres of land dated 10/3/last past, twenty one acres was afsigned by the s'd Holland to James Smith as appears on record. These prefents are to certifie that I **George Yate**, Deputy Surveyor, hath laid out a parcell of land for the s'd Smith called Jacob's Point beginning at a bound Oak of **Ed Towning** lying on the south side of the South River at the head of Jacob's Cr. *Also adjoins land owned by George Puddington.* Note: No patent was found. This tract is included because of the many references to it. It was most likely patented at some point.

John's Cabbin Ridge (Richard Beard) 9/18/1666 – 30/30 acres. L10/748 SR7352

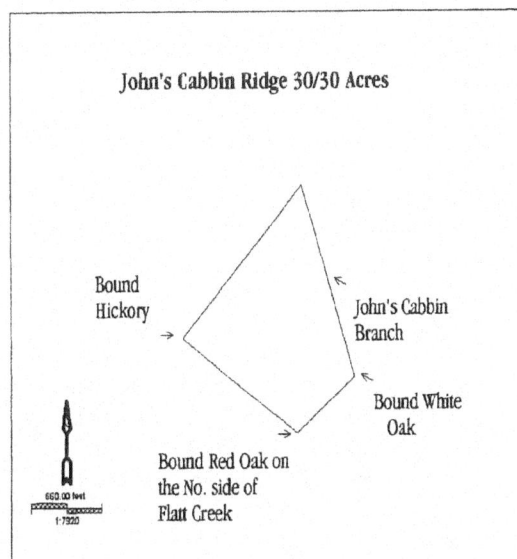

Know yee that for and in consideration that Richard Beard of our Province of Maryland, Boatwright, hath due unto him thirty acres of land within our s'd Province out of his warrant for six hundred twenty acres as appears on record. Upon such considerations and terms as are exprefsed in our Conditions of Plantation of our s'd Province of Maryland, doe hereby grant unto the s'd Richard Beard a parcell of land called John's Cabbin Ridge lying in Ann Arundell County beginning at a bound Red Oake standing on the north side of the main branch of a creek called The Flatt Creek. *Also adjoins John's Cabbin Br. (of Flatt Cr.).*

Jones His Lott (William Jones) 8/8/1673 – 350/332 acres. L13/43 SR7355

Know yee that for and in consideration that William Jones of the County of Calvert in our s'd Province of Maryland hath due unto him three hundred fifty acres of land within our s'd Province the remainder of a warrant for one thousand seven hundred fifty acres to him formerly granted as appears on record. Upon such considerations and terms as are exprefsed in our Conditions of Plantation of our s'd Province of Maryland doe hereby grant unto the s'd William Jones a parcell of land called Jones His Lott lying in Ann Arundell County in the woods beginning at a bound Oak being the northernmost bound tree of land laid out for the **Stockets** of the s'd County, Gents. *Also adjoins tracts owned by Robert Franklin and Richard Beard.*

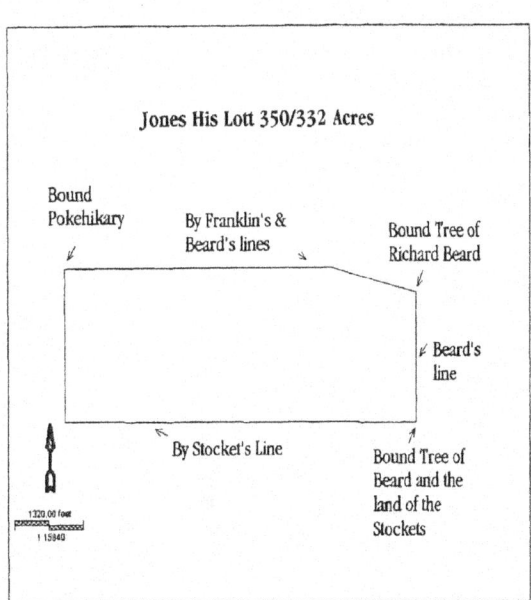

King's Venture (Joseph King) 10/10/1704 – 50/51 acres. LDSF/528 SR7373-2

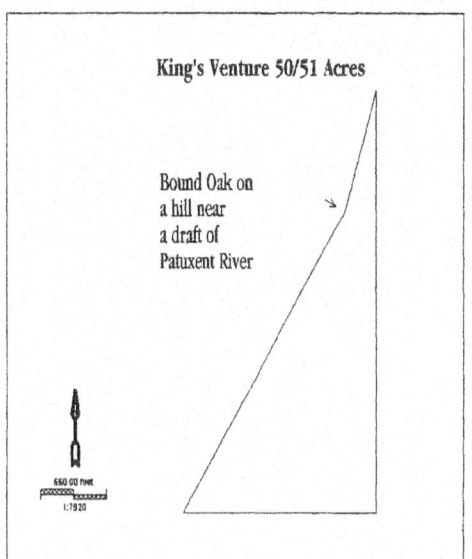

Know yee that for and in consideration that Joseph King of Ann Arundell County in our s'd Province of Maryland hath due unto him fifty acres of land within our s'd Province by virtue of a warrant for the same quantity granted 5/20/1704, as appears on record in our Land Office. Upon such considerations and terms as are exprefsed in our Conditions of Plantation of our Province of Maryland, wee doe therefore hereby grant unto him the s'd Joseph King all that tract or parcel of land called King's Venture lying in the s'd County on the Forke of Patuxent River beginning at a bounded Oak upon a hill near a draft of the s'd River. *Note: Liber DSF has three adjoining yet different versions of folio 528 (with the third version included twice). This patent is found on the "middle," or second, version.*

Lappston (Adam De Lapp) 2/16/1659 – 300/283 acres. L4/509 SR7346

Know yee that we for and in consideration that Adam De Lapp of this Province, Planter, hath due unto him one hundred acres of land in this Province afsigned unto him by **Thomas Emerson** of this Province. Upon such considerations and terms as are exprefsed in our Conditions of Plantation in our s'd Province of Maryland, do hereby grant unto the s'd Adam De Lapp a parcel of land called Lappston lying on the West side of Chesapeake Bay near the mouth of a river called the South River next adjoining to the land of **William Pennington** *(Pennington's Pound).* Begins at a marked Oak by a pond called Pennington's Pond.

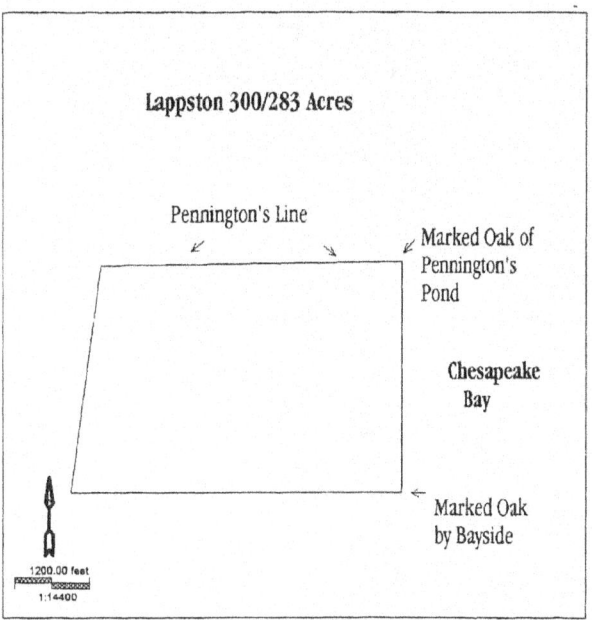

Lappston (Adam De Lapp) 8/5/1664 – 50/50 acres.   L7/340 SR7349

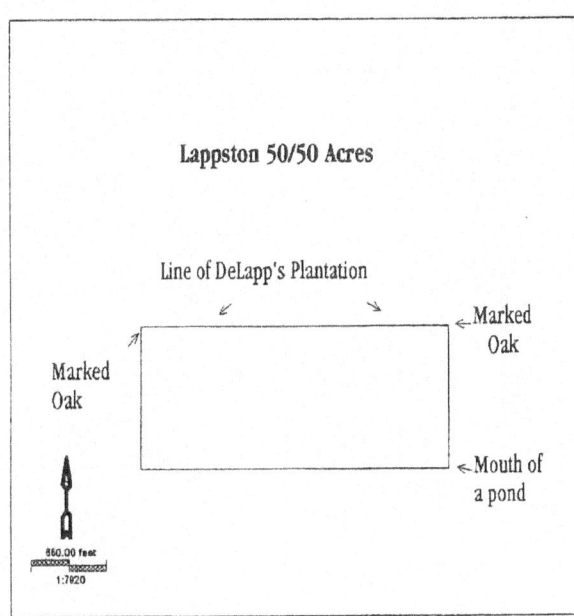

Know yee that wee for and in consideration that Adam De Lapp of this Province, Planter, hath due unto him fifty acres of land within our s'd Province by afsignment of **Phillip Allamby**. Upon such considerations and terms as are exprefsed in our Conditions of Plantation of our s'd Province of Maryland, do hereby grant unto the s'd De Lapp a parcel of land called Lappston lying in the s'd County on the south side of the South River beginning at a marked Oak. *Adjoins a plantation already owned by DeLapp also called Lappston.*

Larkin's Choice (John Larkin) 8/12/1670 – 311/311 acres. L14/44 SR7356

Know yee that we for and in consideration that John Larkin of the County of Ann Arundell in our s'd Province of Maryland, Planter, hath due unto him three hundred eleven acres of land within our s'd Province by afsignment from **George Yate** out of a warrant formerly granted to the s'd Yate for eight hundred sixty five acres, as appears on record. Upon such considerations and terms as are exprefsed in our Conditions of Plantation of our s'd Province of Maryland, doe hereby grant unto the s'd John Larkin a parcell of land called Larkin's Choice beginning at a bound Oake, it being the south by west boundary of a parcel of land the aforesaid Larkin bought from **John Champe.**

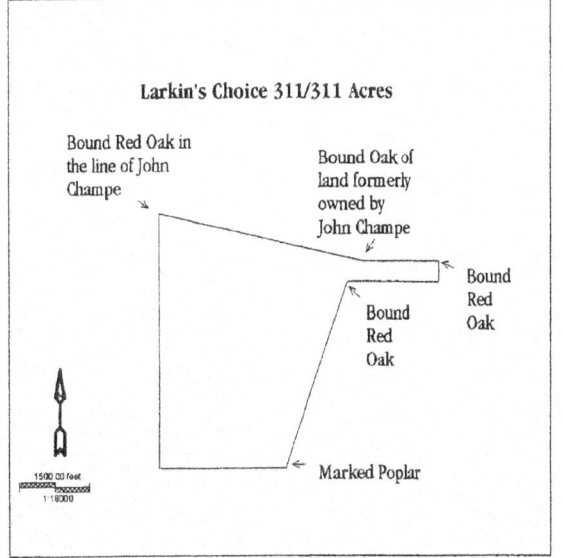

Larkington (John Brewer) 9/2/1663 – 300 acres. L5/462 SR7347

Know yee that wee for and in consideration that **Ellis Brown** of this Province, Planter, hath due unto him three hundred acres of land within our s'd Province for transporting himself, **Edward Stone,** and **John Macubbin** into this Province here to inhabit in Anno 1649, which land the s'd Ellis Brown afsigned unto **John Larkin,** Planter, and the s'd Larkin afsigned it again unto John Brewer, of this Province, Gent, as appears on record. Upon such conditions and terms as are exprefsed in our Conditions of Plantation of our Province of Maryland, do hereby grant unto the s'd John Brewer a parcell of land called Larkinton lying on the west side of Chesapeake Bay on the south side of the South River beginning at a marked Oak by a creek called Pyther's Creek. *Also adjoins the South River and Edward Selby's land. Note: The tract cannot be drawn because only one of the five courses specified include both distance and direction data.*

Lark's Hill (John Larkin) 6/26/1663 450/296 acres. L5/359 SR7347

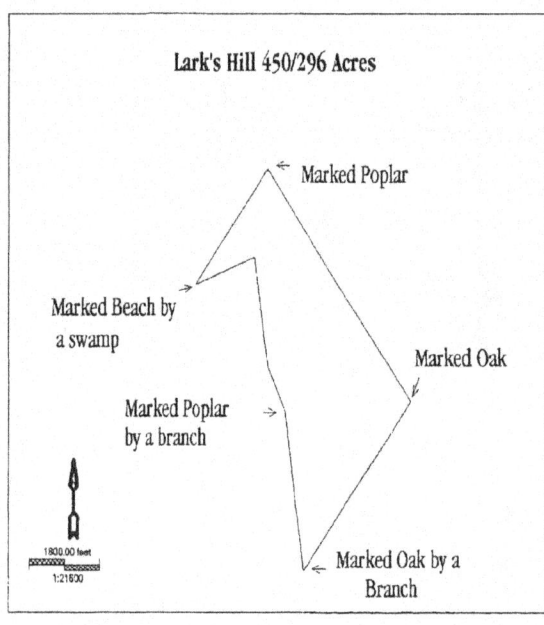

Know yee that wee for and in consideration that John Larkin of this Province, Planter, hath due unto him four hundred fifty acres of land within our s'd Province afsigned him from **Thomas Taylor** of Ann Arundell County, Planter, as appears on record. Upon such considerations and terms as are exprefsed in our Conditions of Plantation of our s'd Province of Maryland, doe hereby grant unto the s'd John Larkin a parcell of land called Lark's Hill lying in Ann Arundell County to the westward of a creek in the Road River called Muddy Creek about two miles from the s'd creek in the woods upon the branches of the Patuxent River beginning at a marked Beach tree by a swamp.

Lavall (Marin Duvall) 1658 - 100/100 acres. L4/259 SR 7346

Marin DuVall demands fifty acres of Land having performed his time of Service with **John Covill** (*after being*) brought and (*transported*) by **William Burges**. Warrant for 50 acres (*to*) return December 25th next. (*July 20, 1659, L4/60*). Upon such conditions and terms as are exprefsed in our Conditions of Plantation doe hereby grant unto the s'd Duvall a tract called Lavall, lying on the West side of Chesapeake Bay and on the West side of a River called the South River and on the Westernmost Branch of the said River near the head, respecting the land of **John Freeman** (*Freeman's Fancy*) on the north, beginning at a marked Oak by a Branch (Western Branch of South River) and

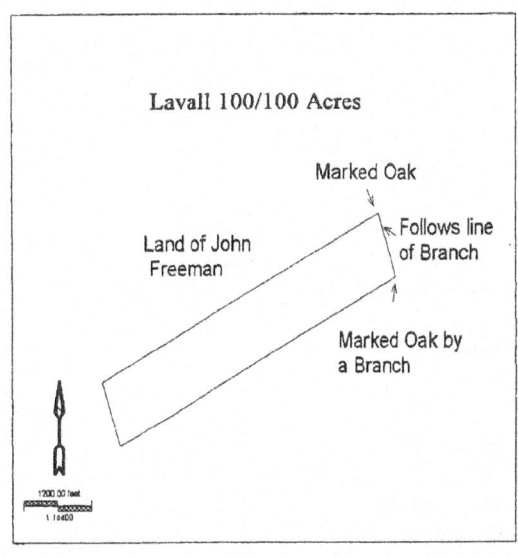

running down to the main Branch. *Note 1: The Certificate for Lavall (January 20, 1659, L4/431) states that, "Marin Duvall hath performed his time of Service within this our Province and hath fifty acres more afsigned unto him by Tobias Butler due to the said Butler for performing his (own) time of Service in accordance with Conditions of Plantation. Note 2: This tract was eventually resurveyed into Godwell.*

Lawe's Chance (William Lawe) 5/27/1675 – 46/44 acres. L19/16 SR7360

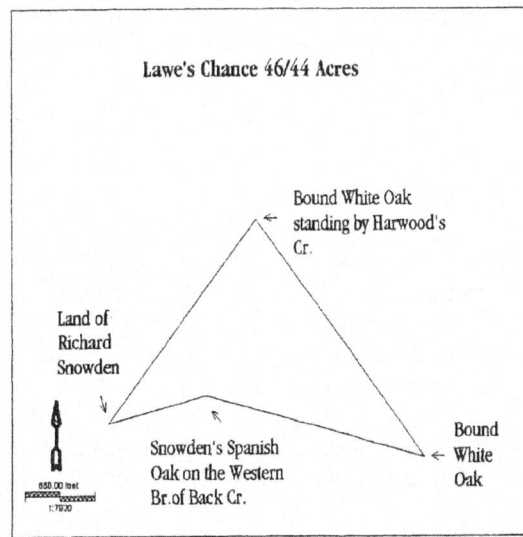

Know yee that wee for and in consideration that William Lawe of Ann Arrundell County in our s'd Province of Maryland hath due unto him forty six acres of and within our s'd Province by afsignment of **George Yate**, parte of a warrant for twelve hundred acres of land granted to the s'd Yate 10/1/1673, as appears on record. Upon such considerations and terms as are exprefsed in our Conditions of Plantation of our s'd Province of Maryland, doe hereby grant unto the s'd William Lawe all that parcell of land called Lawe's Chance in the County of Ann Arundell on a branch of the Road River beginning at a bound Spanish Oak of **Richard Snowden** on the western branch of a creek called Back Creek. *Also adjoins Harwood's Cr.*

Linham's Search (John Linham) 6/12/1688 – 38/41 acres. LNSB2i/718 SR7371

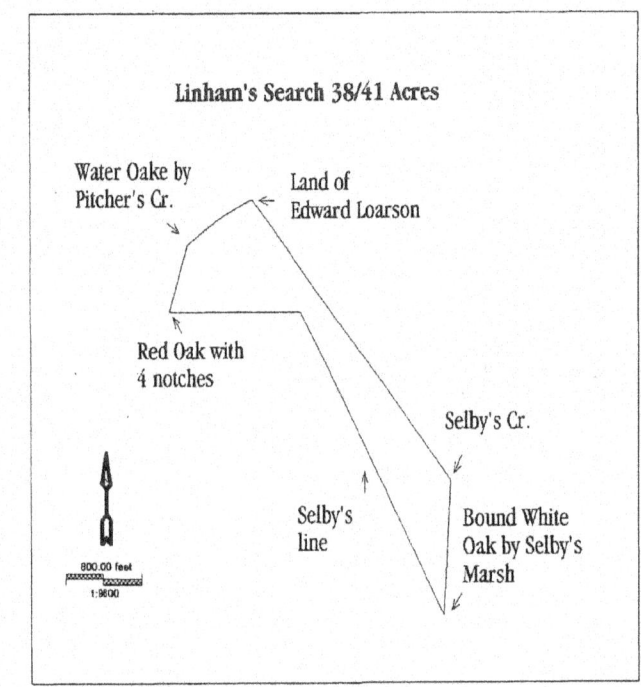

Linham's Search 38/41 Acres

Know yee that we for and in consideration that John Linham of Ann Arundell County in our s'd Province of Maryland hath due unto him thirty eight acres of land within our s'd Province by afsignment of **Thomas Richardson** of Baltimore County, part of a warrant for two thousand eight hundred eighty two acres granted unto the s'd Richardson 2/27/1677, as appears on record. Upon such considerations and terms as are exprefsed in our Conditions of Plantation of our s'd Province of Maryland, wee doe therefore hereby grant unto the s'd John Linham all that tract or parcell of land called Linham's Search lying on the south side of the South River on the north side of Selby's Creek beginning at a bound White Oake by a marsh called Selby's Marsh. *Also adjoins Pyther's Creek and tracts owned by **Edward Selby, John Brewer**, and **Edward Loarson**.*

Linnescomb's Lott (Thomas Linnescomb) 5/22/1679 – 70 acres. L20/256 SR7361
Know yee that wee for and in consideration that Thomas Linnescomb of Ann Arundell County in our s'd Province of Maryland hath due unto him seventy acres of land within our s'd Province by afsignment from **George Yate,** parte of a warrant for five hundred acres granted to the s'd Yate 10/21/1678, as appears on record. Upon such considerations and terms as are exprefsed in our Conditions of Plantation of our s'd Province of Maryland, doe hereby grant unto the s'd Thomas Linnescomb all that parcell of land called Linnescomb's Lott lying in the s'd County on the north side of Three Island Bay beginning at a bound White Oak standing at the head of a pond called The Great Pond. *Also adjoins Back Cr., Deep Cr., and the land of **Adam DeLapp**.*

Linthicum Walks (Thomas Linthicum)   10/10/1704 – 631/624 acres.   LRYi/368 SR7468

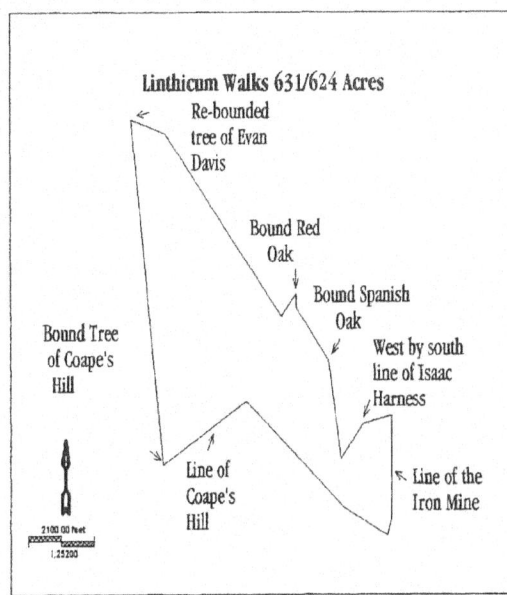

Whereas Thomas Linthicum of Ann Arundell County by his humble petition to our Agent taken this day of September 1701, was seized in fee simple of two severall tracts of land in the s'd County called *Davis's Rest* containing two hundred acres and *Gray's Addition* containing three hundred acres and both contiguous one to the other within the bounds hereinafter thereof and adjacent thereto. The s'd Thomas concedes there might be land surplus and vacancy. Whereupon he humbly prays a Speciall Warrant to resurvey them with the power to include all surplus land and to add any contiguous vacancy and that upon return of a certificate of any such resurvey and upon making good rights for such vacancy and corresponding for the surplus (if any) he might have our Letters Pattents for the whole if we thought fitt to condiscend unto *(him)*.

Accordingly, such warrant did issue by value of which it is certified to our Land Office *(that)* there is no surplus contained in any of the tracts but that there is a quantity of one hundred thirty acres of vacant land added thereunto and he, the s'd Thomas, made rights by paying unto **Coll Henry Darnall**, our Agent in our Province, of twenty five pounds. Wee doe therefore grant unto the s'd Thomas Linthicum both tracts together with the vacancy all reduced into one tract called Linthicum Walks. *Note: The patent is dated 10/10/1701. However, the Certification (FF7/103, 9/10/1716) includes a note at the end as follows, "Then issued Pat for the above land to the s'd Tho pursuant to the foregoing cert."*

Littletown (John Sumers)   10/10/1704 – 280/269 acres.   LDSF/518 SR7373-2

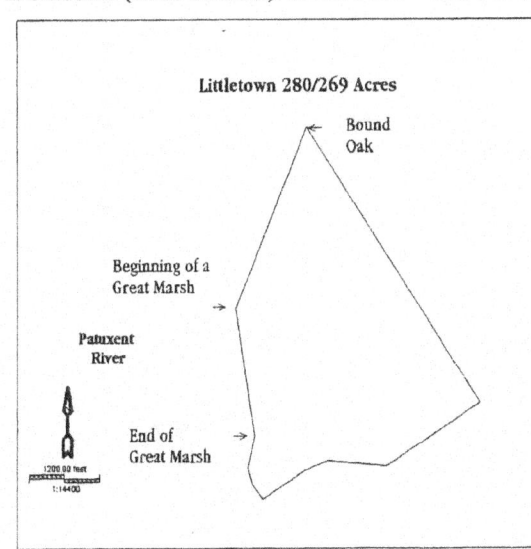

Know yee that for and in consideration that John Sumers of Ann Arundell County in our s'd Province of Maryland hath due unto him two hundred and eighty acres of land within our s'd Province being due unto him by virtue of a warrant for the same quantity granted 1/2/1703, as appears on record in our Land Office. Upon such considerations and terms as are exprefsed in our Conditions of Plantation of our s'd Province, wee doe therefore hereby grant unto the s'd John Sumers all that tract or parcell of land called Littletown lying in the forke of Patuxent River to the North of the North Branch beginning at a bounded Oak.

Love's Neck (Robert Love) 8/12/1664 – 50/45 acres. L7/246 SR7349

Know yee that wee for and in consideration that Robert Love of this Province, Planter, hath due unto him fifty acres of land within our s'd Province by afsignment from **Robert Loyd**, as appears on record. Upon such considerations and terms as are exprefsed in our Conditions of Plantation of our s'd Province of Maryland, do hereby grant unto the s'd Robert Love a parcell of land called Love's Neck lying on the north side of the Road River in Ann Arundell County adjoining the land he now liveth upon between Shaw's Creek and Wollman Creek beginning at a marked Red Oak standing by the side of Shaw's Cr.

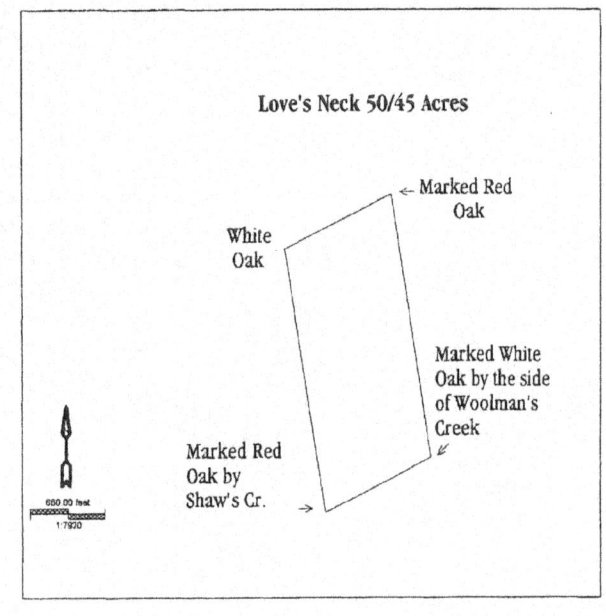

Lugg Ox (John Duvall) 7/9/1702 – 780/1,010 acres. LCD/82 SR7376

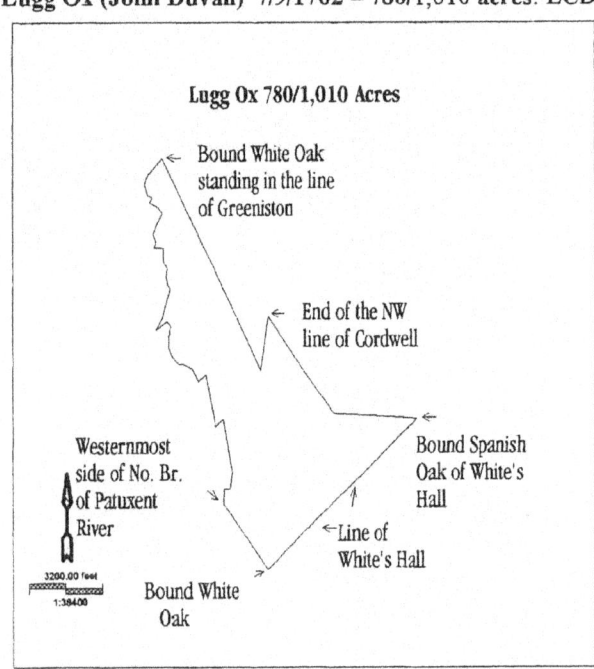

Know yee that for and in consideration that John Duvall of Ann Arundell County in our s'd Province of Maryland hath due unto him seven hundred eighty acres of land within our s'd Province being due unto him by virtue of a warrant for one thousand acres of land granted him 9/29/1701, as appears on record in our land office. Upon such considerations and terms as are exprefsed in our Conditions of Plantation wee doe therefore hereby grant unto the s'd John Duvall all that tract or parcell of land called Lugg Ox lying on the east side of the No. Branch of Patuxent River beginning at a bound Spanish Oake of White's **(Jerome White)** land called *White's Hall*.

Maddox Adventure (Thomas Maddox) 6/4/1683 – 148/147 acres. LSDA/422 SR7369

Know yee that for and in consideration that Thomas Maddox of Ann Arundell County in our s'd Province of Maryland hath due unto him one hundred forty eight acres of land by afsignment of **George Yate,** parte of a warrant for one thousand and fifty acres of land granted to the s'd Yate 6/19/1678, as appears on record. Upon such considerations and terms as are exprefsed in our Conditions of Plantation of our Province of Maryland, doe hereby grant unto the s'd Thomas Maddox a parcel of land called Maddox Adventure lying on the south side of South River in the woods beginning at a bound Oak of land called *Roper's Range. Also adjoins branches of Patuxent River and a meadow called Long Meadow.*

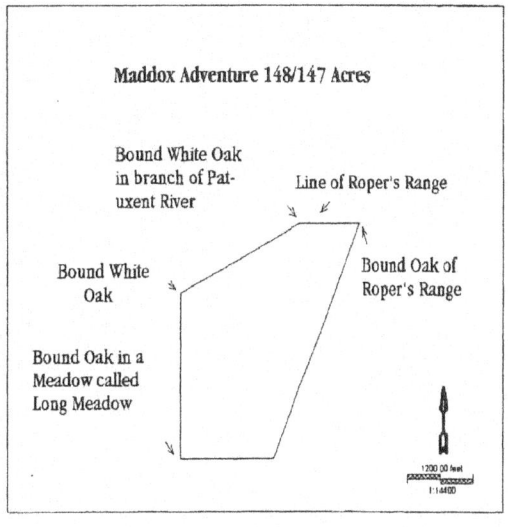

<u>Margaret's Fields Res.</u> **(George Saughier) 7/14/1670 – 280/264 acres. L12/590 SR7356**
Whereas by our deed of grant of 27 August 1658, for the considerations therein, granted unto **William Pell,** afsignee of **William Pennington,** a parcell of land formerly conveyed to the s'd Pennington lying near the mouth of the South River containing by estimate two hundred and eighty acres of land. And whereas the s'd parcell of land by severall means afsignments to is Vested and Sotted in George Saughier of Ann Arundell County within our Province of Maryland. Whereas the s'd Saughier hath since resurveyed the same parcel of land, we doe hereby grant unto the s'd George Saughier all that parcel of land resurveyed called Margaret's Field lying in Ann Arundell County beginning at Pennington's Ponds near the mouth of the s'd ponds as near as an East Course will carry from the North side of a point called Bene's Point and running from the South River west over the ponds near unto Hasting's *(probably Haslin's)* Creek. *Note 1: This resurvey and grant resulted from a dispute caused by an error in a survey in 1650, issued to William Pennington and assigned to and patented by William Pell, who sold the tract to George Saughier. Upon Pell's death the conflicting boundary was discovered by his executor who brought the matter to the attention of **Jerome White Esq.**, Surveyor General. White recommended that his cousin Deputy Surveyor **George Yate,** who was familiar with the matter, resurvey the land and recommend corrected boundaries to the Commissioners to determine and order corrective measures (L12/550). Following the resurvey, the decision was made to grant this resurveyed parcel to Saughier, the person determined to be the most affected by the boundary error. On July 13, 1670, Saughier sent word to **M. Blomfield,** Chief Clerk of the Land Office, that he would pay double rent if he may have his patent "now immediately." Phillip Calvert then issued the following to Mr. Blomfield, "Do order you to dispatch it immediately to be sent to him by the bearer **Richard Mascole**" (L12/590). Note 2: The tract cannot be drawn because the boundary courses are incomplete. However, the tract has been drawn from the courses specified in the original patent (to William Pell). See "Unnamed Patent, William Pell" (8/27/1658 LQ/116/SR7345).*

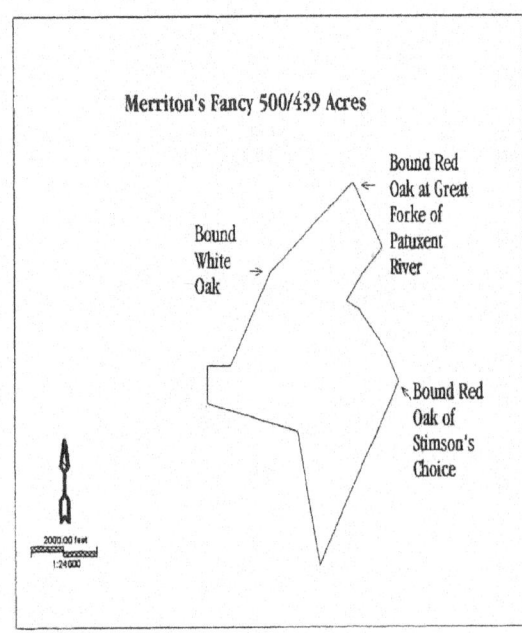

Merriton's Fancy (John Merriton)
6/5/1687 – 500/439 acres. LIB&ILC/268 SR7368-1

Know yee that wee for and in consideration that John Merriton of Ann Arundell County in our Province of Maryland hath due unto him five hundred acres of land within our s'd Province being due to the s'd Merriton by a warrant for the same quantity grant unto him on 10/6/1685, as appears on record. Upon such considerations and terms as are exprefsed in our Conditions of Plantation of our Province of Maryland, wee doe hereby grant unto the s'd John Merriton all that tract or parcel of land called Merriton's Fancy lying in the forke of the North Great Branch of the Patuxent River. Begins at a bounded Red Oak, a bound tree of **John Stinson**, by the s'd Branch.

Middle Plantation (Marin Duvall) 9/4/1664 – 600/585 acres. L7/451-3 SR7349

Know yee that wee for and in consideration that Marin Duvall of this Province hath due unto him two hundred fifty acres of land within this Province by afsignment of **John Ewan** and fifty acres more by afsigment of **Thomas Pierson** and three hundred acres more by afsignment of a warrant from **Andrew Skinner,** as appears on record. Upon such considerations and termes as are exprefsed in our Conditions of Plantation of this our Province of Maryland, wee doe therefore grant unto the s'd Marin Duvall all that tract or parcell of land called Middle Plantation lying in the s'd County on the south side *(actually, the west side)* of the South River between the lands formerly laid out for **George Nettlefold, Ann Covill, George Walker,** and **George Puddington.**

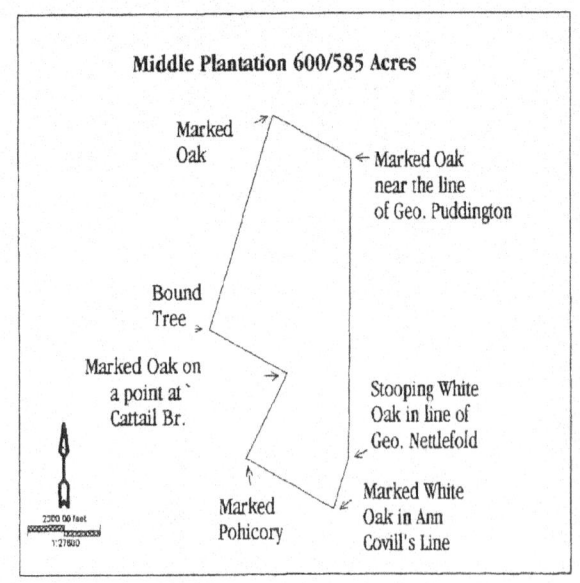

Middle Plantation Res. (Lewis Duvall) 10/10/1708 - 844/1,217 acres. LDD5i/511 SR7378

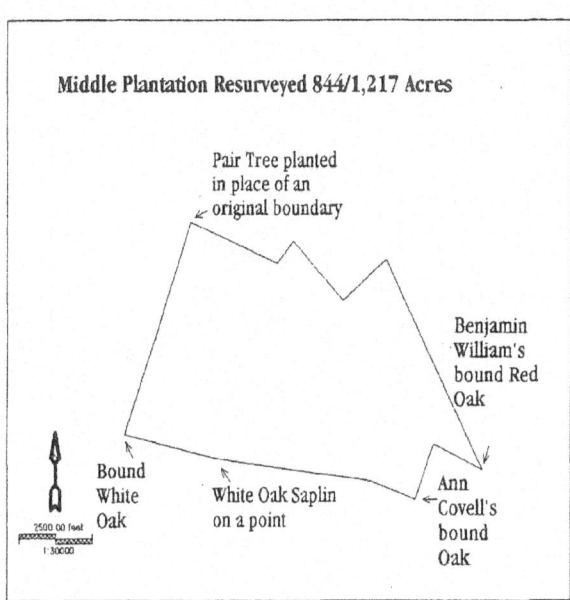

Whereas Lewis Duvall of Ann Arundell County, Gent, did obtain a Speciall Warrant for the resurvey of a tract called Middle Plantation originally surveyed for his father **Marin Duvall** in two parcells but inserted into one grant and, whereas there is found to be two omissions in the survey and the s'd Lewis requested upon resurvey that the s'd tract might be one these are to certify that I have resurveyed the s'd Middle Plantation according to the bounds to me showne beginning at a bounded Red Oak on a parcell of land of one **Benjamin Williams**. Then issued Pattent for the above land to the above Duvall pursuant to the above *(Special Warrant)*.

Mitchell's Addition (William Mitchell) 12/17/1704 – 18.5/18 acres. LDD#5/211 SR7378

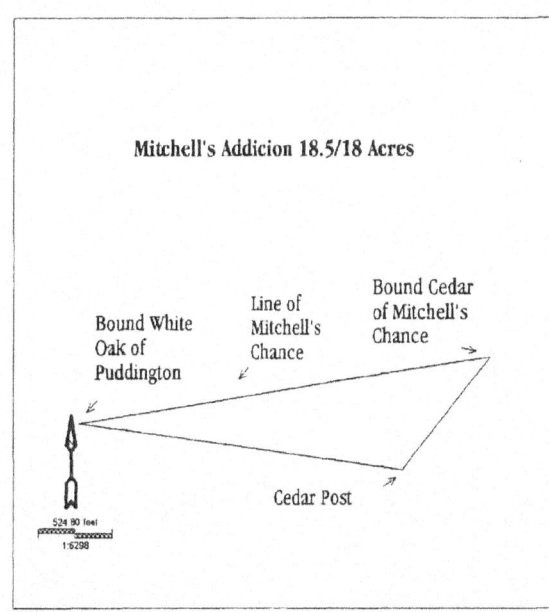

By virtue of a warrant granted to **Thomas Larkin** of Ann Arundell County for one hundred acres of land bearing the date 1704, being due to him by virtue of a warrant for the same quantity granted to him 3/2/1703, eighteen and one half acres of which was afsigned by the s'd Larkin to William Mitchell of Ann Arundell County as appears on record. These are to certify that I Thomas Larkin, Deputy Surveyor, hath laid out a parcel of land called Mitchell's Addition lying in Ann Arundell County on the south side of the South River beginning at a bound White Oak of a tract called *Puddington* and also a bound tree of a land called *Mitchell's Chance*, and also a bound tree of a land called *Poplar Neck*. Then issued patt for the above land to the s'd Mitchell pursuant to the above warrant.

Morley's Grove (**Joseph Morley**) 7/10/1674 – 320 acres. L14/270 SR7356
Know yee that for and in consideration that Joseph Morley of Ann Arundell County in our s'd Province of Maryland hath due unto him three hundred twenty acres of land within our s'd Province by virtue of a warrant for one thousand two hundred fifty acres granted to the s'd Morley and *(to)* **Marin Duvall** 6/20/1670, as appears on record. The s'd Duvall hath afsigned, sold, and made over unto the s'd Morley all his right, title, and interest in and of the s'd warrant, as appears on record. Upon such considerations and terms as are exprefsed in our Conditions of Plantation of our s'd Province of Maryland, wee doe hereby grant unto the s'd Joseph Morely all that parcell of land called Morley's Grove lying in Ann Arundell County on a branch of the Patuxent River.
Note: The tract cannot be drawn because the seventh course lacks direction.

Morley's Lott (Joseph Morley) 7/10/1671 – **450/471 acres.** L16/260 SR7357
Know yee that wee for and in consideration that Joseph Morley of Ann Arundell County in our s'd

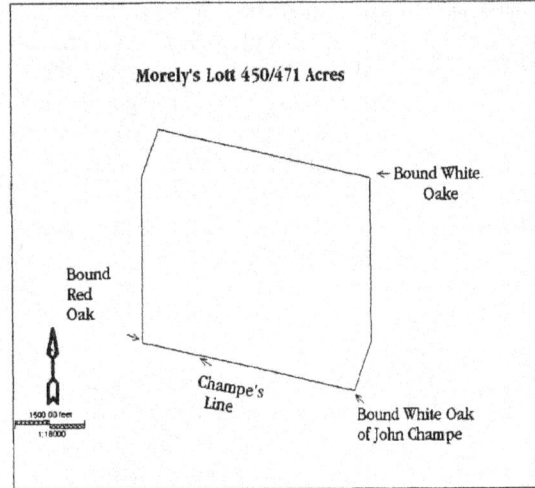

Province of Maryland hath due unto him four hundred fifty acres of land within our s'd Province part of a warrant for twelve hundred fifty acres to the s'd Morley and **Marin Duvall** afsigned 6/9/1670, as appears on record. The s'd Duvall hath afsigned to the s'd Morley all right, title, and interest in and to the same as appears on record. Upon such considerations and terms as are exprefsed in our Conditions of Plantation of this our Province of Maryland, wee doe therefore hereby grant unto the s'd Joseph Morley all that parcel of land called Morley's Lott lying about three miles in the woods at the west side of the South River beginning at a bounded White Oak.
*Adjoins Champe's Adventure and Soldier's Delight. Note (from MSA Tract Index 73): Devised to **Robert Proctor** & **John Gaither** for their lifetimes. Then, to heirs at law (of Morley) or to escheat. Chancery Court ruled for Proctor and Gaither who sold the tract for 6,000 lbs tobacco in 1679 (IH#2/1).*

Nettlefold (George Nettlefold) 9/17/1666 - **200/200 acres.** L5/289 SR7347
Know yee that wee for and in consideration that George Nettlefold of this Province, Planter, hath due unto him two hundred acres of land in this Province as appears on record. And, upon such considerations and terms as are exprefsed in our Conditions of Plantation of our Province of Maryland, doe hereby grant unto the s'd George Nettlefold a parcell of land located in Ann Arundell County on the west side of the South River near the head. *Note: The patent shows two adjoining 100-acre*

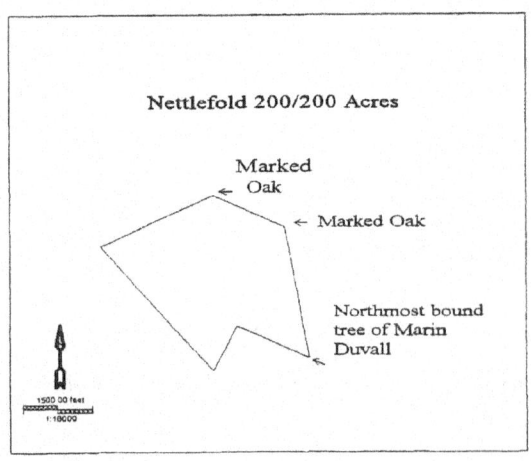

*parcels each with its own boundary courses. I have plotted these as one parcel, as it is named. Tract one begins at the northmost bound tree of land laid out for **Marin Duvall** (Middle Plantation). Tract two begins at the westernmost bound tree (Oak) of the westnorthwest line of tract one. These tracts were later included in Godwell Resurveyed (10/13/1679 LC/21SR7362).*

Obligation (Thomas Stockett) 1/20/1670 663 acres. L16/483 SR7353
Know yee that wee for and in consideration that Thomas Stockett of the County of Ann Arundell in our s'd Province of Maryland hath due unto him six hundred sixty three acres of land within our Province part of a warrant for two thousand acres granted to the s'd Thomas, **Francis, and Henry Stockett** 4/20/1669, as appears on record. Upon such considerations and terms as are exprefsed in our Conditions of Plantation of this our Province of Maryland, wee doe hereby grant unto him the s'd Thomas Stockett all that parcel of land called Obligation lying in Ann Arundell County in the woods beginning at the northmost corner Oak of *Taylor's Choice*. Also adjoins *Brewerston, Bessonton, Lark's Hill, Hale, Hooker's Purchase,* and *Dodon.*

Owen Wood Thickett (Leonard Wayman) 2/18/1688 – 200/174 acres. LNDBI/289 SR7370
Know yee that for and in consideration that Leonard Wayman of Ann Arundell County in our s'd Province of Maryland hath due unto him two hundred acres of land within our Province by virtue of an afsignment of the same quantity from **John Duvall** of the County aforesaid, parte of a warrant for seven hundred acres granted to the s'd Duvall 6/16/1688, as appears on record. Upon such considerations and terms as are exprefsed in our Conditions of Plantation of this our Province, wee doe hereby grant unto the s'd Leonard Wayman all that tract or parcel of land called Owen Wood Thickett lying in a forke of the Patuxant River. Begins at a bounded Swamp Oak by the northernmost branch of the s'd river.

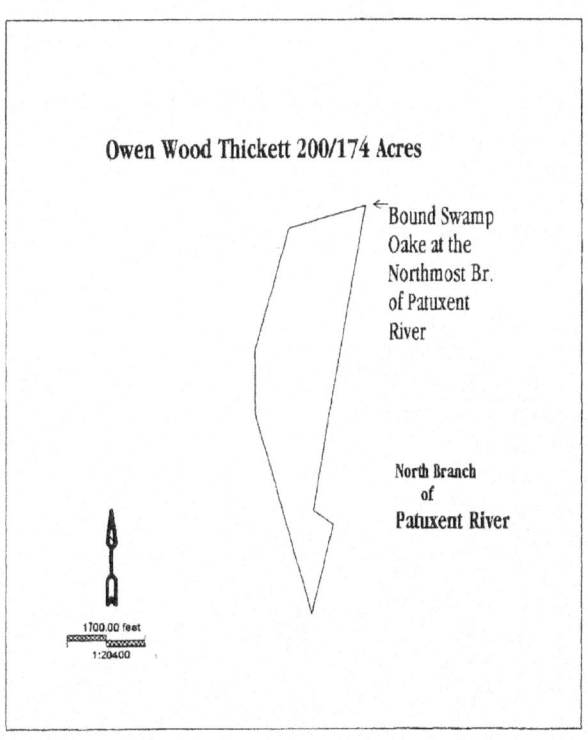

Parrishes Purchase (John Parrish) 6/1/1700 – 50/52 acres. LIB&ILC/402 SR7368-3

Know yee that we for and in consideration of fifty lbs. of current money of England to us paid or to be paid by John Parrish of Ann Arundell County in our s'd Province of Maryland, we doe hereby give and grant unto him the s'd John Parrish all that tract or parcell of land called Parrishes Purchase being part of *Ann Arundell Manor* beginning at a bound Hickory with nine notches it being a bound tree of **Soloman Sparrow**.

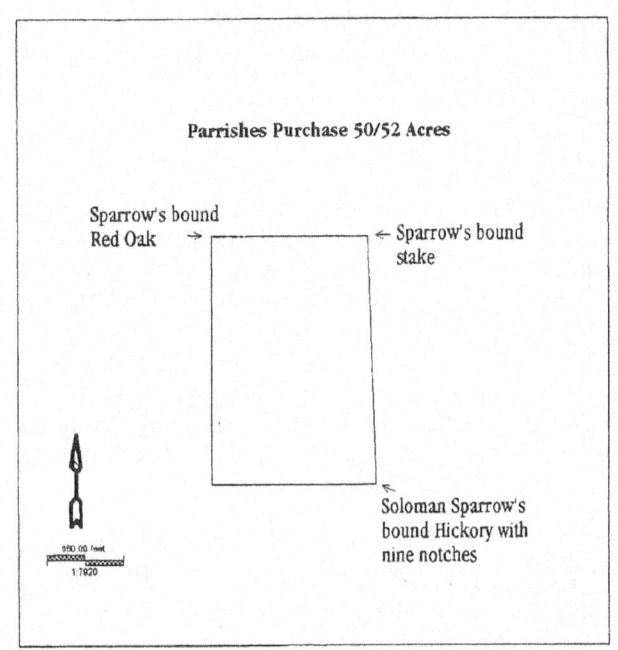

Phelps His Choice (Walter Phelps) 6/1/1685 – 200/197 acres. LNS2i/97 SR7371

Know yee that for and in consideration that Walter Phelps of our s'd Province of Maryland hath due unto him two hundred acres of land within our s'd Province by a warrant for the same quantity granted unto him 6/25/1684, as appears on record. Upon such considerations and terms as are exprefsed in our Conditions of Plantation of this our Province, wee doe hereby grant unto the s'd Walter Phelps all that tract or parcell of land called Phelps His Choice lying in the s'd County on the west side of the northmost Great Branch of Patuxent River. Begins at a bounded Gum tree standing by the s'd Branch.

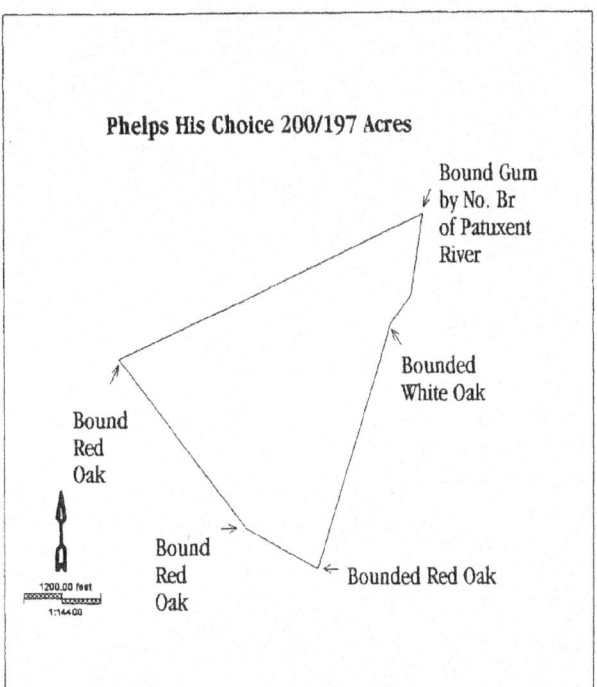

Phelps His Luck (Walter Phelps) 9/1/1687 – 83/56 acres. LNS2i/397 SR7371

Know yee that for and in consideration that Walter Phelps of Ann Arundell County in our s'd Province of Maryland hath due unto him eighty three acres of land within our s'd Province by afsignment of **John Dorsey** of the s'd County, part of a warrant for two hundred acres granted to the s'd Dorsey on 10/4/1684, as appears on record. Upon such considerations and terms as are exprefsed in our Conditions of Plantation of our s'd Province of Maryland do therefore grant unto the s'd Walter Phelps all that tract or parcell of land called Phelps His Luck lying on the south side of the South River beginning at a bounded Red Oak. *Adjoins a branch of Flatt Cr., the land of **Richard Cheney**, and the land of **Archer Arbuckle**.*

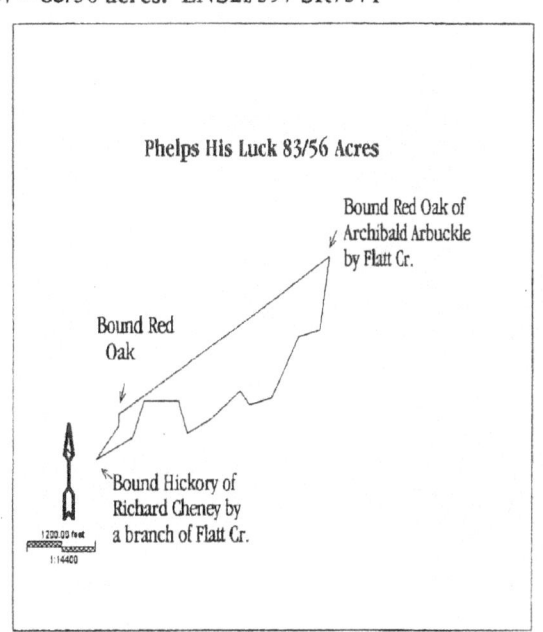

Pierpoint's Branch (Henry Pierpoint) 6/1/1673 – 40/38 acres. L17/198 SR7358

Know yee that wee for and in consideration that Henry Pierpoint of Ann Arundell County in our s'd Province of Maryland, Planter, hath due unto him forty acres of land within our s'd Province by afsignment of **Robert Wilson** the afsignee of **William Burges** part of a warrant for three hundred fifty acres granted to the s'd Burges 12/16/1669, as appears on record. Upon such considerations and terms as are exprefsed in our Conditions of Plantatioin of our s'd Province of Maryland, wee doe hereby grant unto the s'd Henry Pierpoint a parcel

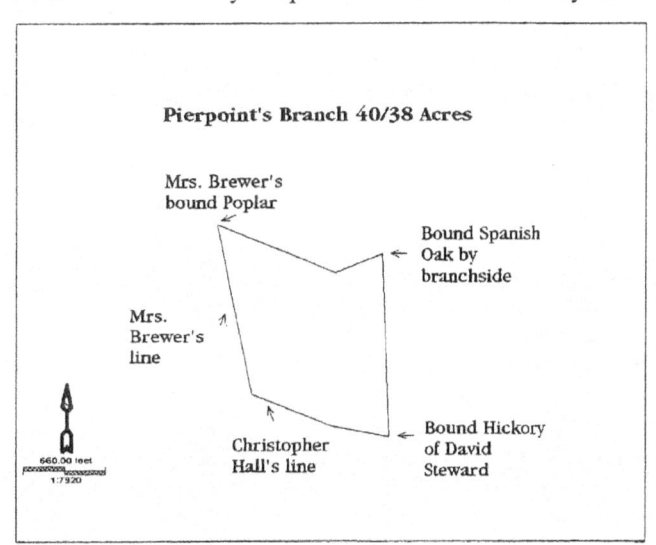

of land called Pierpoint's Branch lying on the Ridge in the s'd County of Ann Arundell beginning at a bound Poplar of land belonging to **Mrs. Brewer**. *Also adjoins land of **Christopher Hall** and land of **David Steward**.*

Pinkston's Folly (Peter Pinkston) 10/1/1700 – 180/174 acres. LDD5i/4 SR7378

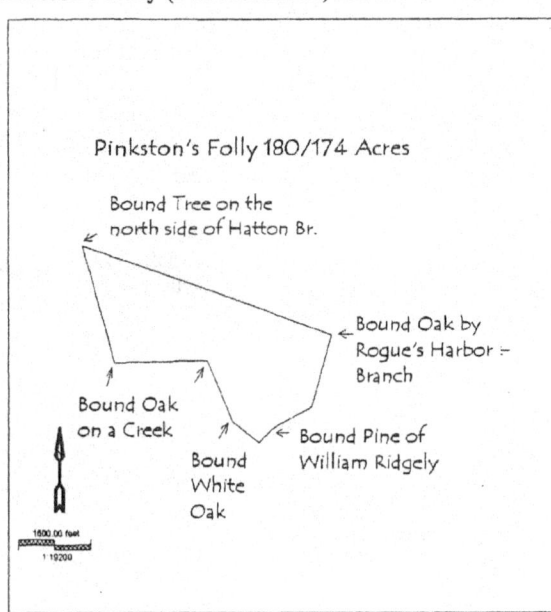

By virtue of a warrant for one hundred acres granted unto Peter Pinkston of Ann Arundell County 2/9/1699, also by virtue of a warrant for eighty acres granted unto Peter Pinkston 6/13/1700, as appears on record. These are to certify that I **James Carroll**, Deputy Surveyor of the s'd County have laid out for the s'd Pinkston a parcell of land called Pinkston's Folly lying in the s'd County on a branch *(of the Patuxent River)* called Rogue's Harbor Branch beginning at a bound Oak standing by the s'd branch. Then issued pattent to the above s'd Pinkston for the above s'd land pursuant to the above Cert. *Also adjoins the north side of Hatton's Branch.*

Plumpton (George Walker) 6/22/1663 – 280/280 acres. L5/357 SR7347

Know yee that wee for and in consideration that George Walker of this Province, Planter, hath due unto him one hundred eighty acres of land afsigned to him by **Robert Clarkson** and one hundred acres more from **George Puddington** both of this Province, Planters, as appears on record. Upon such considerations and terms as are exprefsed in our Conditions of Plantation of our Province of Maryland, wee doe hereby grant unto the s'd George Walker a parcell of land called Plumpton lying in the west side of the South River near the land of **Marin Duvall** in the County of Ann Arundell beginning at a marked Oak on a hill by a great swamp. *The grant conveys two adjoining tracts.*

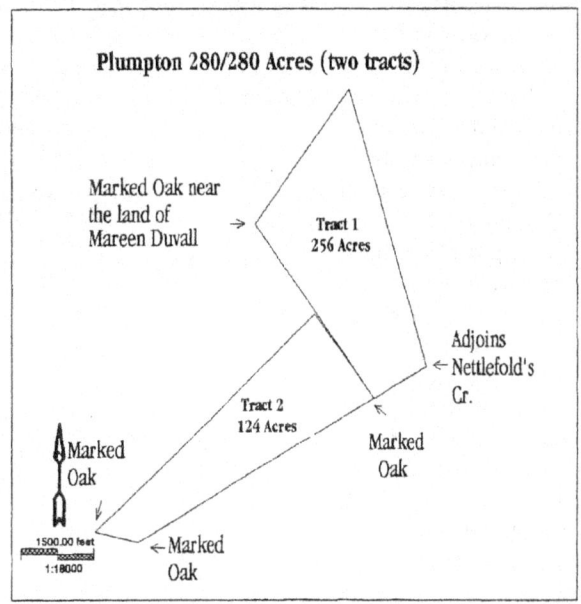

Poll Catt Hill (John Gaither) 9/1/1687 – 391/373 acres. LNS2i/380 SR7371

Know yee that for and in consideration that John Gaither of Ann Arundell County in our s'd Province of Maryland hath due unto him three hundred ninety one acres of land within our s'd

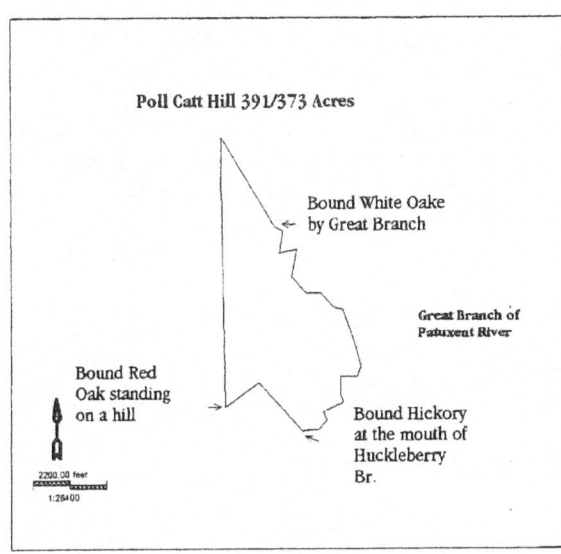

Province by afsignment of two severall parcells of land one of three hundred eighty two acres from **John Stimson** of the s'd County part of a warrant for two thousand acres of land granted to the s'd Stimson 11/27/1684, and the other nine acres from **Richard Beard** of the s'd County part of a warrant for one thousand acres granted the s'd Beard 2/25/1685, as appears on record. Upon such conditions and terms as are exprefsed in our Conditions of Plantation of this our Province, wee doe therefore grant unto the s'd John Gaither all that tract or parcell of land called Poll Catt Hill lying in the forke of the Patuxent River on the North Great Branch beginning at a bounded Oak standing on a hill.

Poplar Hill (Thomas & Edward Selby) 9/15/1665 - 100/100 acres. L8/296 SR7350

Know yee that wee for and in consideration that Thomas and Edward Selby of this Province, Planters, have due unto them one hundred acres of land by afsignment from **George Puddington**, parte of a warrant for five hundred acres of land, as appears on record. Upon such considerations and terms as are exprefsed in our Conditions of Plantation of our Province of Maryland, doe hereby grant unto the s'd Thomas and Edward Selby a parcell of land called Poplar Hill lying on the north side of Road River beginning at

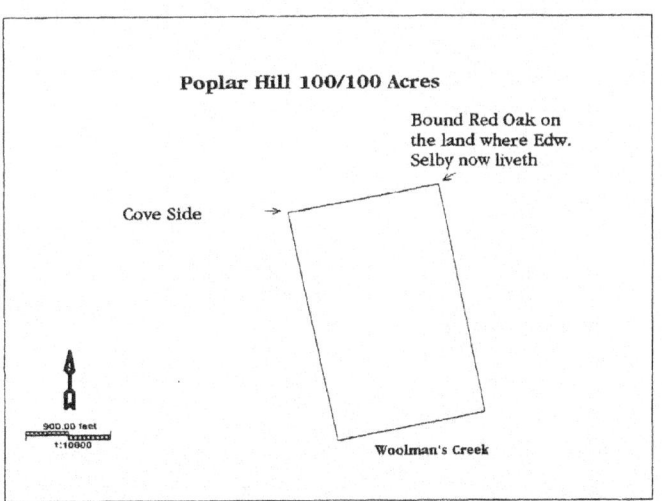

a bounded Red Oak adjoining the land of Edward Selby at which he now liveth. *Also adjoins Woolman's Creek.*

Poplar Neck (**Richard Beard**) 9/20/1663 – 200 acres. L5/588 SR7347
Know yee that we for and in consideration that Richard Beard, Planter, hath due unto him two hundred acres of land for transporting himself and **Rachell**, his wife, into this Province here to inhabit Anno 1650, as appears on record. Upon such considerations and terms as are exprefsed in our Conditions of Plantation of our Province of Maryland, wee doe hereby grant unto the s'd Richard Beard a parcell of land called Poplar Neck lying in Ann Arundell County on the west side of Chesapeake Bay neare to a river called the South River beginning at a marked Oak standing on a point. *Note: The tract cannot be drawn because of incomplete boundary course data.*

Poplar Ridge (Nicholas Gassaway) 8/5/1654 –150/144 acres. L7/269 SR7349
Know yee that we for and in consideration that Nicholas Gassaway of this Province, Planter, hath due unto him one hundred acres of land in this Province by afsignment of a warrant from **George Saughier** and fifty acres more by afsignment of **Robert Loyd** as appears on Record. And, upon such considerations and terms as are exprefsed in our Conditions of Plantation of our Province of Maryland do hereby grant unto the s'd Nicholas Gassaway a parcell of land called Poplar Ridge lying in Ann Arundel County on the south side of the South River adjoining the land of **Capt. Thomas Befson**. Begins at a marked White Oak.

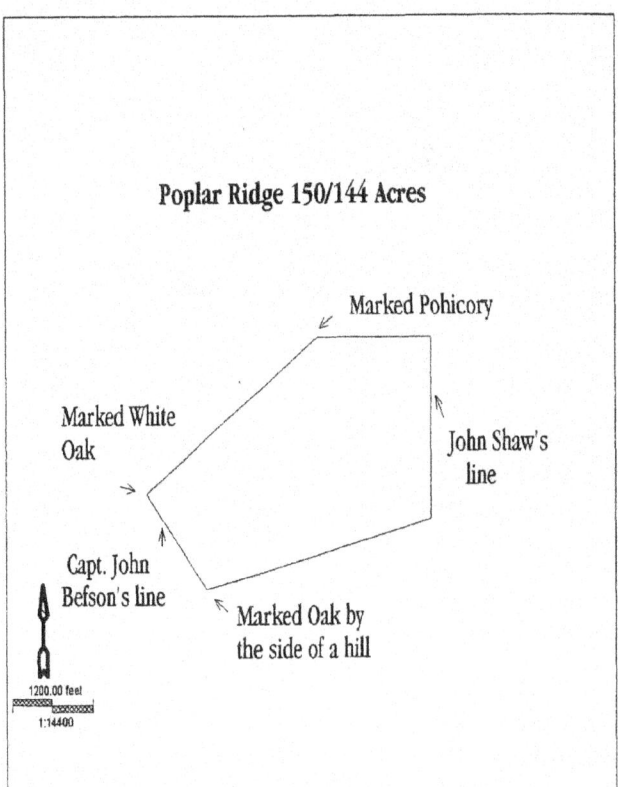

54

Powell's Inheritance (John & Jas. Powell) 4/1/1685 - 125/107 acres. LIB&IL/236 SR7368

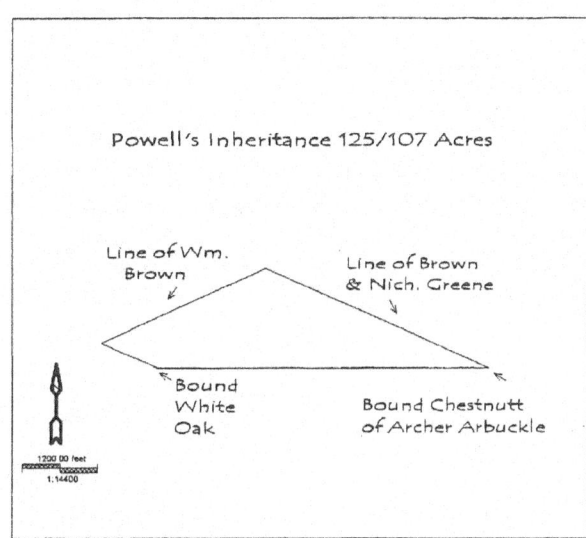

Know yee that **Richard Huggings**, Late, of this Province had granted unto him a parcel of land called Huggings Advantage in Ann Arundell County for fifty acres which s'd parcel of land was *(devised)* from **John Grange** who married with the relict of the s'd Huggings *(whereas)* Huggins lawfully vested and joined *(the rights)* to John and James Powell being of the same County of Ann Arundell. The s'd John and James Powell being seized of aforesaid upon inspection thereof *(found)* a greater quantity than the fifty acres granted as aforesaid and humbly besought us to grant them our Speciall Warrant to resurvey with liberty of making good rights for the surplus, if any, in a Pattent of Confirmation of the whole. Whereas the s'd John & James Powell have caused that the land be resurveyed and made good rights for the surplus of seventy five acres, wee doe hereby grant unto the s'd Powells all that tract now resurveyed and called Powell's Inheritance beginning at a bound Chestnutt of a parcel formerly belonging to **Archer Arbuckle**.

Puddington (George Puddington) 2/7/1650 – 160/165 acres. LQ/393 SR7345

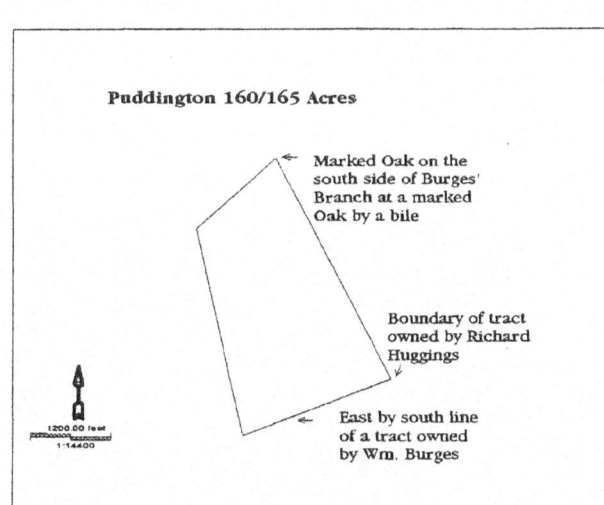

Know yee that wee for and in consideration that George Puddington of this Province, Planter, hath transported himself and **Jane Puddington** into this Province here to inhabit. Upon such considerations and terms as are exprefsed in our Conditions of Plantation of our s'd Province of Maryland, doe hereby grant unto the s'd George Puddington a parcell of land called Puddington lying on the west side of Chesapeake Bay and on the south side of South River beginning at a marked Oak by a bile upon a bank side. *Adjoins land of Richard Huggings and land of William Burges.*

Puddington's Enlargement (George Puddington) 6/30/1662 –300/300 acres. L5/348 SR7347
(Two Tracts)
Know yee that for and in consideration that George Puddington of this Province, Planter, hath due unto him three hundred acres of land within our s'd Province for the transporting of **Thomas Hipsley, John Burrage,** and **Margaret Joy** into this Province here to inhabit in Anno 1649, as appears on record. Upon such considerations and terms as are exprefsed in our Conditions of Plantation of our s'd Province of Maryland, doe hereby grant unto the s'd George Puddington a parcel of land called Puddington's Enlargement lying on the west side of the South River adjoining the land of **George Nettlefold**. *Note: Tract one, 200/200 acres, begins at the southernmost bound Pokehikary in Nettlefold's ESE line. Tract 2, 100/100 acres, begins at the southernmost bounded Oak in Nettlefold's SE line. However, these tracts do not join each other.*

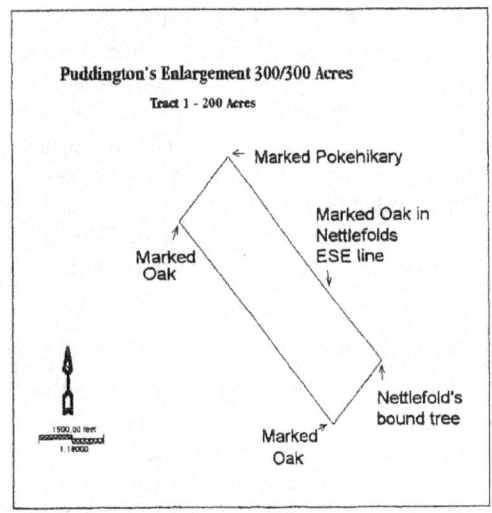
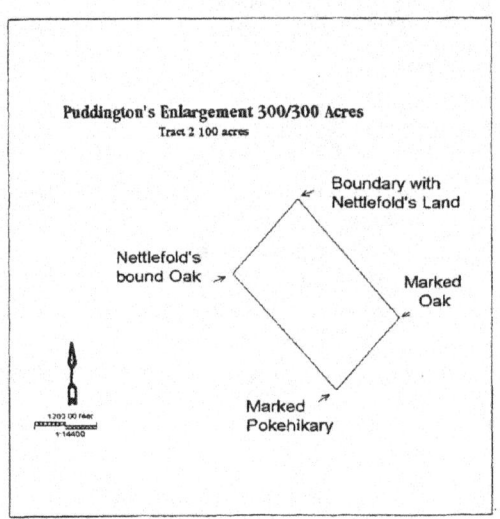

Puddington's Harbor (George Puddington) 9/29/1663 - 700 acres. L5/618 SR7347
Know yee that wee for and in consideration that George Puddington hath due unto him seven hundred acres of land within our s'd Province for the transporting of three persons in Anno 1650, and four persons more in Anno 1651. Also, two hundred acres more afsigned to him by **Richard Huggings**. Upon such considerations and terms as are exprefsed in our Conditions of Plantation of our Province of Maryland, doe hereby grant unto the s'd George Puddington all that parcel of land called Puddington's Harbor being in Ann Arundell County lying on the south side of the South River beginning at Jacob's Creek.. *Also adjoins Puddington's Creek, the South River, and a tract called Puddington. Note 1: Puddington also patented a tract called **Puddington's First** which he lett fall because it was found to be within the bounds of Puddington's Harbor. Note 2: The tract cannot be drawn because of incomplete boundary course data.*

Rachell's Hope (Thomas Maddox) 6/4/1683 – 72/89 acres. LCB#3i/514 SR7367

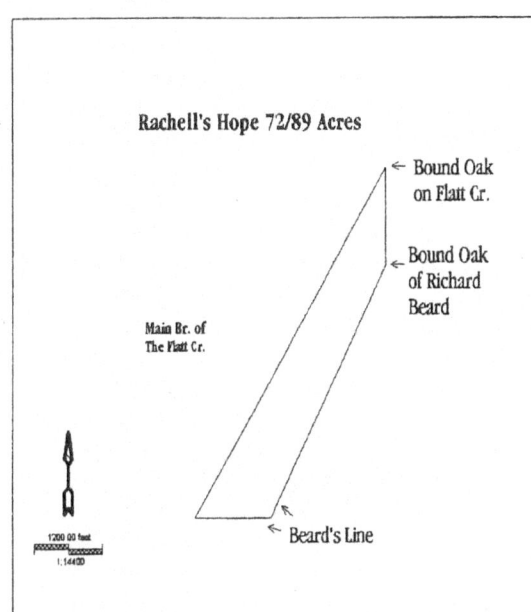

Know yee that for and in consideration that Thomas Maddox of Ann Arundell County in our s'd Province of Maryland hath due unto him seventy two acres of land within our s'd Province by afsignment of **George Yate** part of a warrant for one thousand fifty acres granted the s'd Yate 6/19/1668, as appears on record. Upon such considerations and terms as are exprefsed in our Conditions of Plantation of our Province of Maryland, doe hereby grant unto the s'd Thomas Maddox all that parcell of land called Rachell's Hope lying in Ann Arundell County on the south side of a creek in the South River called the Flatt Creek. *Also adjoins the land of Richard Beard.*

Rich Neck (Wm. Young & Marin Duvall) 8/24/1665 – 200/207 acres. L8/147 SR7350

Know yee that for and in consideration that William Young and Marin Duvall hath due unto them one hundred acres of land by afsignment from **George Puddington** to the s'd Duvall and by afsignment of **Ann Covill** to the s'd Young, as appears on record. Upon such conditions and terms as are exprefsed in our Conditions of Plantation of our s'd Province of Maryland, doe hereby grant unto the s'd Young and Duvall a parcell of land called Rich Neck lying in Ann Arundell County on the south side of the South River and on the west side of Jacob's Creek beginning at a marked Red Oake at the head of a valley in the line of the land of **John Clark**. *Also adjoins land of Richard Cheney*.

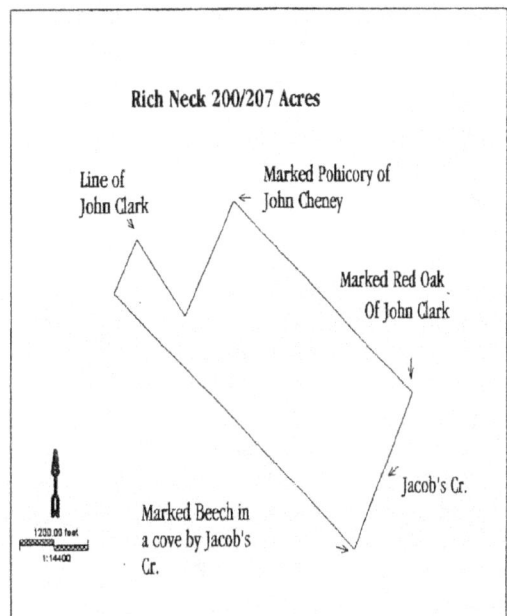

Ridgely's Chance (William Ridgely) 10/2/1694 – 305/302 acres. LC3/412 SR7377

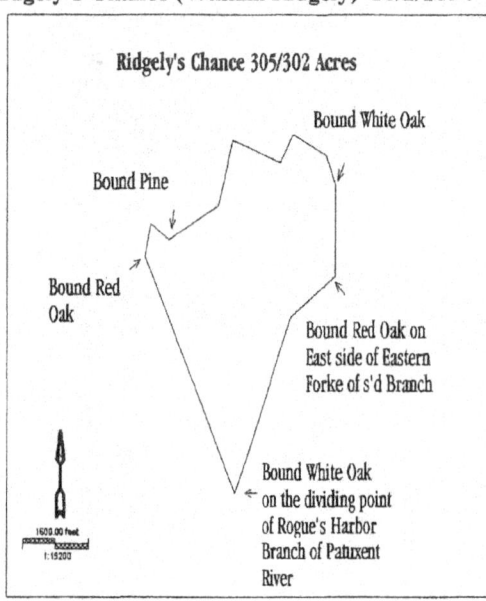

Whereas William Ridgely of Ann Arundell County has in his humble petition to us sett forth that he did have surveyed for him three hundred acres of land on 10/1/1694, by virtue of a warrant duly obtained and the Certificate thereof returned but that this grant for the s'd land has been stopped because there was improvements made by building and clearing and by our Instructions *(that improved land)* could not be taken up by Common Warrant. He humbly prayed that we would issue our letter patent for the s'd land according to the survey. We have thought fitt to condescend unto the *(petitioner)* rather for that the improvements were made by himself. Know yee that for and in consideration that the s'd Ridgely hath due unto him three hundred five acres of land within our s'd Province being due him by afsignment of that quantity from **Henry Ridgely Jr**, out of a warrant for eighteen hundred acres granted him 6/9/1694, as appears on record in our Land Office. Upon such considerations and terms as are exprefsed in our Conditions of Plantation of this our Province, wee doe therefore hereby grant unto the s'd William Ridgely all that tract or parcell of land lying in Ann Arundell County on the Forke of a branch of Patuxent River called Rogue's Harbor Branch beginning at a bound White Oak standing on the point of the dividing of the branch.

Robin Hood's Forrest (Rich Snowden) 8/1/1686 – 1,976/1,684 acres. LIB&ILC/230 SR7368

Know yee that wee for and in consideration that Richard Snowden of Ann Arundell County in our Province of Maryland hath due unto him one thousand nine hundred and seventy five acres of land within our s'd Province being due unto him the s'd Richard Snowden by our severall warrants containing five hundred acres granted to him 2/25/1685, as appears on record. Upon such considerations and terms as are exprefsed in our Conditions of Plantation of this our Province of Maryland, wee doe therefore hereby grant unto the s'd Richard Snowden all that tract or parcell of land called Robin Hood's Forrest lying in the Forke of the Patuxent River beginning at a bounded

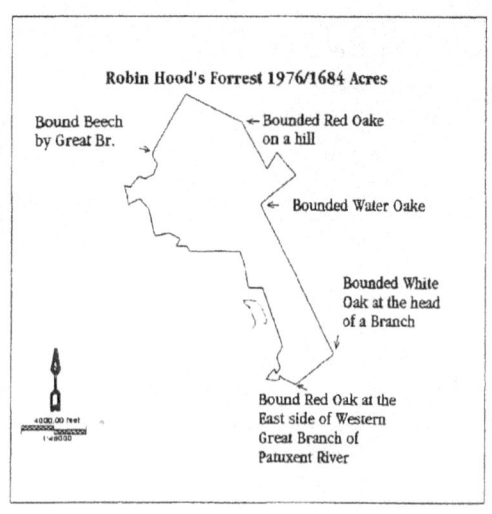

White Oak standing at the head of a branch. *Note 1: The "rights" certified are vague in that they are based on an unspecified number of "our" 500-acre warrants given him. It is assumed that "our" refers to the Lord Proprietor via the Land Office. No further explanation found. Note 2: This tract is located in what is now Prince George's County in the general area of the*

intersection of I 295 and Route 197. Note 3: According to the Rent Rolls (1707) there was also another tract (150 acres) called Robin Hood's Forrest located at the head of Swan Creek on the north side of the Severn River.

Roedown Security (Thomas Taylor Esq.) 6/20/1675 – 477/369 acres. L19/28 SR7360
Know yee that for and in consideration that Thomas Taylor of Ann Arundell County in our s'd Province of Maryland hath due unto him four hundred seventy seven acres of land within our s'd Province part of his Warrant for five hundred fifty acres granted unto him 7/21/1674, as appears on record. Upon such considerations and terms as are exprefsed in our Conditions of Plantation of our s'd Province of Maryland, wee doe hereby grant unto him the s'd Thomas Taylor all that parcell of land called Roedown Security lying in Ann Arundell County on the east side of the North Branch of Patuxent River beginning at a bound Oak by the s'd Branch. *Adjoins land already patented by Thomas Taylor.*

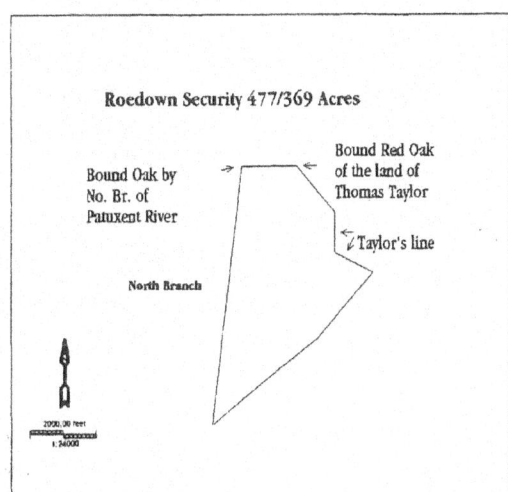

Roper Gray (Wm. Roper & John Gray) 8/2/1683 – 480/487 acres. LSDA/410 SR7369
Know yee that for and in consideration that William Roper and John Gray hath due unto them four hundred eighty acres of land within our s'd Province. Two hundred acres thereof by bequest of **David Fry**, Deceased, of the same County and forty acres more due to the s'd Fry by afsignment of **Henry Hanslap** the afsignee of **Coll Thomas Taillor** on 4/30/1683, and the other two hundred forty acres due to the s'd Roper from the s'd Hanslap afsignee of the s'd Taillor part of the s'd Warrant, as appears on record. Upon such considerations and terms as are exprefsed in our Conditions of Plantation of our late father **Cecilius**, of noble memory, wee doe hereby grant unto the s'd Roper and Gray all that tract or parcell of land called Roper Gray lying in the s'd County in the woods beginning at a bound Red Oake by the North

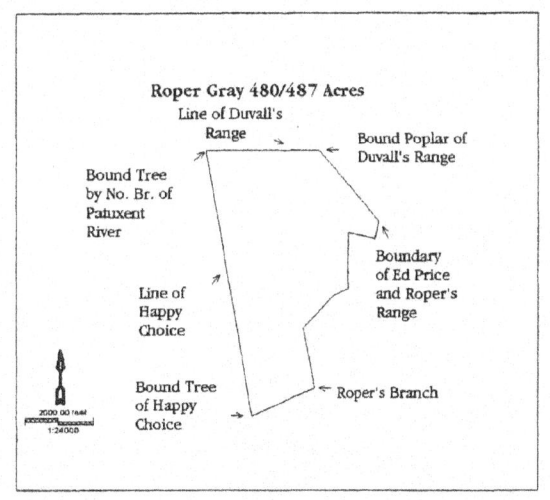

Branch of Patuxent River and running east with the line of land of **Marin Duvall** called *Duvall's Range.* *Also adjoins Roper's Range and The Happy Choice.*

Roper's Range (William Roper) 9/6/1670 – 420/419 acres. L14/54 SR7356

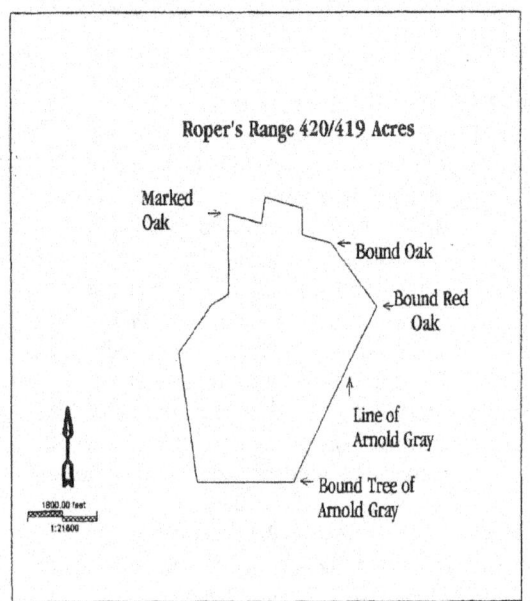

Know yee that for and in consideration that William Roper of the County of Ann Arundell hath due unto him four hundred twenty acres of land within our s'd Province by afsignment of **Robert Wilson** the afsignee of **Coll Wm. Burges** parte of a warrant for three hundred ninety acres. Also, 30 acres more from **Jerome White, Esq.**, parte of a warrant for twenty one hundred and fifty acres formerly granted to the s'd White, as appears on record. Upon such considerations and terms as are exprefsed in our Conditions of Plantation of this our s'd Province of Maryland, wee doe hereby grant unto the s'd Roper all that parcell of land called Roper's Range lying in the aforesaid County beginning at a bound White Oak. *Adjoins Roper Gray.*

Roundabout Hill (John Gaither) 9/1/1687 - 120/120 acres. LNS2i/396 SR7371

Know yee that for and in consideration that John Gaither of Ann Arundell County in our s'd Province of Maryland hath due unto him one hundred twenty acres of land by afsignment of **Robert Proctor** of the s'd County part of a warrant for two hundred acres granted the s'd Proctor 2/25/1685, as appears on record. Upon such considerations and terms as are exprefsed in our Conditions of Plantation of this our Province, wee doe therefore grant unto the s'd John Gaither all that tract or parcell of land called Roundabout Hill lying in the s'd County on the west side of the South Runn beginning in the northwest by north line of a parcell of land called *Free Manston*.

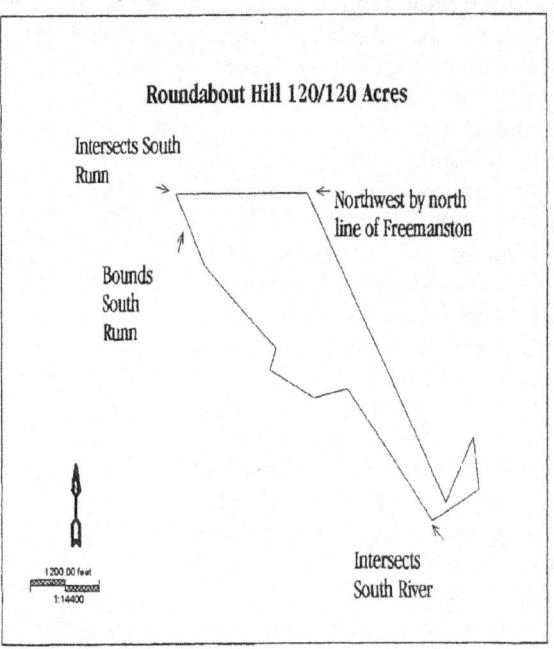

Rowdown (Thomas Taylor) 12/12/1670 – 800/775 acres. L6/34 SR7377

Know yee that wee for and in consideration that **George Yate** of Ann Arundell County, Gent, hath due unto him eight hundred acres of land within our s'd Province part of a warrant for one thousand five hundred twenty three acres to him granted 5/25/1669, whose right, title, and interest in and to were made over to Thomas Taylor, Gent, as appears on record. Upon such considerations and terms as are exprefsed in our Conditions of Plantation of our Province of Maryland, doe hereby grant unto the s'd Thomas Taylor a parcell of land called Rowdown lying in the s'd County beginning at **Stocket's** land on the north side of Stocket's Runn. *Also adjoins The Friend's Choice (**Jones & Gray**), and Yate's Branch.*

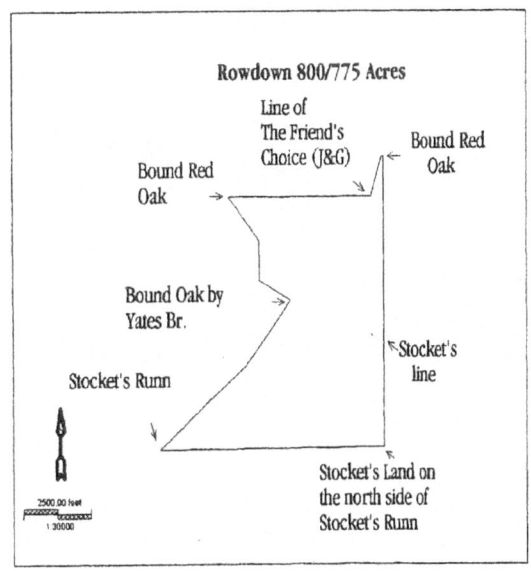

Rutland's Enlarged (Thos. Rutland) 4/19/1700 – 260/300 acres. LDD5i/788 SR7378

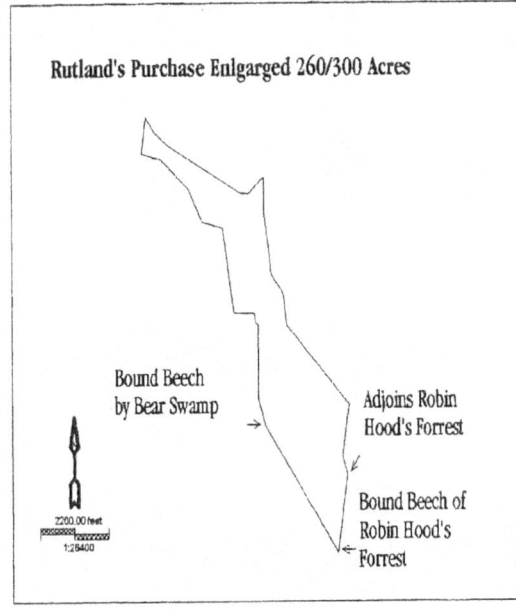

By virtue of a Speciall Warrant granted unto Thomas Rutland of Ann Arundell County 9/30/1709, to resurvey for and in the name of the s'd Rutland a tract of land originally called Timber Neck lying in the s'd County and partly in Prince Georges County and to add therefore the vacant land contiguous. These are to certify that I have laid out that parte thereof in the s'd County and by an *Epistolarry* power from Mr. **Clement Hill**, Surveyor Generall of the Western Shore, I have surveyed that parte lying in Prince George's County and next above a tract called *Robin Hood's Forrest* on a branch of Patuxent River called Snowden's River. Begins at a bound Beach in or near the line of Robin Hood's Forrest. Then issued Pattent for the above land to the above named Thomas Rutland pursuant to the above Cert.

Scornton (George Westhill) 5/2/1659 – 800/715 acres. L4/39 SR7346

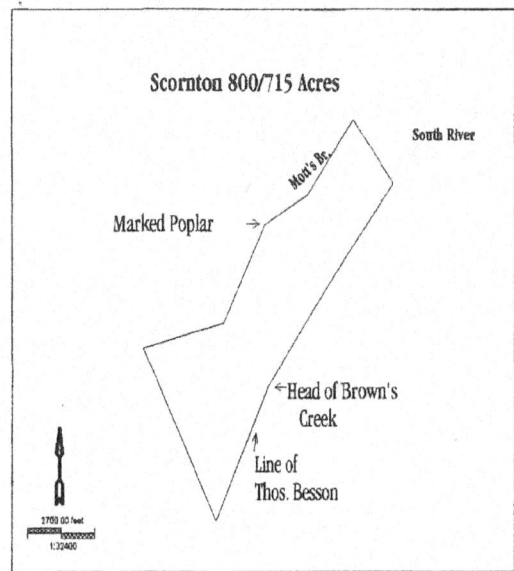

Know yee that we for and in consideration that George Westhill of the County of Ann Arundell hath transported himself, **George Hisson**, and six severall other persons more into this Province here to inhabit. Upon such considerations and terms as are exprefsed in our Conditions of Plantation of our s'd Province of Maryland, doe hereby grant unto the s'd George Westhill a parcell of land called Scornton lying on the west side of Chesapeake Bay and on the south side of the South River beginning at a marked Oak at the head of Brown's Cr. *Also adjoins Mott's Branch and the land of Thomas Besson.*

Selby (Edward Selby) Undated – 490/262 acres. LQ/23 SR7345

Know yee that wee for and in consideration that Edward Selby of Ann Arundell County hath due unto him four hundred ninety acres of land and upon such considerations and terms as are exprefsed in our Conditions of Plantation of our s'd Province of Maryland, do hereby grant unto the s'd Edward Selby all that tract or parcell of land called Selby lying on the west side of Chesapeake and on the west side of Road River beginning at a marked Oak standing in a marsh of the s'd river called Selby Marsh.

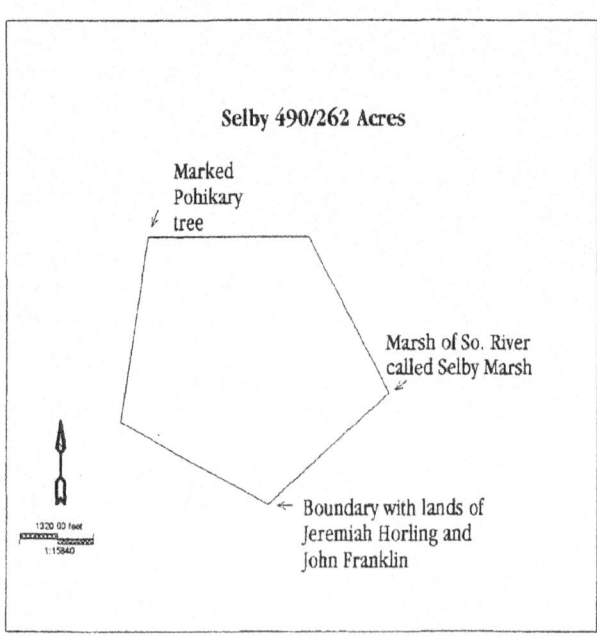

Selby's Stopp (Edward Selby Jr.) 6/12/1688 – 201/202 acres. LNS#2/730 SR7371

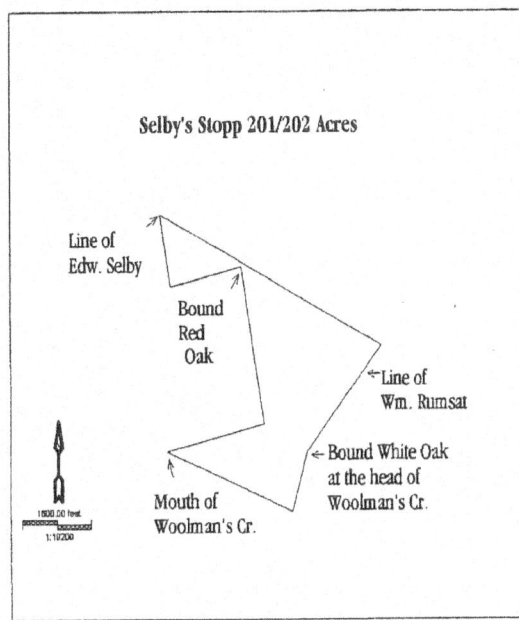

Know yee that for and in consideration that Edward Selby Junior of Ann Arundell County in our s'd Province of Maryland hath due unto him two hundred and one acres of land within our s'd Province due to the s'd Selby by afsignment of parte of three severall warrants of 180 acres from **Richard Beard,** of the s'd County parte of a warrant for four thousand acres to the s'd Beard afsigned 2/27/1686. Sixty seven acres more from **John Hall** of Baltimore County, parte of a warrant for twelve hundred acres granted unto him 2/25/1686, and ten acres more from **Madame Ursala Burges** of Ann Arundell County out of the goods and chattels of **Coll Wm. Burges** late of the s'd County being parte of a warrant for three hundred acres granted to him the s'd Burges 10/30/1686, as appears on record. Wee doe hereby grant unto the s'd Edward Selby all that tract or parcell of land called Selby's Stopp lying on the north side of Road River beginning at mouth of Woolman's Creek. *Also adjoins other property owned by* ***Edw. Selby****, and property owned by* ***Wm. Rumsay****.*

Sharp Pointe (Andrew Roberts) 11/30/1666 (Cert) – 30/23 acres. L10/205 SR7352

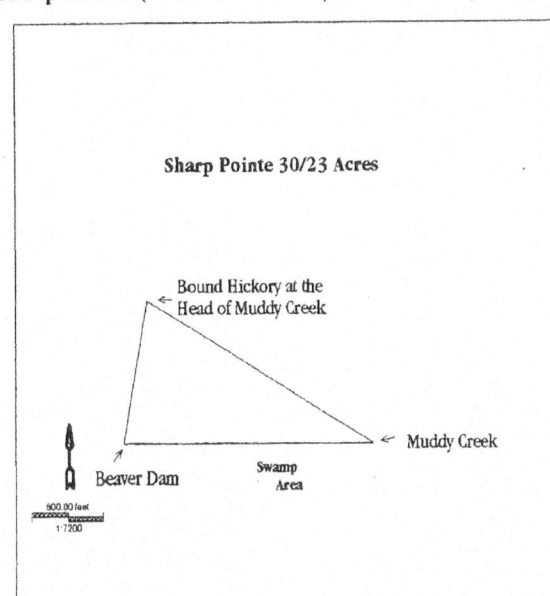

Laid out for Andrew Roberts, Taillor, of the County of Ann Arundell, a parcel of land lying in Ann Arundell County at the head of the Road River and the head of a creek called the Muddy Creek beginning at a bound Hickory. *Adjoins the Beaver Dam Swamp or Creek. Note: From RR 1651-1774 AA County Pg. 44, " I do not find that Roberts ever paid rent for this nor did I find any new claim. Supposed (it) to be a miftaken Survey." However, due to the many references to this tract in other patent documents I have included it.*

Shaw's Folly (John Shaw) 9/15/1666 – 260/275 acres. L10/108 SR7352

Know yee that wee for and in consideration that John Shaw of our Province of Maryland, Planter, hath due unto him two hundred sixty acres of land within our s'd Province out of a warrant for four hundred acres formerly granted to him as appears on record. Upon such considerations and terms as are exprefsed in our Conditions of Plantation of our s'd Province of Maryland, doe hereby grant unto the s'd John Shaw a parcell of land called Shaw's Folly lying in Ann Arundall County on the west side of Chesapeake Bay and on the west side of the Road River beginning at a bound Locust by a creekside. *Note: The following note was written in the margin of the patent document: "This parcell delivered into the office. The land therein mentioned lett fall. Warr to resurvey granted to the s'd Shaw in Liber GG360 Folio 477."*

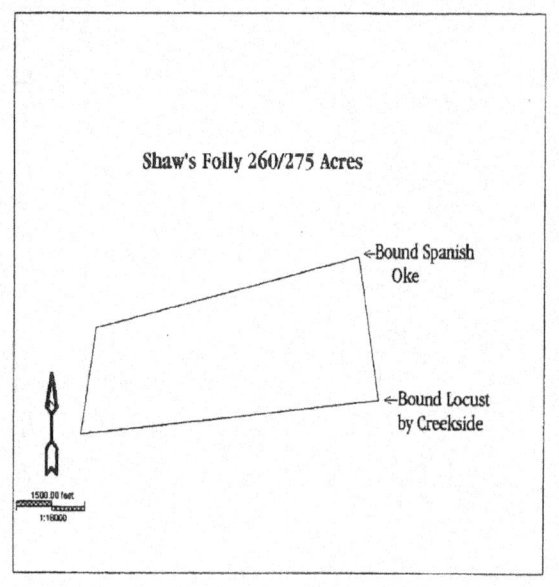

Shaw's Folly Resurveyed (John Shaw) 4/1/1672 – 360/394 acres. L16/554 SR7357

Know yee that whereas we did grant on 9/5/1672, unto John Shaw of Ann Arundell County a parcell of land called Shaw's Folly containing and then laid out for two hundred sixty acres of land. And, the s'd John Shaw, finding that the s'd parcell did containe a greater quantity then certified did surrender the pattent and cause the grant to be vacated upon record. By virtue of a warrant of resurvey bearing the date 11/8/1668, the tract was determined to containe three hundred sixty acres and whereas the s'd John Shaw hath due unto him one hundred acres of land within our s'd Province by afsignment of **George Yate** the afsignee of **Capt. James Connaway**, part of a warrant for twenty five hundred fifty acres to the s'd Connaway granted, we doe therefore grant and confirm unto him the s'd John Shaw all that tract or parcell of land now resurveyed called Shaw's Folly lying in the County of Ann Arundell on the west side of Road River beginning at a bounded Locust standing on the point of Shaw's Creek.

Slatbourne (Robert Proctor) 5/10/1676 – 380/340 acres. L19/329 SR7360

Know Yee that Wee for and in consideration that Robert Proctor of Ann Arundell County hath due unto him three hundred and eighty acres of land within our Province of Maryland by afsignment of **George Yate,** part of a warrant for five hundred acres granted to the s'd Yate on the 12th day of August, 1674, as appears on record. Upon such considerations and terms as are exprefsed in our Conditions of Plantation of our Province of Maryland, doe hereby grant unto the s'd Robert Proctor all that parcel of land called Slatbourne lying in the s'd County between the main branches of the South River in the woods. Begins at a bound White Oak of the land called *Freeman's Fancy.* Note: From *Rent Rolls Baltimore and Anne Arundel Counties 1700-1707, 1705-1724* page 181, " This land is within the Lines of Abingdon & the Patt therefore surrendered & vacated."

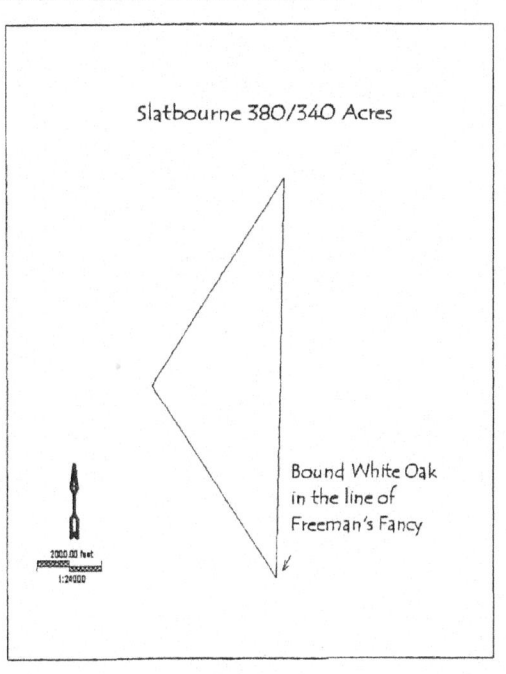

Soldier's Fortune (Christopher Miller) 10/10/1704 - 100/80 Acres LDSF/539 SR7373-2

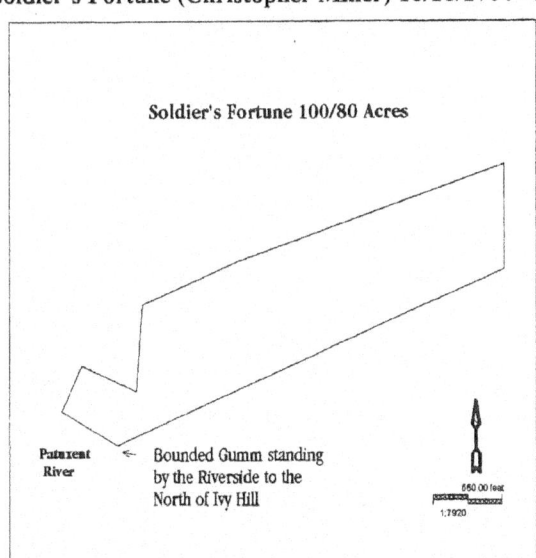

Know yee that for and in consideration that Christopher Miller of Ann Arundell County in our s'd Province of Maryland hath due unto him one hundred acres of land within our s'd Province by virtue of a warrant of the same quantity from **Richard Snowden Jr.** The afsignee of **James Carroll** out of a warrant for seven hundred eleven acres granted the s'd Carroll and afsigned by him to the Snowden as appears on record. Upon such conditions and terms as are exprefsed in our Conditions of Plantation of our s'd Province, wee doe therefore hereby grant unto the s'd Christopher Miller all that tract or parcell of land lying on the North Branch of the Patuxent River in the place called The Forke beginning at a bounded Gumm standing to the north of Ivy Hill. *Note: AA Co. Rent Rolls (pg. 190) indicates that this tract was re-patented by Richard Snowden Jr. on 10/8/1707.*

Soloman's Purchase (Soloman Sparrow) 1/15/1695 – 150/150 acres. LWD/274 SR7372-2

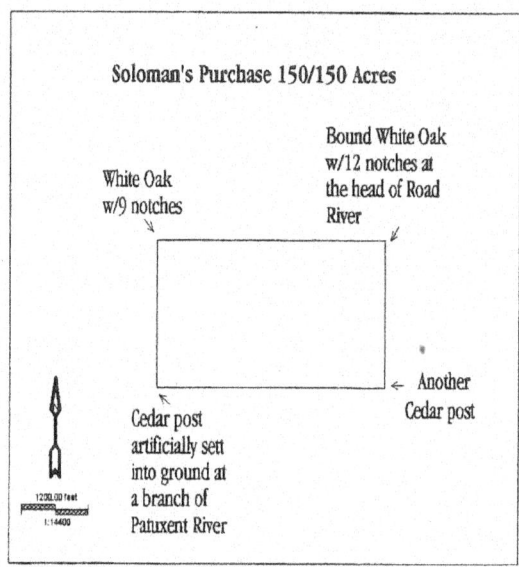

Know yee that for and in consideration of the full summ of one hundred fifty pounds, current money of England, to us in hand paid or to be paid before the passing of this our Letters of Pattents by Soloman Sparrow of Ann Arundell County in our s'd Province of Maryland, have given, granted and by this prefents wee doe for us and our heirs give and grant unto him the s'd Soloman Sparrow all that parcell of land called Soloman's Purchase being parte of our *Ann Arundell Manor,* beginning at a bound White Oak marked with twelve notches at the head of the Road River.

Sparrow's Addition (Thomas Sparrow) 5/28/1675 – 100/48 acres. L19/8 SR7360

Know yee that wee for and in consideration that Thomas Sparrow of Ann Arundell County in our s'd Province of Maryland hath due unto him one hundred acres of land within our s'd Province part of a warrant for four hundred acres granted to him 10/15/1673, as appears on record. Upon such considerations and terms as are exprefsed in our Conditions of Plantation of our Province of Maryland doe hereby grant unto him the s'd Thomas Sparrow all that parcell of land called Sparrow's Addition lying in Ann Arundell County on the Road River beginning at the end of the northeast by north line of the land of the s'd Sparrow on the river called the Road River and by a branch called Nettlefold's Branch.

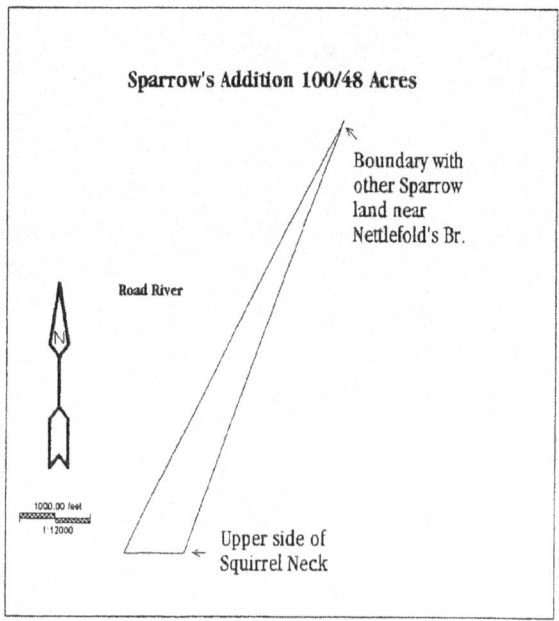

Stinson's Choice (John Stinson) 2/20/1684 – 618/695 acres. IB&ILC/227 SR7368-1

Know yee that wee for and in consideration that John Stinson of Ann Arundell County in our Province of Maryland hath due unto him six hundred and eighteen acres of land within our s'd Province being part of a warrant for one thousand acres of land granted unto him 11/27/1684, as appears on record. Upon such considerations and terms as are exprefsed in our Conditions of Plantation of this our Province of Maryland, wee doe hereby grant unto the s'd John Stinson all that tract or parcell of land called Stinson's Choice lying in the forke of Patuxent River on the south side of the North Great Branch. Begins at a bounded Red Oak on a Hill. *Adjoins Merriton's Fancy.*

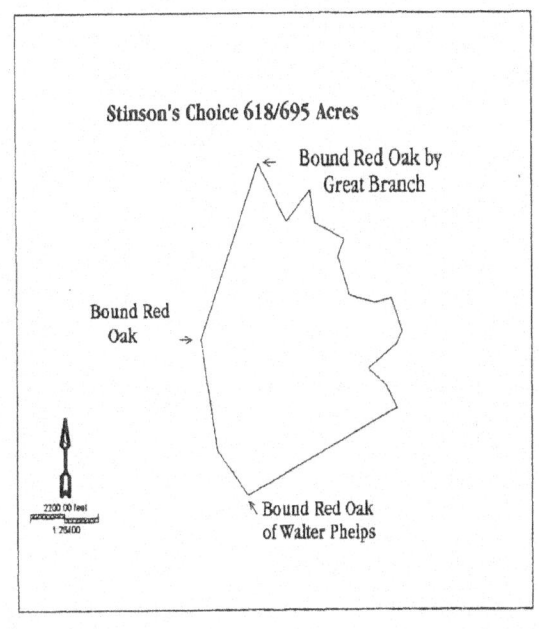

Surplus Land Within Cheney's Neck (Wm. & Ann Burroughs) 6/1/1696 – 80/82 acres. LC3i/390 SR7377

Know yee that whereas William Burroughs and his wife Ann by their humble petition have sett forth that one **Ann Barnett**, the daughter of the s'd Ann Burroughs by a former husband was seized in fee simple of a certaine tract of land in the s'd County called *Cheney's Neck* originally patented by **Richard Cheney** for one hundred ten acres. And the s'd Ann, while solo did grant unto the s'd Ann Burroughs, her mother, free liberty to compound with us for what surplus land should, upon resurvey, be found within the s'd tract. This grant of the s'd Ann Barnett was confirmed and consented to by one **John Horring** with whom she afterwards intermarried as appears. And whereas upon resurvey it is certified that there is a surplus of eighty acres within the bounds of the s'd tract we do therefore, in consideration of the quantity of 1,330 lbs of tobacco to us in hand paid by the s'd William Burroughs, give, grant, and confirm unto him and his wife Ann all that parcell of land as aforesaid "sett apart" out of the aforesaid tract called Cheney's Neck beginning at a Spanish Oak by the river.

Sutton's Addition (Thomas Sutton)
2/11/1688 – 20/19 acres. LNS#B/621 SR7370

Know yee that for and in consideration that Thomas Sutton of Ann Arundell County hath due unto him twenty acres of land within our s'd Province being due by afsignment of **Thomas Richardson** of Baltimore County in our Province aforesaid, parte of a warrant for two thousand eight hundred eighty three acres granted to the s'd Richardson 2/27/1687, as appears on record. Upon such considerations and terms as are exprefsed in our Conditions of Plantation of this our s'd Province of Maryland, wee doe hereby grant unto the s'd Thomas Sutton all that parcell of land called Sutton's Addition lying on the south side of the South River beginning at a bound

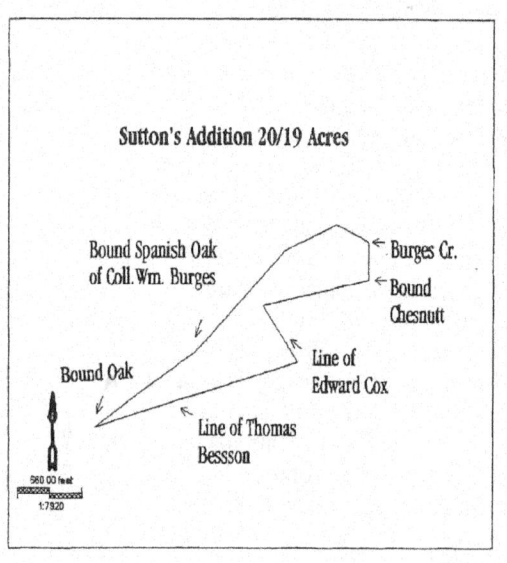

Chestnutt. *Adjoins Burge's Cr, and tracts owned by* **Wm. Burges, Edw. Cox,** *and* **Thos. Besson.**

Tangerine (Leonard Wayman) 10/10/1695 – 10/10 acres. L23/317 SR7365

Know yee that for and in consideration that Leonard Wayman of Ann Arundell County in our s'd

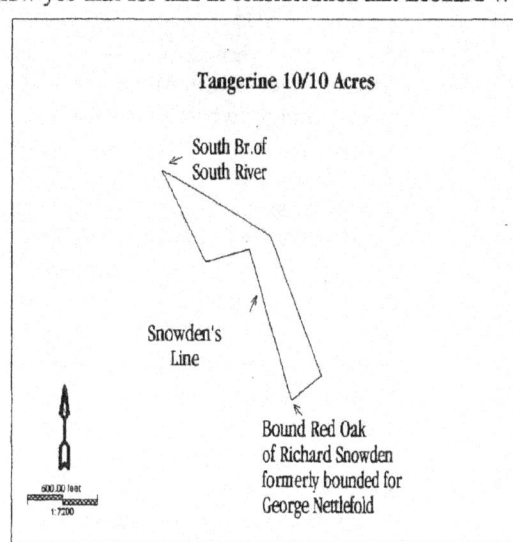

Province of Maryland hath due unto him ten acres of land within our s'd Province by virtue of a warrant granted unto **Daniel Eliott** of Charles County *(dated)* 9/4/1694, as appears on record in our Land Office. Upon such considerations and terms as are exprefsed in our Conditions of Plantation of this our Province of Maryland, wee doe hereby grant unto the s'd Leonard Wayman all that tract or parcell of land called Tangerine lying in Ann Arundell County on the south side of the head of the South River beginning at a bound Red Oak of **Richard Snowden**, formerly bounded for **George Nettlefold's** land near the mouth of Walker's Branch.

Taylor's Addition (Thomas Taylor) 9/10/1672 100/107 acres. L17/299 SR7352
Know yee that for and in consideration that Thomas Taylor of Ann Arundell County, Gent, hath due unto him one hundred acres of land within our s'd Province by afsignment from **George Yate** the afsignee of him the s'd Thomas Taylor, attorney for **Jerome White Esq.**, part of a warrant for nine hundred acres granted to the s'd White 4/9/1672, as appears on record. Upon such considerations and terms as are exprefsed in our Conditions of Plantation of our Province of Maryland, doe hereby grant unto the s'd Thomas Taylor a parcell of land called Taylor's Addition lying in the s'd County beginning at a bounded Red Oake being the southeasternmost bound tree of a parcell called *Taylor's Choice*. *Also adjoins Hale and land owned by **Thomas Mills**.*

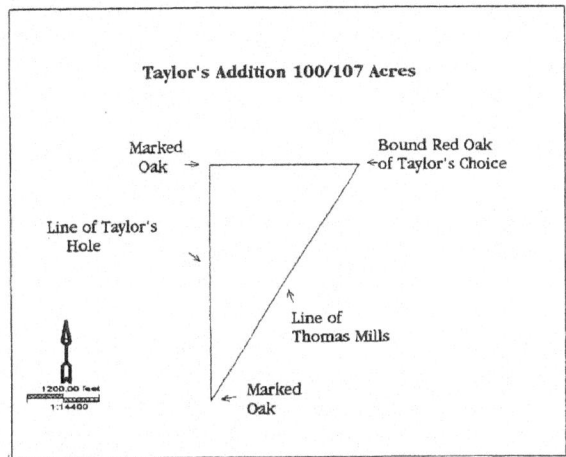

The Addition (James Chillcott) 8/8/1670 – 90/111 acres. L14/24 SR7356
Know yee that for and in consideration that James Chillcott of the County of Ann Arundell in our s'd Province of Maryland hath due unto him one hundred thirty acres of land within our s'd Province by afsignment of **George Yate** the afsignee of **David Poole** for his, the s'd Pooles, transporting of severall persons to this Province as appears on record. Upon such conditions and terms as are exprefsed in our Conditions of Plantation of this our Province of Maryland, wee doe hereby grant unto the s'd Chillcott all that parcell of land called The Addition lying in the s'd County of Ann Arundell on the west side of South River about three miles from the river beginning at a bound Chestnutt by a great branch side. *Adjoins West Puddington and Arnold Gray.*
Note: Two adjoining tracts were granted in this document. The second tract, which is unnamed and described as a "small adjoining tract," could not be drawn because the boundary course data was insufficient.

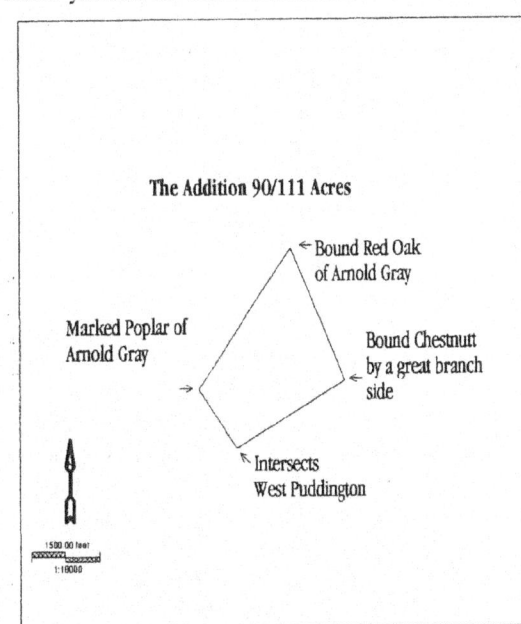

The Addition (Nicholas Gassaway) 9/8/1688 – 70 acres. L12/135 SR7354
Cecilius. Grant for seventy acres of land to Nicholas Gassaway of the County of Ann Arundell, Gent, bearing date 9/8/1688, considered by afsignment of **George Yate** the afsignee of **James Connaway** part of a warrant for two thousand five hundred five acres formerly granted to the s'd Connaway. Conditions dated 7/2/1651 (alteration 9/22/1658). Cert: Lib GY Fol 439. Name: The Addition, Manor of Ann Arundel. Yearly Rent: one shilling five pence the same for every alienation of the land in the usuall form. Witness: **Charles Calvert Esq.** *Note: The abbreviated patent format did not include location or boundary course information. Location information was eventually found in the Cert (L11 or GG/484 (not 48 9) SR7353), however, the tract cannot be drawn because of incomplete boundary course data.*

The Addition (John Gray) 9/10/1672 300 acres. L17/292 SR7358
Know yee that for and in consideration that John Gray of Ann Arundell County in our s'd Province of Maryland hath due unto him three hundred acres of land within our s'd Province by afsignment of **George Yate** the afsignee of **Thomas Taylor** attorney of Jerome White Esq. Part of a warrant for eleven hundred acres to the s'd White granted 4/9/1672, as appears on record. Upon such conditions and terms as are exprefsed in our Conditions of Plantation of this our Province of Maryland we doe hereby grant unto the s'd John Gray all that tract or parcell of land called The Addition lying in Ann Arundell County on the south side of South River beginning at a Bound Oak standing on a plaine by a great marsh. *Note: The tract cannot be drawn because the second course lacks distance and the fourth course crosses the first course.*

The Burgh (William Burges) 2/9/1650 – 300/249 acres. LQ/403 SR7345

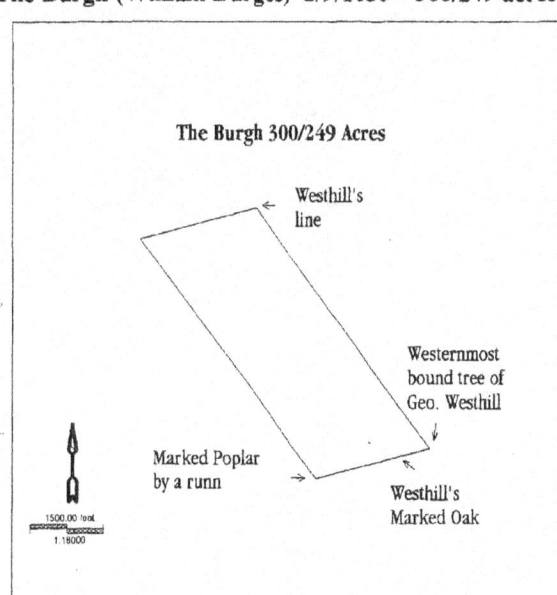

Know yee that for and in consideration that William Burges hath transported himself, **Anthony Holland** and **Thomas Hilliard** into this Province here to inhabit and upon such considerations and terms as are exprefsed in our Conditions of Plantation of our s'd Province of Maryland, do hereby grant unto the s'd William Burges all that parcell of land called The Burgh lying on the west side of Chesapeake Bay and on the south side of the South River next adjoining to land lately laid out for **George Westhill** and **Thomas Befson** of the s'd County, Planters, beginning at Westhill's east by north line. *Adjoins Scornton.*

The Conclusion (Richard Foster) 9/25/1666 – 50/32 acres. L10.152 SR7352

Know yee that wee for and in consideration that Richard Foster, Planter, hath due unto him fifty acres of land within our s'd Province by afsignment from **Richard Beard,** Gent, out of a warrant for six hundred twenty acres as appears on record. Upon such considerations and terms as are exprefsed in our Conditions of Plantation of our s'd Province of Maryland, doe hereby grant unto the s'd Foster a parcell of land called The Conclusion lying in the s'd County on the south side of the South River and on the east side of Flatt Creek beginning at a bound Oak of **Richard Cheney.** *Also adjoins the land of **John Wheeler** and land of **Marin Duvall.***

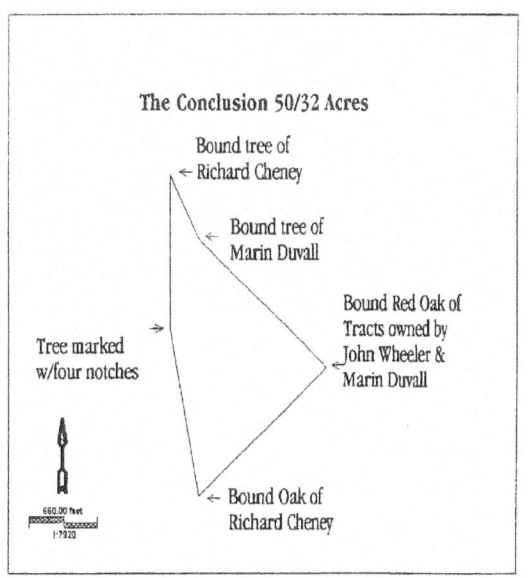

The Diligent Search (William Richardson) 10/1/1678 – 75/69 acres. L20/94 SR7361

By Virtue of a warrant granted unto William Richardson of the County of Ann Arundell, Gent, for two hundred fifty six acres of land bearing the date 5/14/1678, these are in humble manner to certifie that I **George Yate,** Deputy Surveyor under **Baker Brooke,** Surveyor General, hath laid out for the s'd William Richardson a parcell of land called The Diligent Search lying in the s'd County in the branches of the Road River beginning at a bound Poplar of the land of **Ferdinand Batten.** *Also adjoins the land of **Richard Talbott.** Note: This tract is located on the southern boundary between the West River Hundred and the Herring Creek Hundred. It is surrounded by tracts that are shown in various Rent Rolls as being in these Hundreds. However, the same Rent Rolls list this as a South River Hundred Tract so I have included it here.*

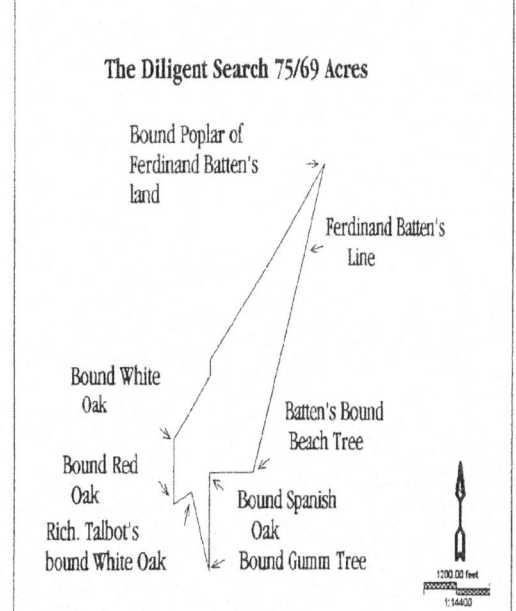

The Enlargement (John Welsh) 5/25/1704 – 50 acres. LDD5i/440 SR7378
By virtue of a warrant for fifty acres of land granted on 1/22/1703 unto **Joseph King** of Ann Arundell County and whereas the s'd warrant was afsigned by the s'd King to the s'd Welsh and also by virtue of two other warrants granted unto the s'd John Welsh the one of thirty acres dated 1/28/1703, the other of seventeen acres dated 5/23/1704. These are to certify that I have laid out for the s'd John Welsh a parcell of land called The Enlargement lying in the s'd County at the head of the South River adjacent to a tract called *Arnold Gray*. Begins at an old bounded Oak of a Parcel of land called *Madoc's (Maddox) Adventure*. *Note: The tract could not be drawn because of erroneous boundary course information. That is to say that some boundary lines cross others toward the middle rather than at the end.*

The Equality (James Sanders) 5/10/1685 – 140/137 acres. LNS#2/138 SR7371
Know yee that wee for and in consideration that James Sanders of Ann Arundell County in our s'd Province of Maryland hath due unto him one hundred forty acres of land within our s'd Province being due unto him by a warrant for the same quantity bearing date 6/25/1684, as appears on record. Upon such considerations and terms as are exprefsed in our Conditions of Plantation of our s'd Province of Maryland, doe hereby grant unto the s'd John Sanders all that tract or parcell of land called The Equality lying in the s'd County in the woods beginning at a bound Oak by John's Cabbin Branch, it being a bound tree of **Richard Cheney**. *Also adjoins a tract called John's Cabbin and The Flatt Cr.*

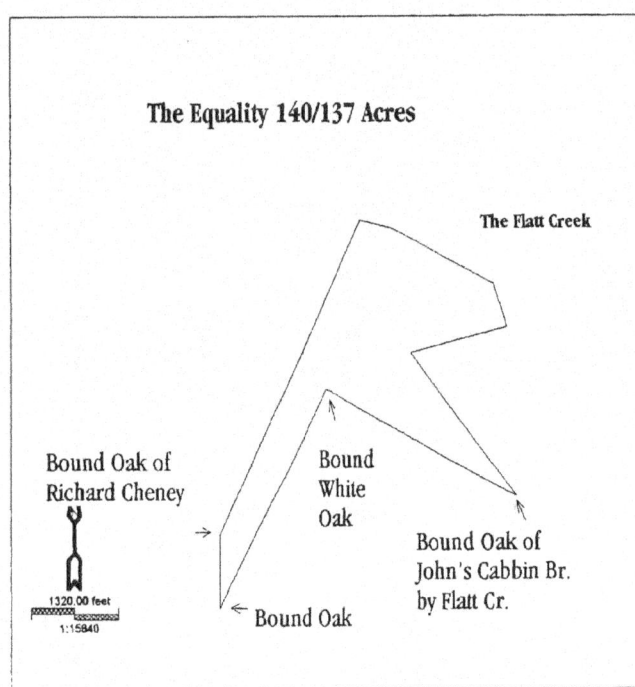

The Friend's Choice (John Gray & William Jones) 8/8/1670 – 340/320 acres.
L14/12 SR7356.

Know Yee that for and in consideration that William Jones and John Gray, Planters, of Ann Arundell County in our Province of Maryland hath due unto them three hundred and forty acres of land in our s'd Province by afsignment of **George Yate** out of a greater number of rights afsigned to the s'd Yate from **David Poole** as appears on record. And, upon such considerations and terms as are exprefsed in our Conditions of Plantation, doe hereby grant unto the s'd Gray and Jones a parcell of land about three miles and a half from the north side of the South River beginning at a bounded Red Oak it being the westernmost bound Oak of the west line of **Robert Franklin** (*Hickory Hills*).

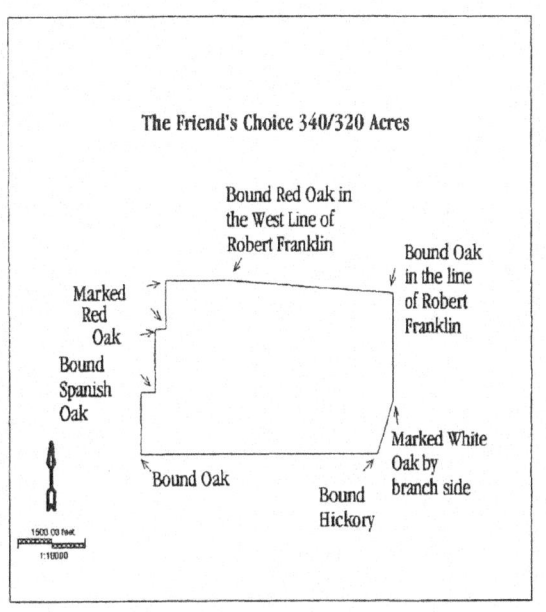

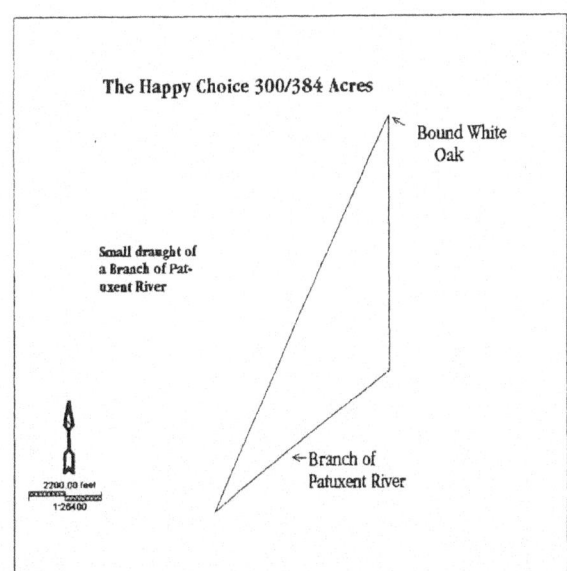

The Happy Choice (George Yate) 5/10/1671 – 300/384 acres.
L16/239 SR7357

Know yee that for and in consideration that George Yate of the County of Ann Arundell hath due unto him three hundred acres of land within our s'd Province by afsignment from **Thomas Knighton** of the s'd County part of a warrant for one thousand and fifty acres *(granted)* to the s'd Knighton 6/9/1670, as appears on record. Upon such considerations and terms as are exprefsed in our Conditions of Plantation of our s'd Province of Maryland, wee doe hereby grant unto the s'd Yate all that parcell called The Happy Choice lying on the east side of Patuxent River branches beginning at a bound White Oak. *Note: The second (of three) courses lacked distance and direction. In order to draw this tract it was necessary to draw the first and third courses (reversing direction on the third) and close on the second course.*

The Indian Range (Robert Franklin) 9/20/1665 – 250/217 acres. L8/4-2 SR7350

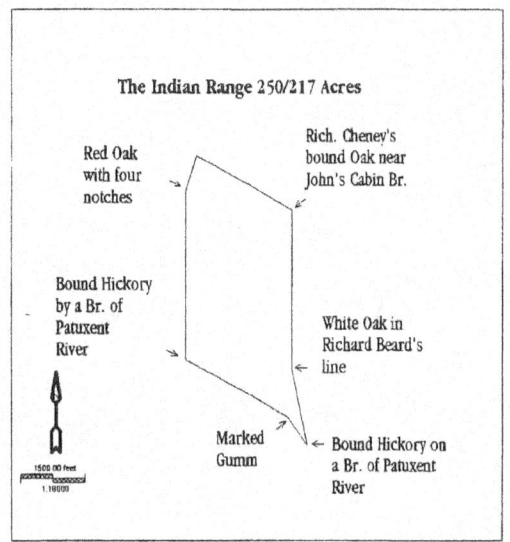

Know yee that for and in consideration that Robert Franklin hath due unto him two hundred fifty acres of land within our s'd Province by afsignment to the s'd Franklin by **George Yate** the afsignee of **John Dartford** for transporting himself, **Francis Clarke, James Blunt, Sarah Oberton,** and **Stephen Harper** into this Province here to inhabit, as appears on record. Upon such considerations and terms as are exprefsed in our Conditions of Plantation of this our Province of Maryland, wee doe hereby grant unto the s'd Robert Franklin all that parcel of land called The Indian Range lying in the s'd County beginning in the woods at a bounded White Oak in **Richard Beard's** line. *Adjoins land of Richard Cheney, John's Cabin Branch, and the Patuxent River.*

The Iron Mine (Jerome White) 4/10/1668 – 500/502 acres. L11/332 SR7353

Know Yee that for and in consideration that Jerome White Esq. of the County of St. Marie's in our Province hath due unto him five hundred acres of land within our s'd Province, part of a warrant for eight hundred acres formerly granted. Doe hereby grant unto him the s'd Jerome White a parcell of land lying in Ann Arundell County and on the head of a River called the South River and in the western side of the South Branch of the s'd River and on the north side of land now in the pofsefsion of **George Nettlefold**.

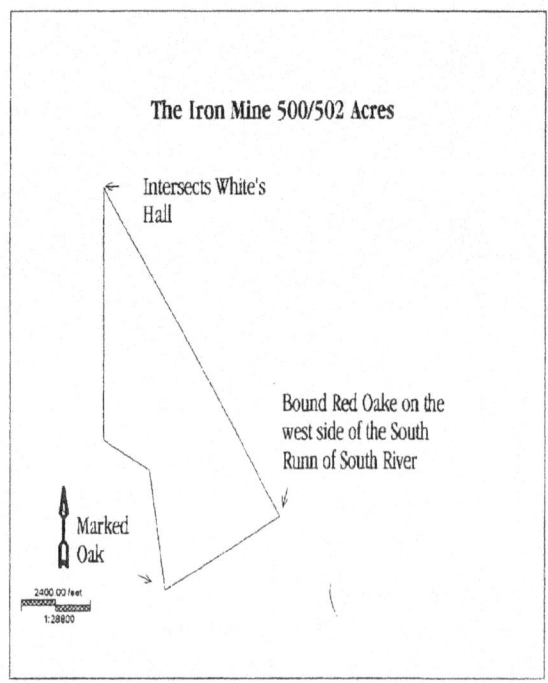

The Landing (Robert Proctor) 9/8/1668 – 70/57 acres. L11/484 SR7354

Grant for seventy acres of land iſsued to Robert Proctor of the County of Ann Arundel, Gent, bearing the date 9/8/1668. Consideration by aſsignment by **William Bateman** part of a warrant for one hundred acres of land formerly granted to the s'd Bateman. Condicions date: 7/2/1649, (with alteracon) 9/22/1658. Yearly rent: 1 shilling, five pence the same for a fine upon every alienacon of the same in the usual form. Witneſsed by **Charles Calvert Esq.** *Note 1: There are two patent references (L11/482 and L12/135) for this tract. Neither provides location or boundary course data. Boundary courses from a later patent were used to make the drawing. Note 2 (from MSA Tract Index 73): Sold in 1673 to George Puddington. Devised in 1674 to Edward Burges*

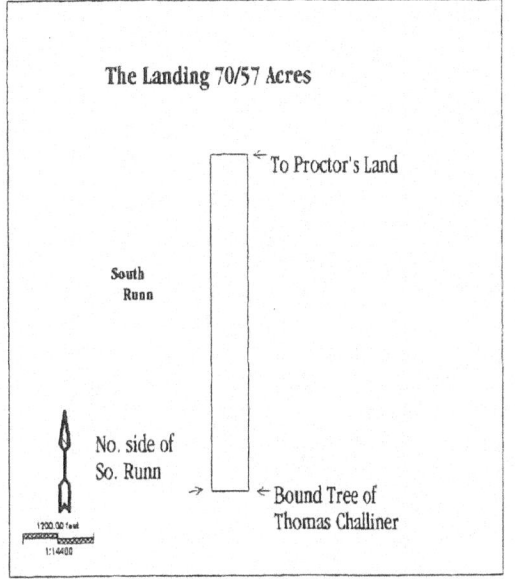

The Plaine (George Yate) 9/26/1677 – 120/117 acres. L20/40 SR7361

Know yee that wee for and in consideration that George Yate of Ann Arundell County in our s'd

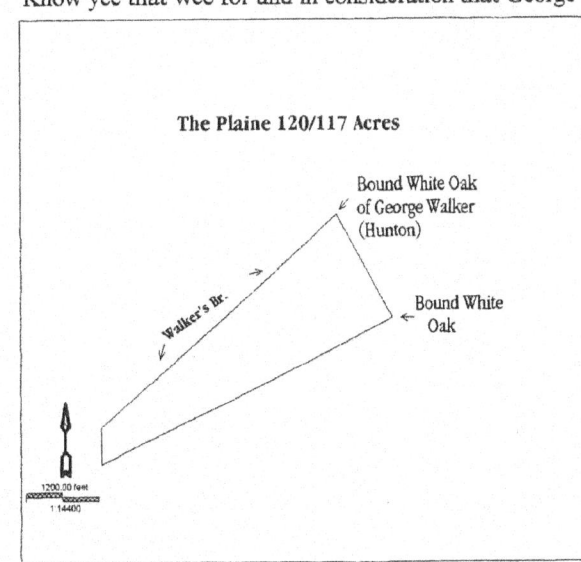

Province of Maryland hath due unto him one hundred twenty acres of land within our s'd Province by aſsignment of **George Holland**, parte of a warrant for three hundred sixty acres of land granted to the s'd Holland 10/3/1676, as appears on record. Upon such considerations and terms as are exprefsed in our Conditions of Plantation of this our s'd Province of Maryland, doe hereby grant unto the s'd Yate a parcell of land called The Plaine lying in the s'd County on the south side of the South River in the woods beginning at a bound White Oake it being a bound tree of land laid out for **George Walker** called *Hunton*, standing by Walker's Branch.

The Plaine (Robert Wilson) 7/10/1671 – 300/294 acres. L16/135 SR7357

Know yee that for and in consideration that Robert Wilson of the County of Ann Arundell in our s'd Province of Maryland hath due unto him three hundred acres of land within our s'd Province by afsignment of **John Pawson**, Merchant, part of a warrant for one thousand acres of land granted 9/30/1670, as appears on record. Upon such considerations and terms as are exprefsed in our Conditions of Plantation of our s'd Province of Maryland, doe hereby grant unto the s'd Robert Wilson all that parcell of land called The Plaine lying on the west side of a branch of the Patuxent River beginning at a bound Oak standing by a great Marsh. *Adjoins the land of **John Howerton**. Note: This tract is probably in what is now Prince George's County.*

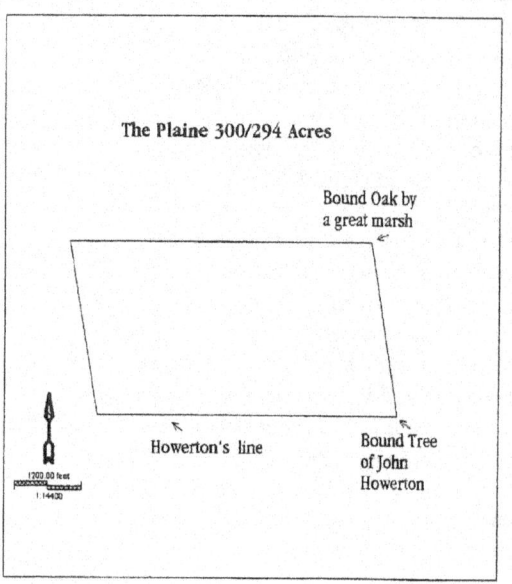

The Schoolhouse (John Grammar) 10/25/1659 – 100/93 acres. L4/151 SR7346

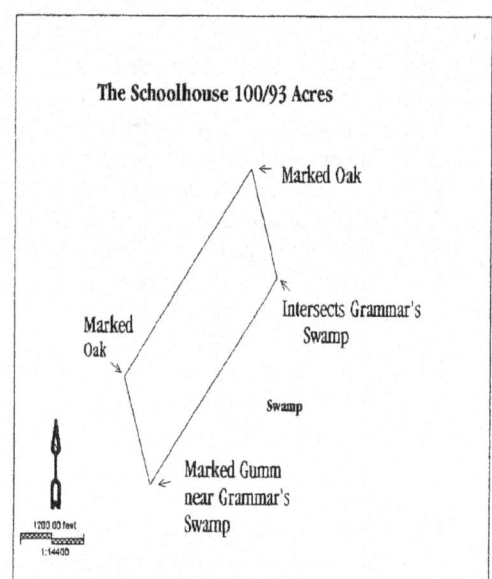

Know yee that for and in consideration that John Grammar and **Lawrence Ward** have transported themselves into this Province here to inhabit and the s'd John Grammar hath one hundred acres more due him by afsignment from **Richard Preston**. Upon such considerations and terms as are exprefsed in our declaration bearing date 7/21/1649, in our Conditions of Plantation, doe hereby grant unto the s'd John Grammar all that parcell of land called The Schoolhouse formerly surveyed for Lawrence Ward on the north side of the Patuxent River near Island Creek beginning at a marked Oak standing near a branch. *Note 1: The patent conveys three tracts. Two of these cannot be drawn because of insufficient boundary course data. Note 2: Although the grant is to Grammar, the rights are based in part on "rights" belonging to Lawrence Ward. The patent neither includes nor makes reference to a transfer or assignment of these rights from Ward to Grammar.*

The Security (John Brewer) 8/5/1664 – 66/49 acres. L7/267 SR7349

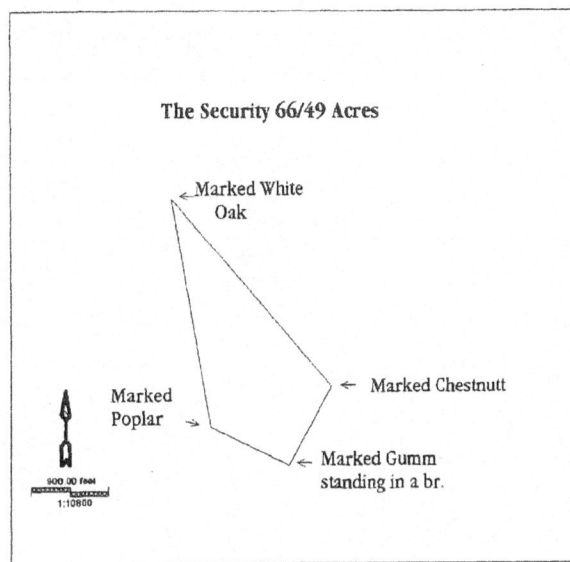

Know yee that wee for and in consideration that John Brewer, Planter, of this Province hath due unto him sixty six acres of land being part of a warrant for four hundred acres as appears on record. Upon such considerations and terms as are exprefsed in our Conditions of Plantation of our Province of Maryland, doe hereby grant unto the s'd John Brewer a parcell of land called The Security lying on the west side of Chesapeake Bay in Ann Arundell County on the south side of the South River beginning at a marked Chestnutt. *Bounded on the east by the land of **William Burges**.*

The Tryangle (Thomas Taylor) 9/10/1672 – 36/36 acres. L17/300 SR7358

Know yee that wee for and in consideration that Thomas Taylor of Ann Arundell County, Gent, hath due unto him thirty six acres of land within our s'd Province by afsignment from **George Yate** the afsignee of him the s'd Thomas Taylor, attorney for **Jerome White, Esq**, parte of a warrant for nine hundred acres to the s'd White granted 4/9/1672, as appears on record. Upon such considerations and terms as are exprefsed in our Conditions of Plantation of our s'd Province of Maryland, doe hereby grant unto the s'd Thomas Taylor a parcell of land called The Tryangle lying in Ann Arundell County beginning at a bounded Red Oak in the land of the s'd Taylor. *Also adjoins a tract owned by **John Larkin** and Beaver Pond Branch.*

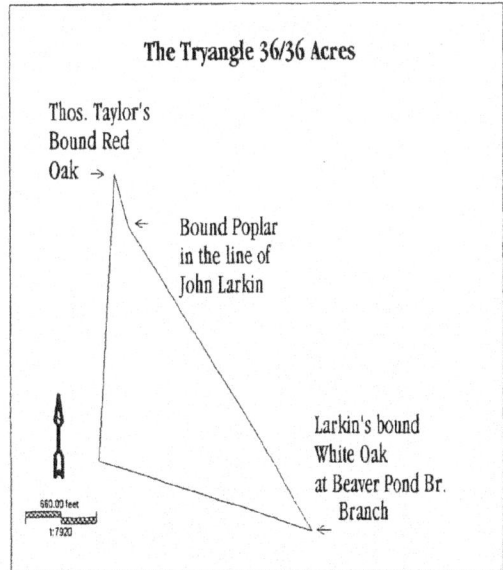

Timber Neck (Rich. Uggams & John Wheeler) 8/20/1665 – 200/199 acres. L8/150 SR7370

Know yee that wee for and in consideration that Richard Uggams and John Wheeler hath due unto them one hundred fifty acres of land within our s'd Province by afsignment from **George Puddington** to the s'd Wheeler out of a warrant for nine hundred acres, and fifty acres more the remainder of a warrant of one hundred acres granted the s'd Uggams as appears on record. Upon such considerations and terms as are exprefsed in our Conditions of Plantation of our Province of Maryland, doe hereby grant unto the s'd Uggams and Wheeler a parcell of land called Timber Neck lying in Ann Arundell County on the south side of the South River and on the west side of Jacob's Creek beginning at a marked Red Oak standing on a point. *Adjoins tracts of **Richard Beard**, **Richard Cheney**, and **Marin Duvall & William Young**.*

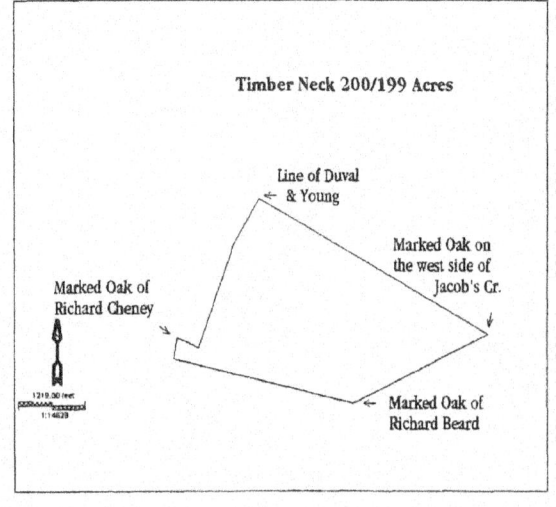

Townehill (Edmond Townehill) 2/16/1659 – 400/393 acres. L4/508 SR7346

Know yee that for and in consideration that Edmond Townhill of this Province, Planter, hath due unto him four hundred acres of land. And, upon such conditions and terms as are exprefsed in our Conditions of Plantation of our Province of Maryland, do grant unto the s'd Edmond Townhill a parcel of land called Townhill lying on the west side of Chesapeake Bay on the west side of a river called the Road River and on the north side of Muddy Branch next adjoining the land of **John Brewer** beginning at Brewer's northmost bound Oak.

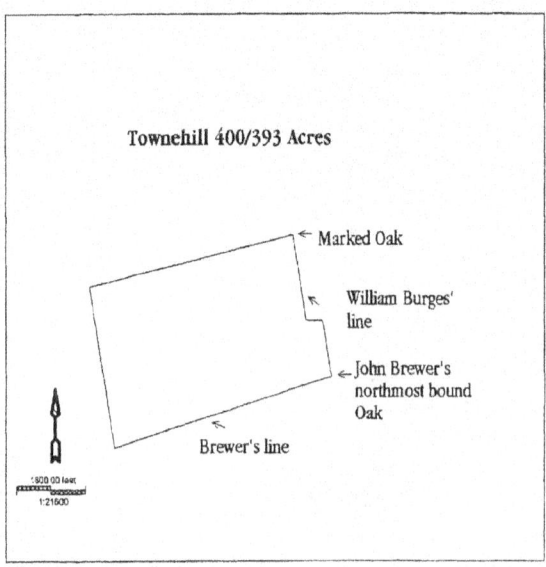

Townhill Choice **(Patrick Gossum)** 6/20/1652 - 180 acres. LAB&H/295 SR7344
Laid out for Patrick Gossum of the County of Ann Arundell, Planter, a parcell of land on the West side of the South River next adjoining the land of **Edmond Townhill** beginning at Townhill's marked Oak. *Note: No patent record has been found, however, a marginal note on the certification document says "pattent viz folio 165." However, this was not correct a patent was not found.*

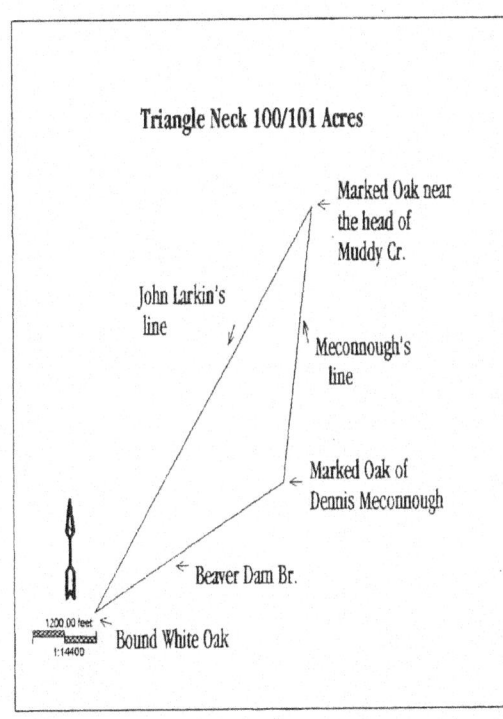

Triangle Neck (Robert Loyd)
8/5/1666 – 100/101 acres. L7/284 SR7349
Know yee that wee for and in consideration that Robert Loyd of this Province, Chrugeon *(Surgeon)* hath due unto him one hundred acres of land within our s'd Province by afsignment of a warrant by **Thomas Games** as appears on record. Upon such considerations and terms as are exprefsed in our Conditions of Plantations of our Province of Maryland, do hereby grant unto the s'd Robert Loyd a parcell of land called Triangle Neck lying on the south side of Road River in Ann Arundell County on the north side of *(a tract called)* Beaver Dam Neck beginning at a marked Oak of **Dennis McConough's** line.

Turkey Neck (Richard Snowden) 9/10/1698 – 200/188 acres. LCC4/122 SR7375

Know yee that for and in consideration that Richard Snowden hath due unto him two hundred acres of land within our s'd Province being due unto him by virtue of a warrant for the same quantity granted to him 4/21/1697, as appears on record in our Land Office. Upon such considerations and terms as are exprefsed in our Conditions of Plantation of our Province of Maryland, wee doe therefore hereby grant unto the s'd Richard Snowden all that tract or parcell of land lying in the Forke of Patuxent River and on the north side of the s'd Forke beginning at a bounded Red Oake near the s'd branch it being a bound tree of **John Gaither**. *Also adjoins Phelps His Choice.*

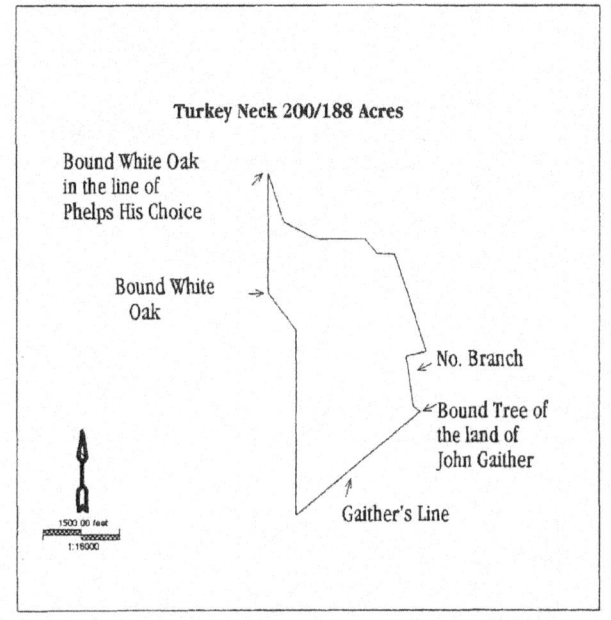

Uggam's Advantage **(Richard Uggams)** 8/5/1664 – 50 acres. L7/294 SR7349
Know yee that wee for and in consideration that Richard Uggams of this Province, Planter, hath due unto him fifty acres of land within our s'd Province by afsignment from **John Hatten** of this Province, Planter, who hath transported **John Verson** Anno 1657, as appears on record. Upon such considerations and terms as are exprefsed in our Conditions of Plantation of our s'd Province of Maryland, doe hereby grant unto the s'd Richard Uggams all that parcell of land called Uggam's Advantage lying in Ann Arundell County and adjoining the plantation he now liveth upon. Begins at a marked Oak standing by the South River. *Adjoins land of **Archer Arbuckle, Ann Covill** and **George Nettlefold**. Note 1: The tract cannot be drawn because of incomplete boundary course data in the patent document. Note 2: This tract resurveyed in 1685 and renamed Powell's Inheritance (RR, AAC, pg. 41 SR7346).*

Unnamed Certification **(Thomas Myles)** Cert 9/21/1652 – 300 acres. LAB&H/276 SR7344
Laid out for Thomas Myles of Ann Arundell County a parcell of land lying on the west side of Chesapeake Bay next adjoining the land of **Roger Grosse** of the s'd place. *Note 1: The tract cannot be drawn because of incomplete boundary course data in the survey document. Note 2: A patent was not found. This tract was included because of the many references to the land of Thomas Myles (Miles) in other patents.*

Unnamed Certification **(Will Pyther)** 6/20/1650 – 250 acres. AB&H/296 SR7344
Laid out for Will Pyther of the County of Ann Arundell a parcel of land on the west side of Chesapeake Bay and on the west *(actually, south)* side of the Severn River next adjoining **Patrick Gossum** beginning at Gossum's bound Oak standing by a creek called Pyther's Cr. *Note 1: The certification does not identify this tract by name. However, MSA Land Records (Index 54)*

*indicate that it was called Pytherston and that it was patented by **John Brewer**. A marginal note on the Cert document confirms this but does not provide a patent reference. Note 2: Will Pyther also owned a smaller (60 acre) tract called Pytherston located on the north side of the Severn River.*

Unnamed Patent (Thomas Emerson) 8/27/1658 - 100 acres. LQ/101 SR7345
Know yee that wee for and in consideration that **Thomas Howell** hath transported one able bodied servant into this Province here to inhabit and upon such considerations and terms as are exprefsed in our Conditions of Plantation of this our s'd Province of Maryland, doe hereby grant unto the s'd Thomas Emerson all that parcell of land formerly surveyed for Thomas Emerson lying on the west side of Chesapeake Bay and near to a bay called the Three Island Bay upon a branch of the s'd Bay called Road River beginning at marked Pine at the mouth of a branch called Howell's Branch. *Note 1: This tract was Certified to Thomas Howell (LQ/107) as Howell and patented as an unnamed tract to Thomas Emerson. A transfer of "rights" from Howell to Emerson was not found. Note 2: The tract cannot be drawn because of incomplete boundary course information.*

Unnamed Patent (**Roger Grosse**) 8/15/1658 - 600 acres. LQ/90 SR7345
Know yee that wee for and in consideration that Roger Grosse of Ann Arundell County hath transported himself, his wife, and two servants into this province here to inhabit and hath due unto him two hundred acres more by afsignment from **Edward Lloyd**, as appears on record. Upon such considerations and terms as are exprefsed in our Conditions of Plantation of our s'd Province of Maryland, doe hereby grant unto the s'd Roger Grosse all that tract or parcell of land lying in the County of Ann Arundell in this Province of Maryland on the west side of Chesapeake Bay near a river called the Road River beginning at a marked Oak in a valley called Grosse's *Valley* by a marsh near the head of the s'd River. *Note: The tract cannot be drawn because of incomplete boundary course information in the patent document.*

Unnamed Patent (Robert Jones) 8/20/1658 – 100/98 acres. LQ/167 SR7345

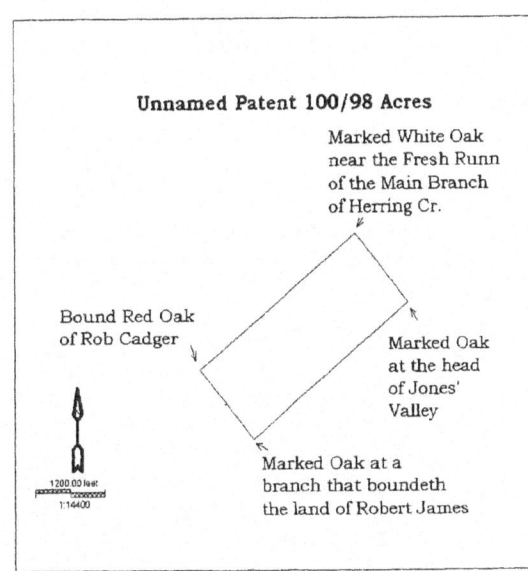

Know yee that wee for and in consideration that **William Stephenson** hath afsigned all right to land for transportation of **Dermott Mahalone** into this Province unto Robert Jones and also for that the s'd Jones hath transported **Annis** his wife into this Province here to inhabit. Upon such considerations and terms as are exprefsed in our Conditions of Plantation of our s'd Province of Maryland, do hereby grant unto the s'd Robert Jones a parcell of land in the woods adjoining to his own land beginning at a marked Red Oak standing on the boundary of **Robert Cadger**, upon the main branch of Herring Creek.

Unnamed Patent (William Pell) 8/27/1658 – 280/264 acres. LQ/116 SR7345
Know yee that wee for and in consideration that **William Pennington** hath transported himself, **Elizabeth** his wife and one servant into this Province, here to inhabit, and upon such considerations and terms as are exprefsed in our Conditions of Plantation of our s'd Province of Maryland, do hereby grant unto William Pell the afsignee of William Pennington, all that parcel of land formerly surveyed for the s'd Pennington lying on the west side of Chesapeake Bay near the mouth of the South River beginning at a pond called Pennington's Pond. *Note: Although not shown in the Patent Document, at some point this tract became known as Margaret's Fields and a resurvey is included here under that name.*

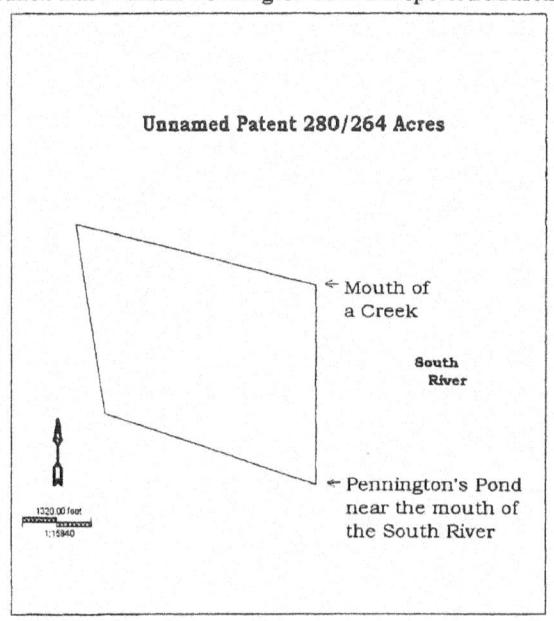

Unnamed Patent (Edward Townhill) 8/9/1658 – 270 acres. LQ/111 SR7345
Know yee that wee for and in consideration that **Patrick Gossum** and **Elizabeth,** his wife hath transported themselves and one servant into this Province here to inhabit and upon such considerations and terms as are exprefsed in our Conditions of Plantation of our s'd Province of Maryland, doe hereby grant unto the s'd Edward Townhill, the afsignee of Patrick Gossum, as appears on record, all that parcell of land formerly surveyed for the s'd Townhill lying on the west side of Chesapeake Bay and on the west side of the West River beginning at a marked Pine near the mouth of a branch called Townhill's Branch. Also another parcel of land formerly surveyed for the s'd Patrick beginning at the s'd Townhill's marked Oak. *Note: The patent conveys two tracts. Neither can be drawn because of incomplete boundary course data.*

Velmeade (John Dearing) 1/11/1667 – **400/400 acres.** L11/214 SR7353
Know yee that for and in consideration that John Dearing of Ann Arundell County in our s'd

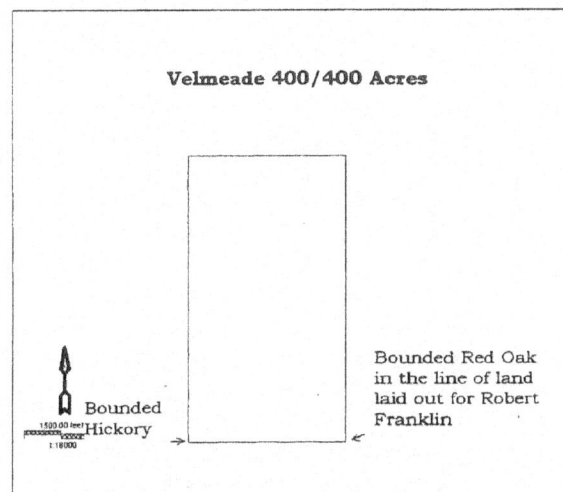

Province of Maryland hath due unto him two hundred acres of land by afsignment of **Charles Boetler** part of a warrant for two hundred and fifty acres formerly granted to the s'd Boetler, and fifty acres more by afsignment of **George Green** for his, the s'd Green's time of service performed in our s'd Province. Also, fifty acres more by the *letfall* of a parcell of land formerly sett forth under him called *The Choice* unto him granted which he, the s'd Dearing, hath delivered unto our Secretary's Office. And also, one hundred acres by afsignment from **John Blomfield** the afsignee of **John Gillum** and **Francis Richardson** for their transporting of themselves into our Province here to inhabit, all of which appears on record. Upon such considerations and terms as are exprefsed in our Conditions of Plantation of our s'd Province of Maryland, wee doe hereby grant unto the s'd John Dearing all that tract or parcell of land called Velmeade lying on the south side near the head of South River about four miles into the woods beginning at a bounded Red Oak in the line of land laid out for **Robert Franklin.** *Note 1: Either the surveyor or the clerk involved in transcribing the surveyor's notes was incorrect about Velmeade being located near the head of the South River. It is not. Note 2: "Velmeade lies near to the bridge over the Patuxent."* <u>Abstracts of Anne Arundel County Land Records, Vol 1, pg 105.</u>

Wade's Encrease (Robert Wade) 5/18/1679 – **75/73 acres.** L20/257 SR7361

Know yee that wee for and in consideration that Robert Wade of Ann Arundell County in our s'd Province of Maryland hath due unto him seventy five acres of land within our s'd Province part of a warrant for one hundred acres granted him 7/29/1678, as appears on record. Upon such conditions and terms as are exprefessed in our Conditions of Plantation of our Province of Maryland, doe hereby grant unto the s'd Robert Wade all that parcell of land called Wade's Encrease lying in Ann Arundell County on the south side of the South River in the woods beginning at a bound

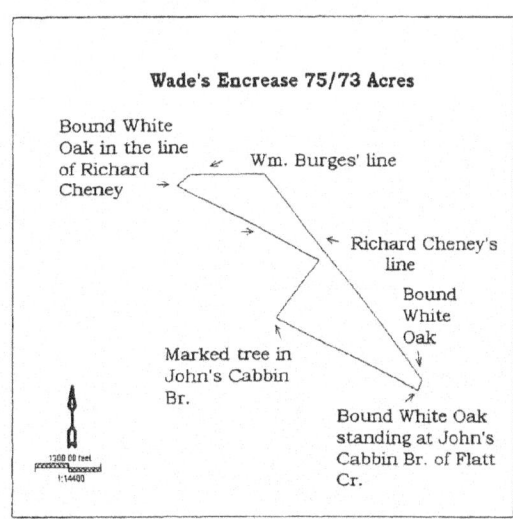

at a bound White Oak standing at a John's Cabbin Branch of a creek called The Flatt Creek. *Adjoins the lands of **Richard Cheney** and **William Burges**.*

Waterford (William Jones) 5/1/1674 – 800/813 **acres.** L19/347 SR7360

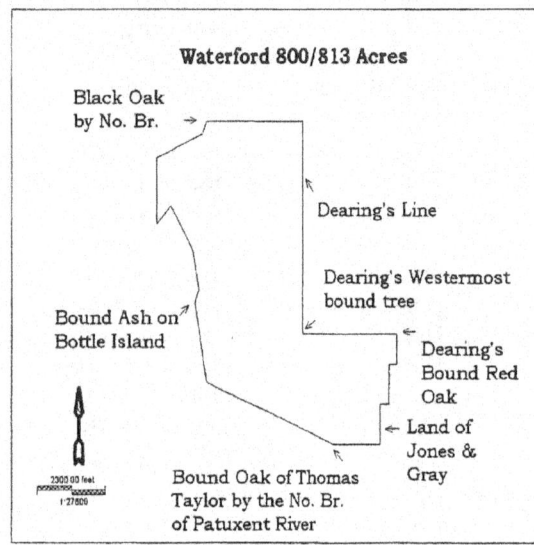

Know yee that for and in consideration that William Jones of Ann Arundell County in our s'd Province of Maryland hath due unto him eight hundred acres of land within our s'd Province part of a warrant for one thousand one hundred acres granted him 7/27/1675, as appears on record. Upon such considerations and terms as are exprefsed in our Conditions of Plantation of our late father **Cecilius**, of noble memory, wee doe hereby grant unto him the s'd William Jones all that parcell of land called Waterford lying in the s'd County on the North Branch of Patuxent River beginning at a bound tree of the land of **Thomas Taylor** standing by the North Branch. *Also adjoins the land of **John Dearing**.*

Walters His Lott (Richard Snowden) 10/10/1704 – 611/594 **acres.** LDSF/514 SR7373-2

Know yee that Richard Snowden in our Province of Maryland hath due unto him six hundred and eleven acres of land within our s'd Province being part of a warrant for seven hundred acres afsigned to him by **James Carroll** and granted unto the s'd Carroll 12/17/1703, as appears on record. Upon such considerations and terms as are exprefsed in our Conditions of Plantation wee doe grant unto the s'd Richard Snowden all that parcell of land called Walter's His Lott lying in the s'd County on the Great Forke of the Patuxent River and on the north side of a tract called *Robin Hood's Forrest* beginning at a bound Red Oak and a bound White Oak on a ridge to the north of a road leading to the falls of Patuxent River.

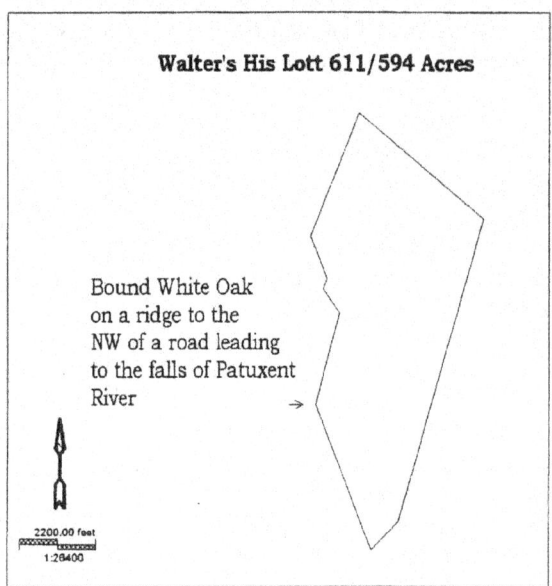

Wayman's Marsh (Leonard Wayman) 6/10/1706 – 55/45 acres. LCD/298 SR7376

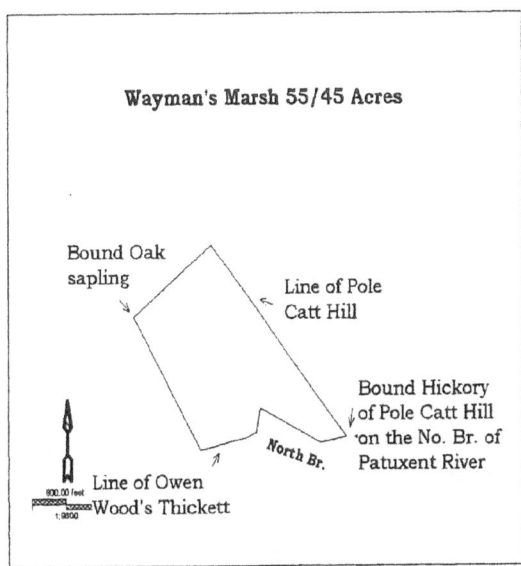

Know yee that for and in consideration that Leonard Wayman of Ann Arundell County in our Province of Maryland hath due unto him fifty five acres of land within our s'd Province being due unto him by virtue of a warrant for that quantity afsigned to him by **James Carroll** of the s'd County part of a warrant for two thousand acres granted him 5/15/1700, as appears on record in our Land Office. Upon such considerations and terms as are exprefsed in our Conditions of Plantation of this our Province, wee doe therefore hereby grant unto the s'd Wayman all that tract or parcell of land called Wayman's Marsh lying in the s'd County on the North Branch of Patuxent River beginning at a bound Hickory of the land called *Pole Catt Hill. Also adjoins Owen Wood's Thickett.*

West Puddington – (George Puddington) 2/8/1650 – 340/340 acres. LQ/395 SR7345

Know yee that for and in consideration that George Puddington hath transported **Mary** and **Comfort Puddington** and **Elizabeth Robins** in Anno 1649, here to inhabit and upon such considerations and terms as are exprefsed in Conditions of Plantation of our s'd Province of Maryland, we doe hereby grant unto the s'd George Puddington all that parcell of land called West Puddington lying on the west side of the Chesapeake Bay and on the south side of the South River on the north side of Burges' Branch beginning at a marked Oak on the west side of the swamp of the branch.

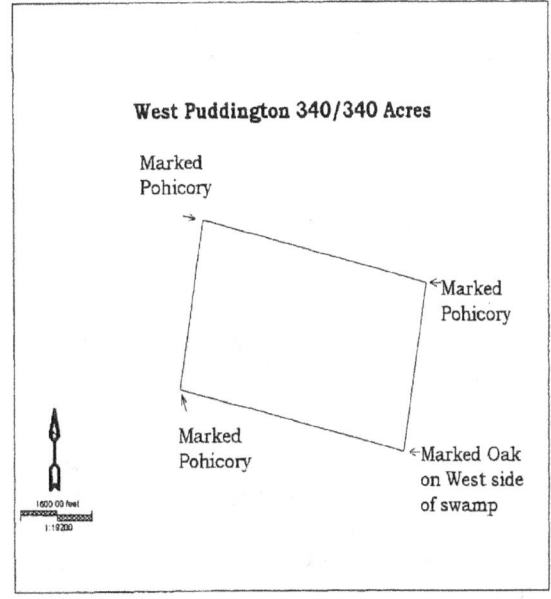

What You Will (John Duvall) 6/1/1700 – 373/379 acres. LIB&ILC/344 SR7368-1

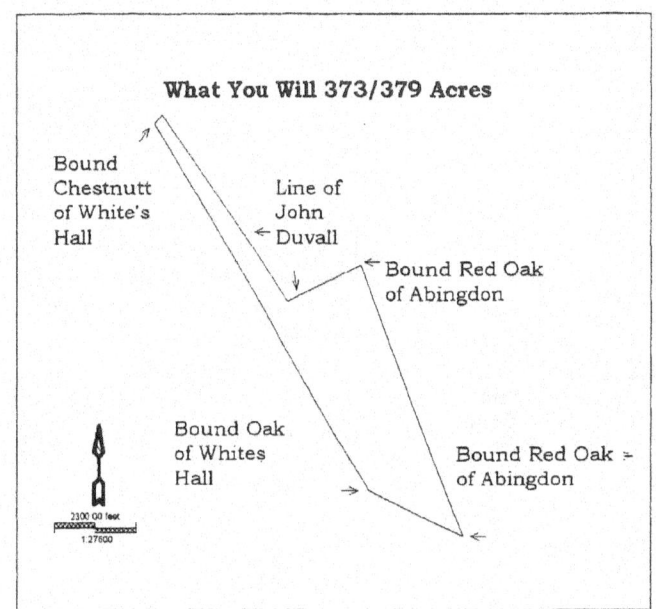

Know yee that wee for and in consideration that John Duvall of Ann Arundell County in our s'd Province of Maryland hath due unto him three hundred and seventy three acres of land within our Province by virtue of a warrant for foure thousand acres granted to him 10/15/1699, as appears on record. Upon such considerations and terms as are exprefsed in our Conditions of Plantation of this our Province of Maryland, wee doe therefore hereby grant unto the s'd John Duvall all that tract or parcell of land called What You Will lying in Ann Arundell County above the South River beginning at a bounded White Oak it being the first bound tree of *White's Hall* standing on the South side of the South Runn of the aforesaid river.

White's Ford (**Jane Gates**) 7/20/1693 – 800 acres. LB23i/147 SR7365
On July 20, 1693, **Charles Baltimore,** *in a Special Warrant that did not specify boundary courses, made two separate grants (L23/44 and 45, SR7364) of land described as "formerly" belonging to* **Jerome White Esq,** *(White's Hall) and lying at or near the head of the South River in Ann Arundell County. Eight hundred acres was granted by virtue of his affectionate special favor for his beloved God Daughter* **Ann Gates***, daughter of* **Joseph Gates***. One thousand acres adjoining was granted to her mother* **Ann Gates the Elder***.*

White's Ford Part Of (**Jane Gates** the elder) 7/20/1693 – 1,000 acres LB23i/147 SR7365
On July 20, 1693, **Charles Baltimore,** *in a Special Warrant that did not specify deed courses, granted the larger portion of White's Ford to Jane Gates (the elder), the wife of* **Joseph Gates** *and mother of* **Jane Gates***. The property is described only as being a one thousand acre parcel lying at or near the head of the South River in Ann Arundell County. Note 1:* <u>Maryland Rent Rolls Baltimore and Anne Arundel Counties 1700-1707, 1705-1724</u> *(pg. 167) states that White's Hall a 1,800 acre tract (not White's Ford), located near the head of the South River was in the possession of Joseph Gates of London in right of his wife Jane and his daughter Jane. On 9/28/1714, Joseph Gates of London and his wife Jane sold their 1,000-acre portion of White's Ford to one* **Gerrard Hopkins** *and* **Samuel Galloway** *of Ann Arundell County. The same day, Jane Gates, Junior, Seamstress of London, also sold her 800- hundred acre portion to Hopkins and Galloway (*<u>Abstracts of Anne Arundel Land Records,</u>*Vol. 3, pgs 109 and 110). thereby consolidating the former White's Hall along with adjoining tracts called What You Will and The Angle, under their ownership.*

White's Hall (Jerome White)
5/29/1665 - 1,800/1,800 acres. L7/587 SR 7349.
Know Yee that Wee for and in consideration that Jerome White Esq., of this Province hath due unto him eighteen hundred acres of land out of our Special Warrant for two thousand acres of land granted the s'd Jerome White bearing the date the eighth day of December 1662, as appears on record. Upon such considerations and terms as are exprefsed in our Conditions of Plantation of our Province of Maryland, do hereby grant unto the s'd Jerome White a parcell of land called White's Hall lying on the south side of the South Run of the South River beginning at a marked Red Oak upon a point respecting the land formerly laid out for **John Freeman** called

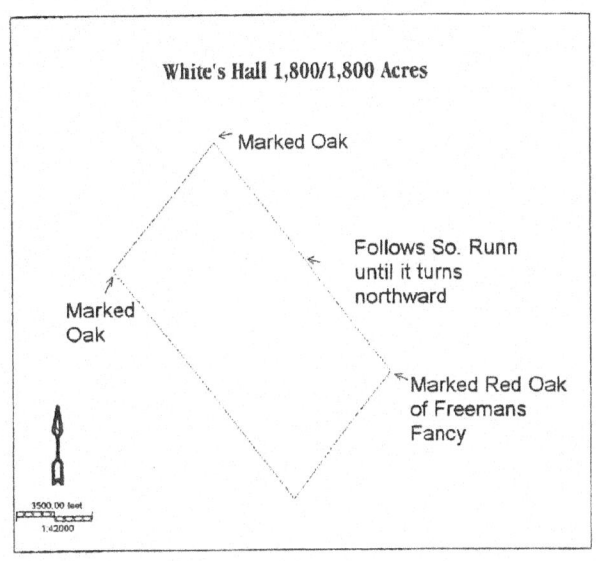

*Freeman's Fancy. Also adjoins Harness' Range. Note 1: Regranted to **Joseph Gates** of London by the rights of his wife (**Jane**) and his daughter (**Jane**). See footnotes for White's Ford and White's Ford Part Of.*

White's Plaines (Jerome White)
8/8/1669 –2,000/2,012 acres. L12/401 SR7354
For and in consideration that Jerome White Esq., of our s'd Province of Maryland hath due unto him 2,000 acres of land formerly granted to him as appears on record. Conditions, 1649, and 1633. *Note 1: This abbreviated patent document may have been influenced by White's position as Surveyor General. Note 2: The patent document does not specify boundary courses. The tract was drawn from courses found in the certification (L12/409 SR7354).*

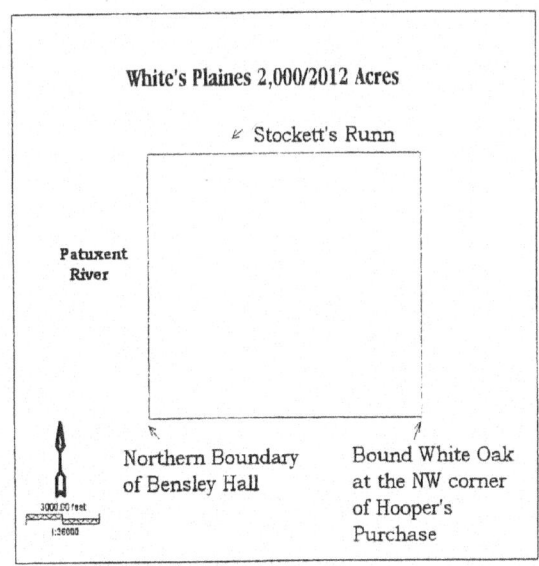

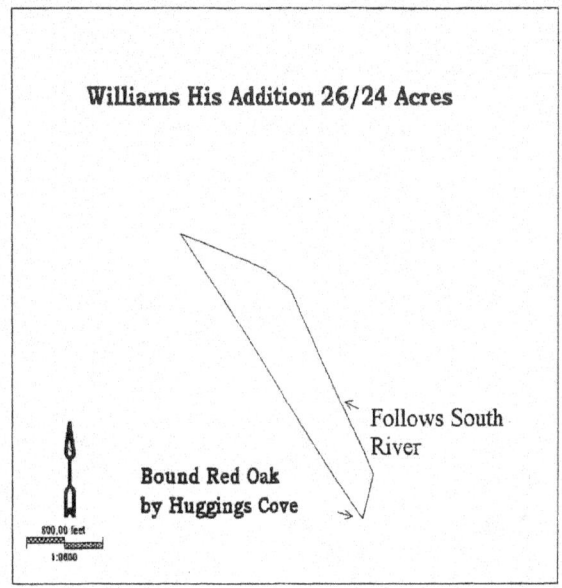

Williams His Addition (Benjamin Williams) 6/12/1687 -26/24 acres. LNS2i/732 SR7371
Know yee that for and in consideration that Benjamin Williams of Ann Arundell County in our s'd Province of Maryland hath due unto him twenty six acres of land within our s'd Province by afsignment of **Charles Gorsuch** of the s'd County parte of a warrant for six hundred acres granted to the s'd Gorsuch 1/10/1687, as appears on record. Upon such considerations and terms as are exprefsed in our Conditions of Plantation of our s'd Province of Maryland, wee doe therefore grant unto the s'd Benjamin Williams all that tract or parcell of land called Williams His Addition lying on the south side of the South River beginning at a bound Red Oak by a cove called Huggin's Cove. *Also adjoins the South River.*

Williams His Angle (Benjamin Williams) 6/1/1688 - 15/15 acres. LNS2/597 SR7371
Know yee that for and in consideration that Benjamin Williams of Ann Arundell County in our s'd Province of Maryland hath due unto him fifteen acres of land within our s'd Province by afsignment of **John Dorsey** of the s'd County out of a warrant for two hundred acres granted to him 10/4/1684, as appears on record. Upon such considerations and terms as are exprefsed in our Conditions of Plantation of our Province of Maryland, wee doe hereby grant unto the s'd Benjamin Williams all that parcell of land called Williams His Angle lying in the s'd County on the south side of the South River beginning at a bound tree of **Coll William Burges'** land. *Also adjoins land of Richard Cheney and Covell's Folly.*

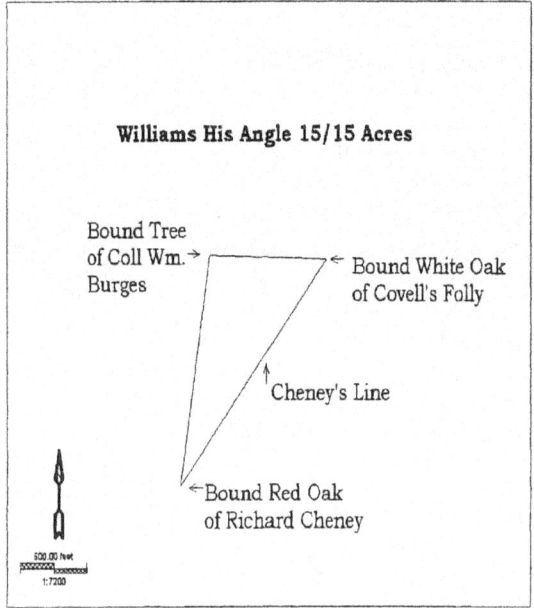

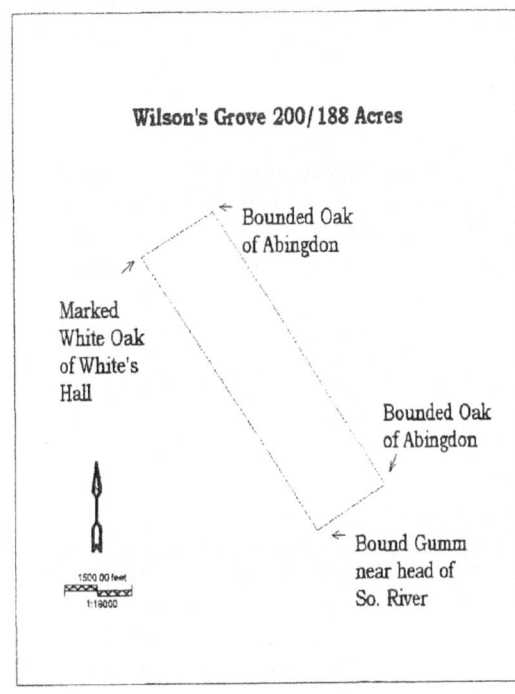

Wilson's Grove (Robert Wilson) 7/5/1672 200/188 acres. L16/385 SR7357.

Know yee that for and in consideration that Robert Wilson, Gent, of Ann Arundell County in our s'd Province of Maryland hath due unto him two hundred acres of land within our s'd Province part of a warrant for six hundred fifty acres to him granted 6/17/1671, as appears on record. Upon such considerations and terms as are exprefsed in our Conditions of Plantation of this our Province of Maryland we doe hereby grant unto the s'd Robert Wilson all that parcell of land called Wilson's Grove lying in the s'd County between the heads of the Severn and South Rivers beginning at a bounded Red Oak of a parcel of land *(Abingdon)* formerly laid out for **Robert Proctor** and **John Gaither** of the s'd County. *Note (from MSA Tract Index 73): Sold to **John & James Powell** and by the Powells to **William Jones** who devised it to **Elizabeth & John Duvall** his daughter and son-in-law (1689- IH#1/66).*

Wrighten (Nicholas Terrett Jr.) 11/10/1697 – 715/703 acres. LCD/6 SR7376

Know ye that whereas **Nicolas Terrett** *(the elder)* of Ann Arundell County in our s'd Province of Maryland , deceased 7/12/1684, being seized in fee simple for a certaine of two hundred acres did obtain our Special Warrant of Resurvey for same including what surplus should be found. Whereas it was certified that there was a quantity of four hundred ninety acres surplus for which the s'd Nicholas Terratt did pay five thousand lbs of tobacco and whereas the s'd Nicholas died before he obtained grant for same first making his LWT in writing wherein he devised one moiety of the s'd tract to his son Nicholas. For the consideration as aforesaid, do give and grant unto the s'd Nicholas the aforesaid tract including surplus land therein contained beginning at a bound tree by the River. *Adjoins His LOP's Mannor (Ann Arundell Manor) and the Patuxent River.*

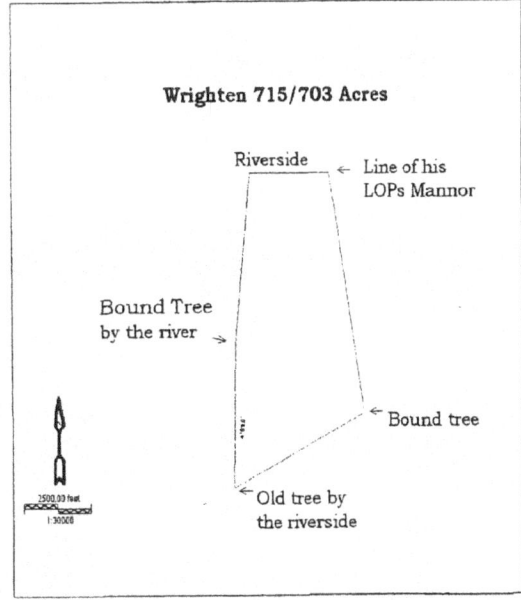

Wrighton (William Taylor) 9/7/1650 – 100 acres. LAB&H/96 SR7346

Know yee that for and in consideration that **Walter Mansfield** hath transported himself into this our Province in Anno 1651, here to inhabit and, upon such conditions and termes as are exprefsed in our Conditions of Plantation of our Province of Maryland, doe hereby grant unto William Taylor, afsignee of Walter Mansfield, a parcel of land formerly surveyed for the s'd Mansfield and now called Wrighton lying on the west side of Chesapeake Bay near to Three Island Bay upon the west side of the Road River beginning at a marked Chestnutt standing on a branch called Harwood's Br. *Also adjoins Mansfield's Cr. Note: The tract could not be drawn because of incomplete boundary course data.*

Wyngate's Rest (Thomas Wyngate) 9/8/1674 – 40/40 acres. L18/215 SR7359

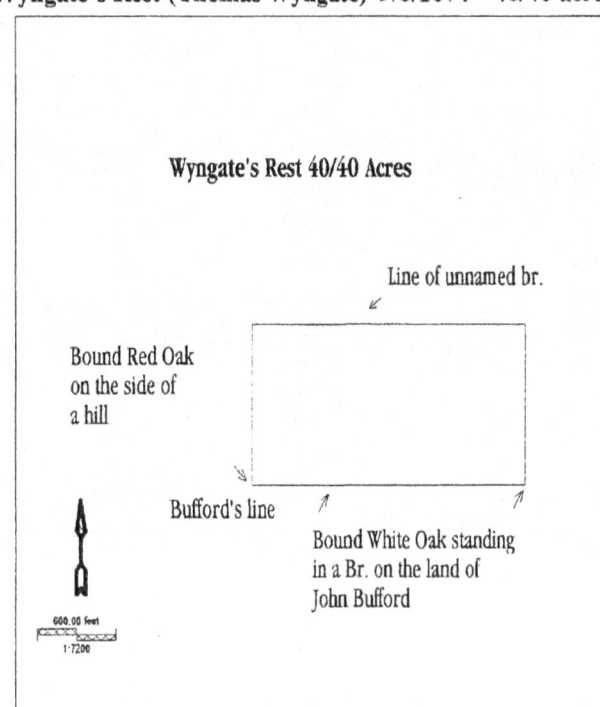

Know yee that for and in consideration that Thomas Wyngate of Ann Arundell County in our s'd Province of Maryland hath due unto him forty acres of land within our s'd Province by afsignment from **George Yate** part of a warrant for twelve hundred acres formerly granted to the s'd Yate, as appears on record. Upon such considerations and terms as are exprefsed in our Conditions of Plantation of our Province of Maryland, doe hereby grant unto the s'd Thomas Wyngate all that parcell of land called Wyneat's Rest lying in the s'd County on the main branch of Road River beginning at a bound White Oak, standing by a branch, on the land of **John Bufford.**

Younger Besson (Thos. Besson the Younger) 2/16/1659 – 50/49 acres. L4/07 SR7346
Know yee that for and in consideration that Thomas Besson (the younger) hath due unto him fifty acres of land and upon such considerations and terms as are exprefsed in our Conditions of Plantation of our Province of Maryland, do hereby grant to the s'd Besson a parcel of land called Younger Besson lying on the west side of Chesapeake Bay on the south side of the South River next adjoining to the land formerly laid out unto **Thomas Befson (the elder)** and land of **George Nettlefold** beginning at the westernmost bound Oak of Nettlefold's line.

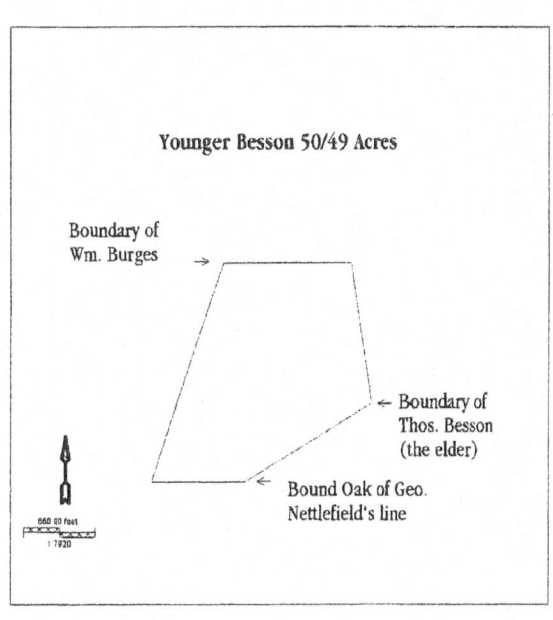

Younger Besson 50/49 Acres

Appendices A-L

The following clusters of adjoined tracts are provided to assist in determining the "relative" location of tracts within the South River Hundred. Without longitude/latitude references in patent documents, determining even the relative location in a given tract is far from an exact science. It is necessary to find a landmark reference a patent document that still exists (even though the current name may have changed). Sometimes finding such a boundary reference may not be enough. Knowing that a tract touched The Flatt Creek without knowing where or, at least, whether the touching point was closer to the mouth or the head, is nothing more than a clue. Once a tract is placed with "relative" accuracy, i.e., on the north side of Pyther's Creek at the mouth, you have a starting point if you disregard three hundred years of erosion. By starting with this "Rosetta Stone" tract and adding tracts outwardly, it is possible to develop a cluster of adjoined tracts that provides a relatively accurate picture of historical tract alignment, within the limitations described above.

The clusters shown in the appendices are scattered in roughly defined areas throughout the South River Hundred. The tracts included are those that are "drawable" and "fitable" to adjoining tracts based on information found in patent documents. A number of tracts, which are drawable and do identify adjoining tracts, are not included because they do not fit. There can be several reasons for this including resurveys or subdivisions that alter the tract footprint and, thereby, adversely affect the fit with adjoining unaltered tracts.

Patent documents for tracts that could not be drawn sometimes provide useful placement information and it may be possible to identify tracts within a cluster that adjoined an "undrawable" tract. It may also be helpful to consult modern day map books or maps for community names, etc., which still bear the names of tracts, creeks, etc. from the targeted period. I have found a number of places in the South River Hundred that are still named as they were. A few examples are: Velmeade, Friend's Choice, Indian Range, Dodon, Waterford, Coxby (Estates), Stocket's Run, Flat Creek, and Selby Bay.

Appendix A

Northern Patuxent River area. Some of these tracts are now located (all or in part) in present day Prince George's County.

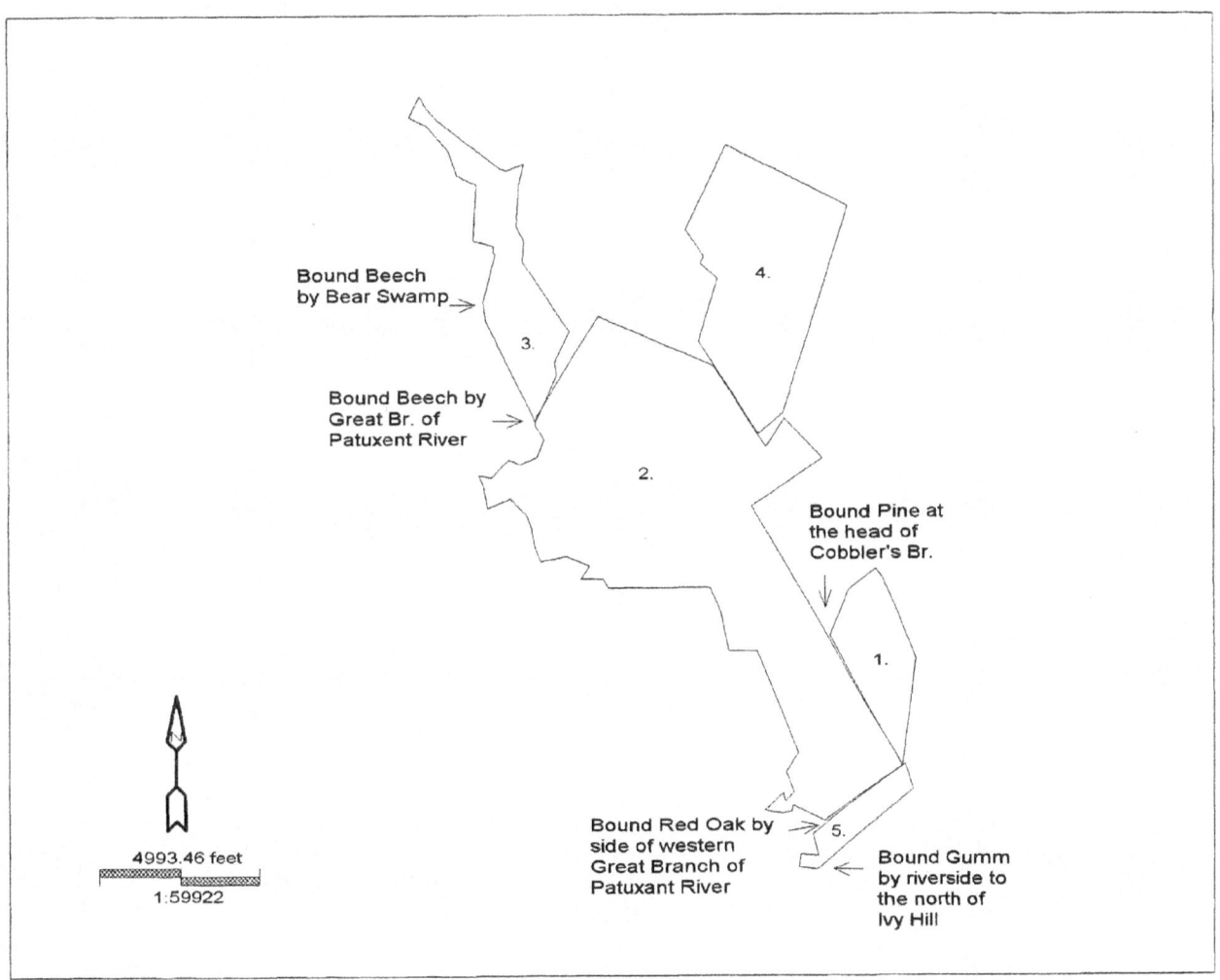

1. Efford's Delight
2. Robin Hood's Forrest
3. Rutland's Purchase Enlarged
4. Walters His Lott
5. Soldier's Furtune

Appendix B

South River at mouths of Western Branch and North and South Runns, northward

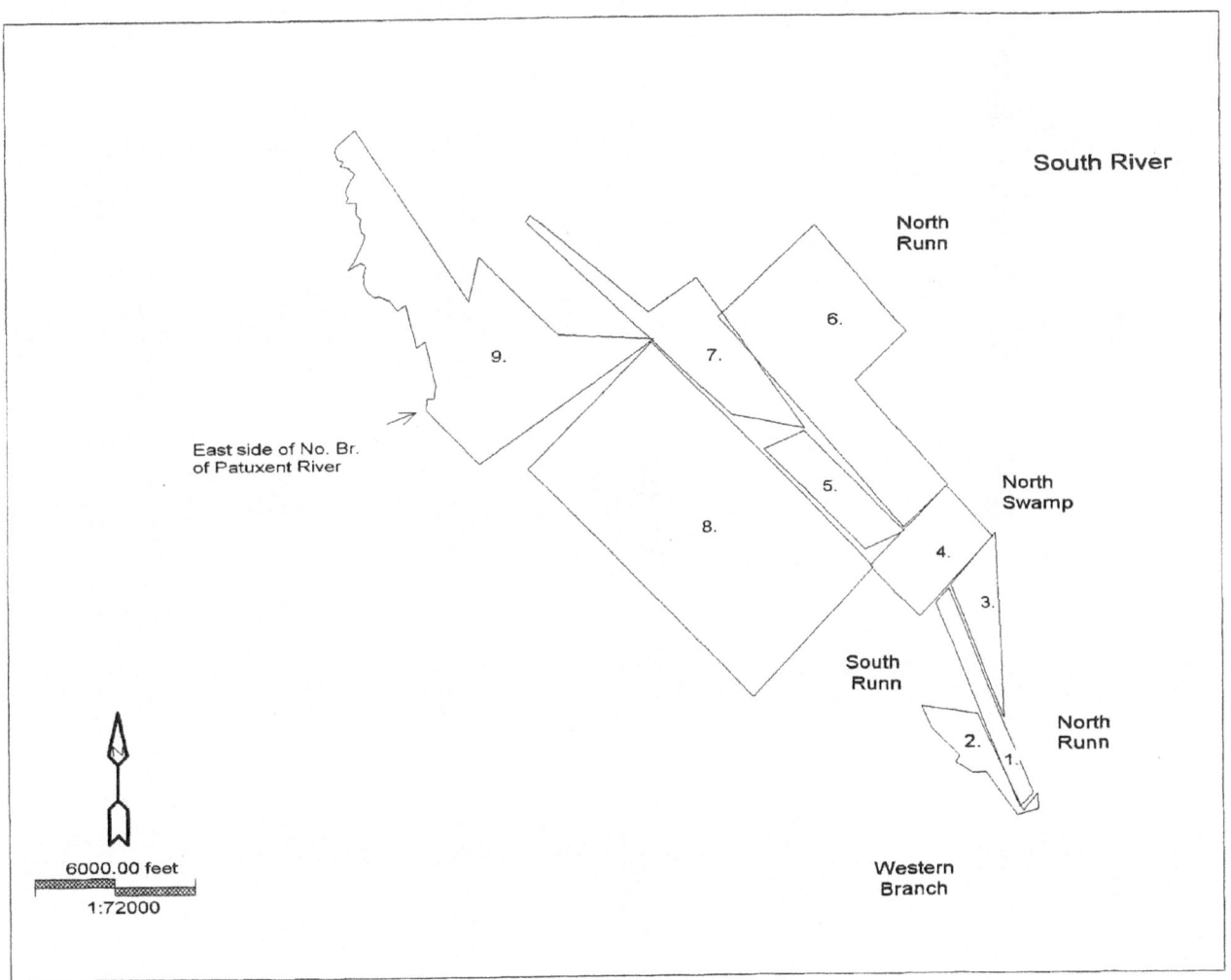

1. Freemanston
2. Roundabout Hill
3. Gater's Range
4. Freeman's Fancy
5. Wilson's Grove
6. Abingdon
7. What You Will
8. White's Hall
9. Lugg Ox

Appendix C

West side of the South Runn of the South River

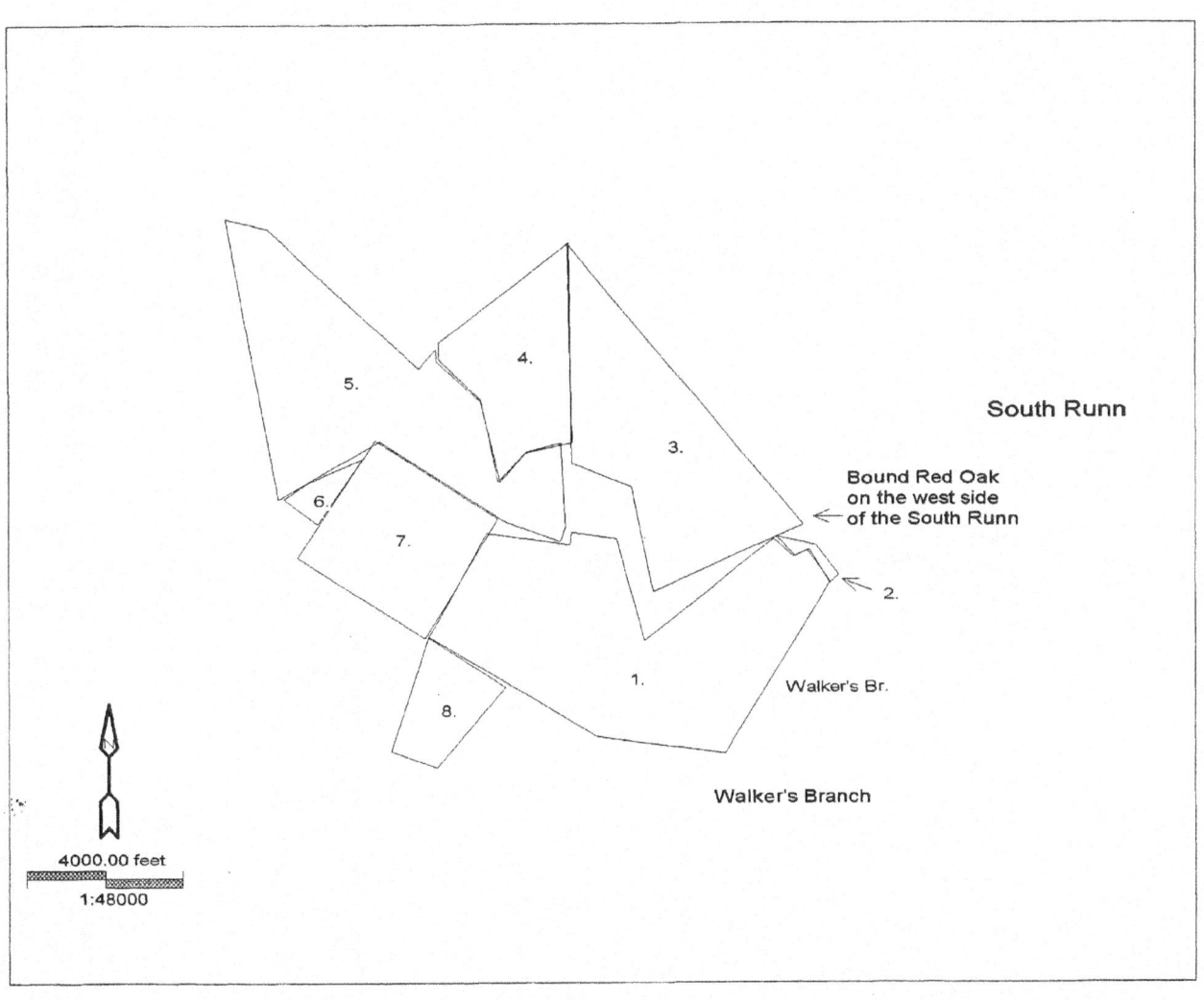

1. Godwell Resurveyed
2. Tangerine
3. The Iron Mine
4. Harness' Range
5. Linthicum Walks
6. Coape's Hill
7. Arnold Gray
8. The Addition (Chilcott)

Appendix D

East side of the North Branch of The Patuxent River

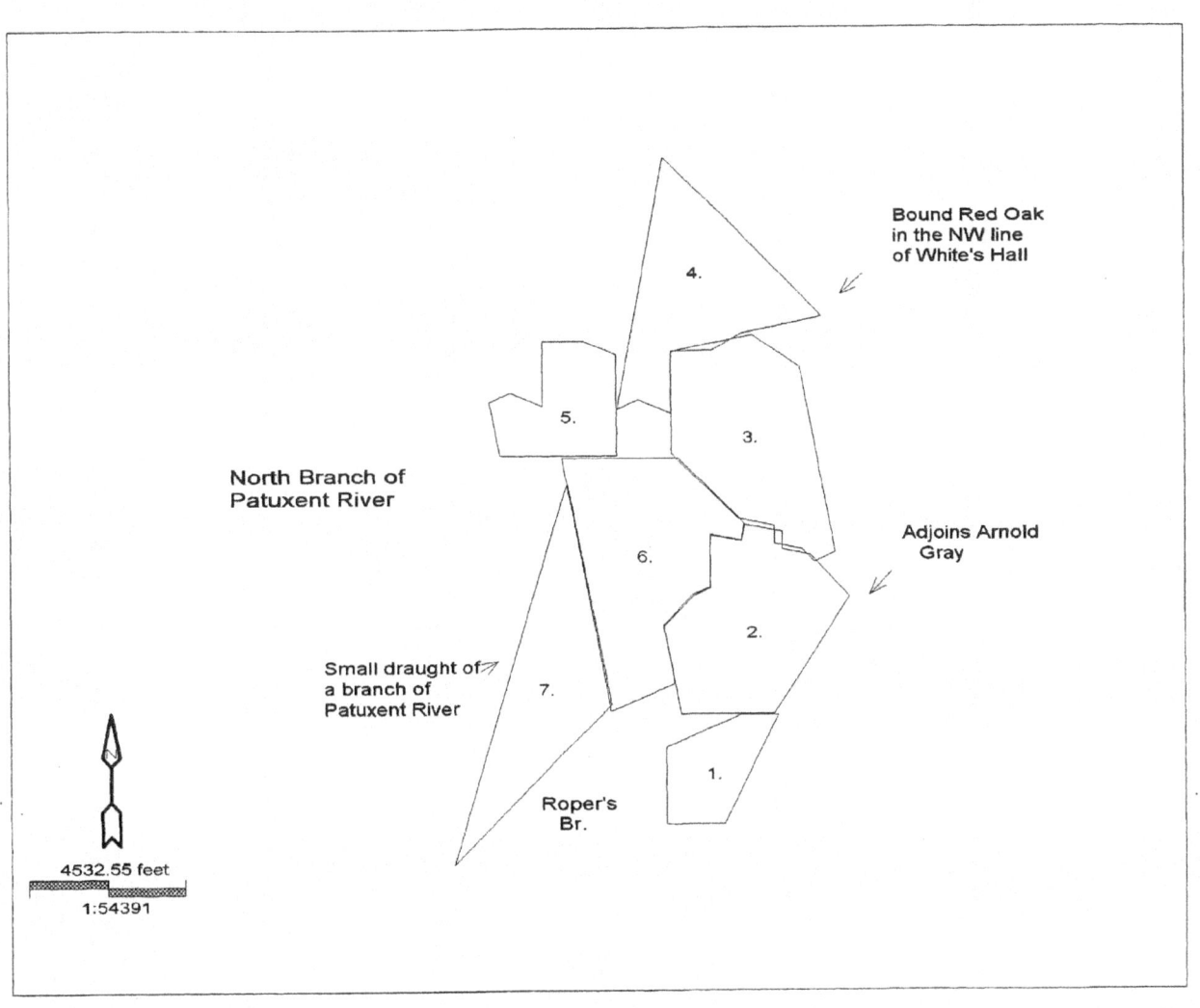

1. Maddox Adventure
2. Roper's Range
3. Bright Seate
4. Ayne
5. Duvall's Range
6. Roper Gray
7. The Happy Choice

Appendix E

The Flatt Creek area near The South River

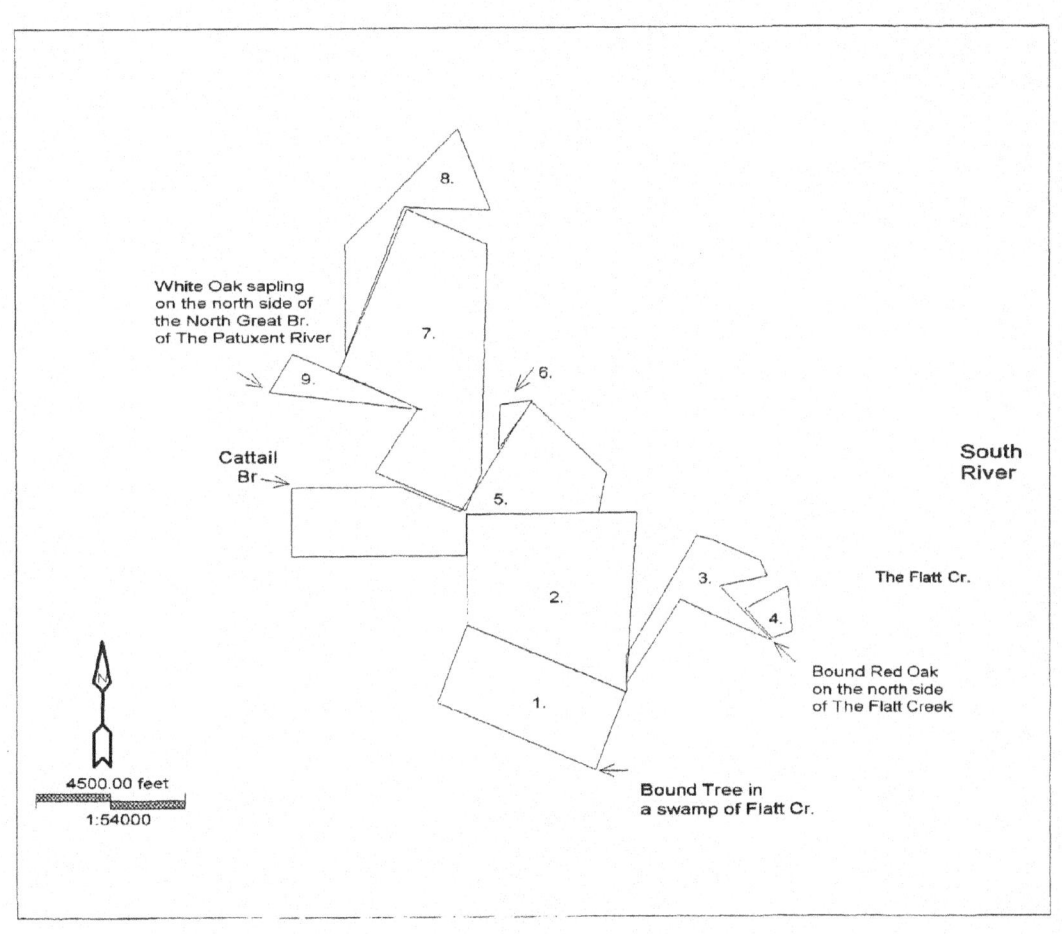

1. Chaney's Rest
2. Cheney's Resolution
3. The Equality
4. Johns Cabbin Ridge
5. Burge's Choice
6. Williams His Angles
7. Middle Plantation
8. Duvall's Addition
9. Duvall's Pasture

Appendix F

The Flatt Creek near the Patuxent River

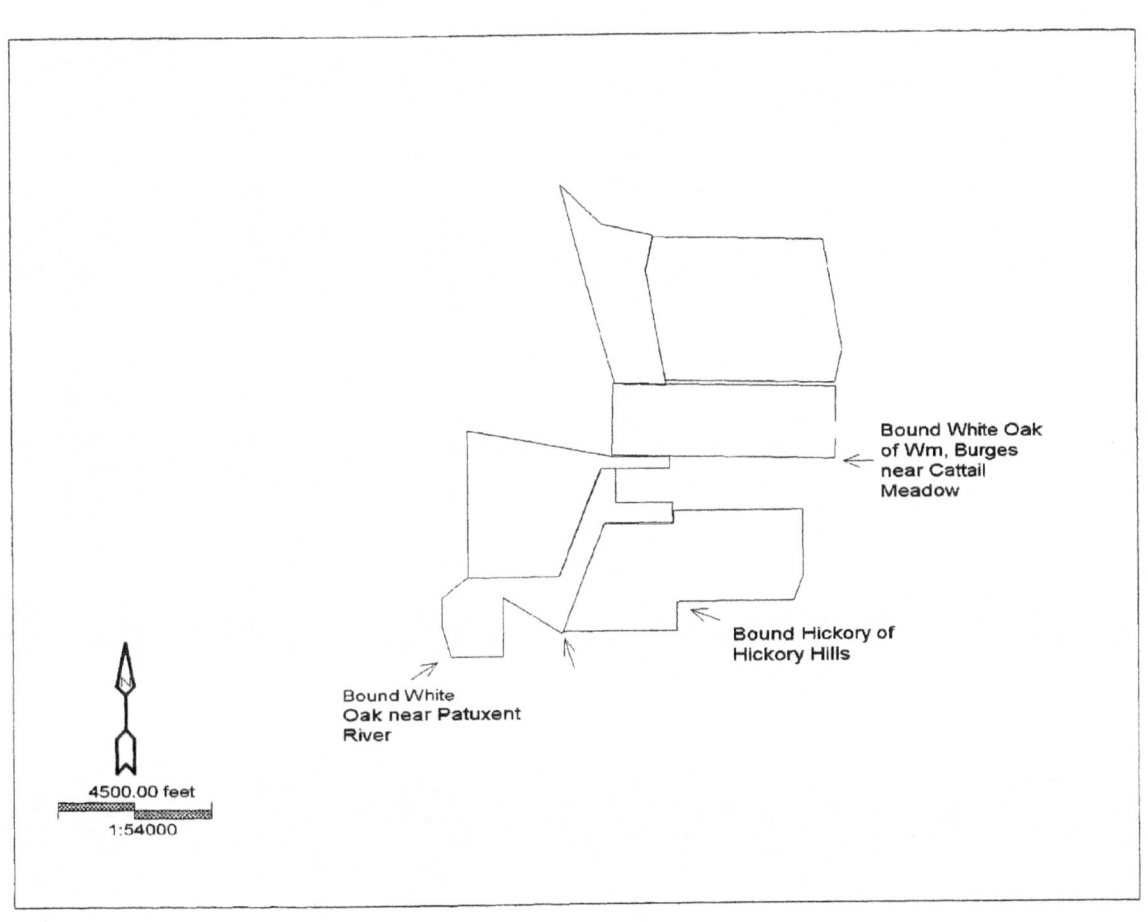

1. Clarke's Inheritance
2. Elizabeth's Fancy
3. Champe's Adventure
4. Morley's Lott
5. Clark of The Councill
6. Larkin's Choice

Appendix G

Area Between Flatt and Beard's/Jacob's Creeks

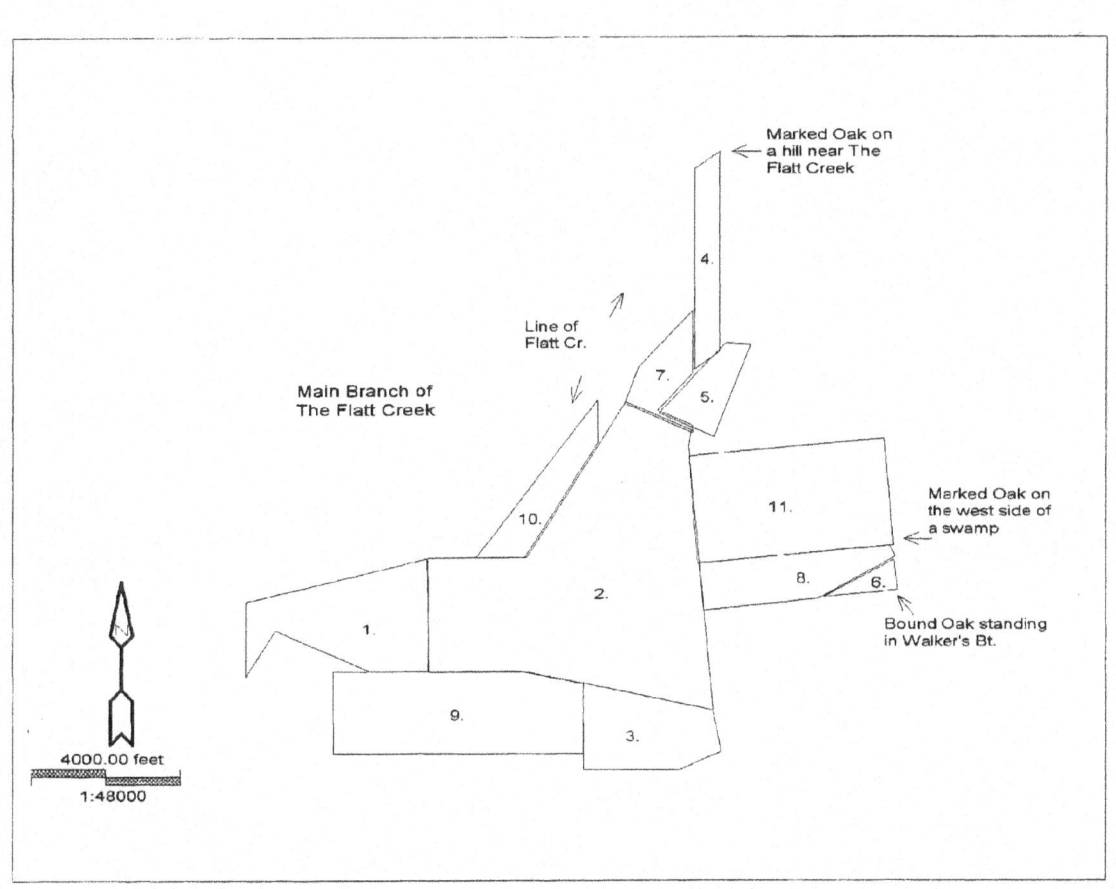

1. Beard's Habitation (1)
2. Beard's Habitation (2)
3. Beard's Habitation (3)
4. Cheney Hill
5. Cheney's Purchase
6. Chilcott's Increase
7. Gray's Chance
8. Hester's Habitation
9. Jones His Lott
10. Rachel's Hope
11. West Puddington

Appendix H
Central area near The Patuxent River

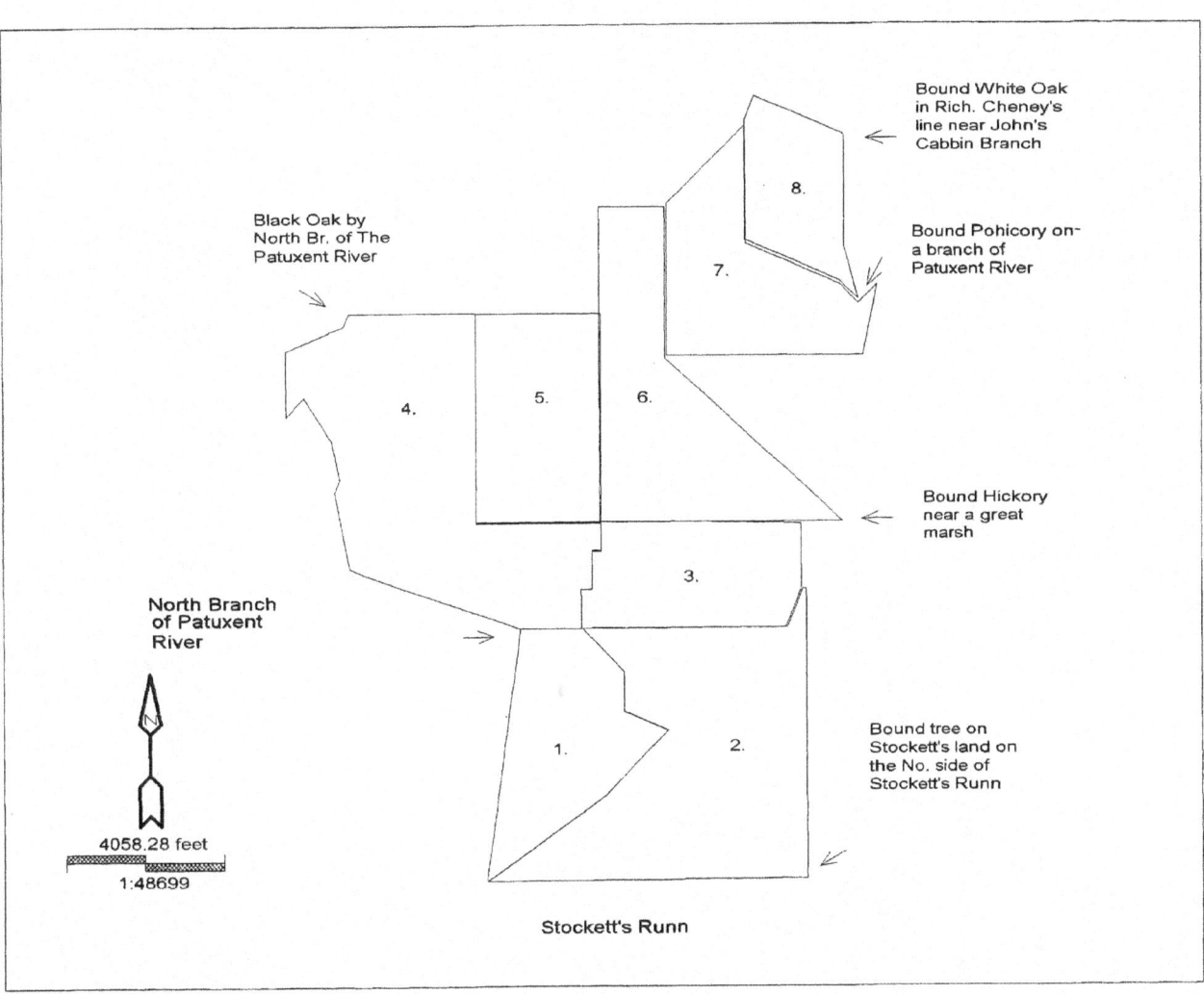

1. Roedown Security
2. Rowdown
3. The Friend's Choice (Jones & Gray)
4. Waterford
5. Velmeade
6. Hickry Hills
7. Franklin's Enlargement
8. The Indian Range

Appendix I

Area between Jacob's/Beard/s Cr. and Burges/ Glebe Cr.

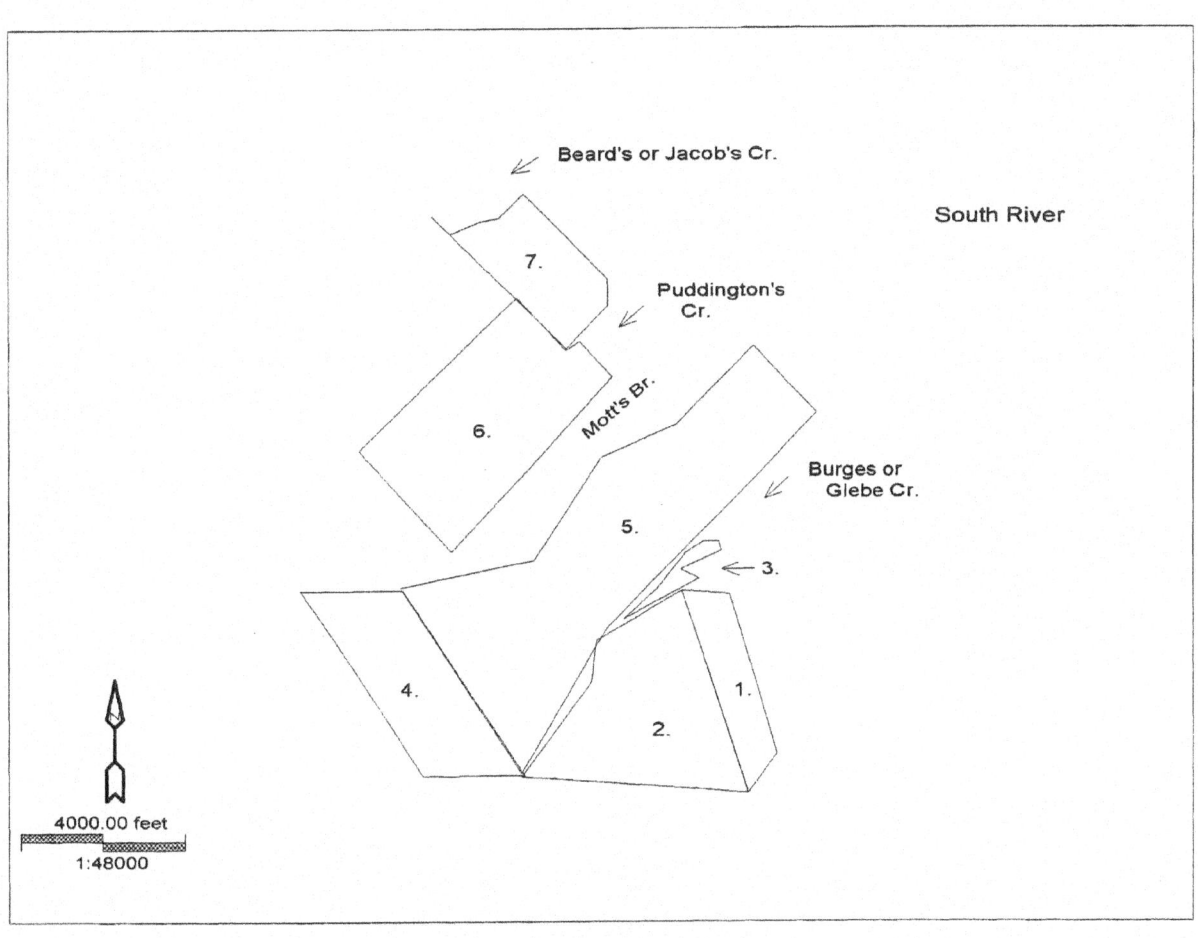

1. Coxby
2. Besson's Den
3. Sutton's Additon
4. The Burgh
5. Scornton
6. Townhill
7. Burges His Right

Appendix J

Mouth of South River Southward down the Chesapeake Bay

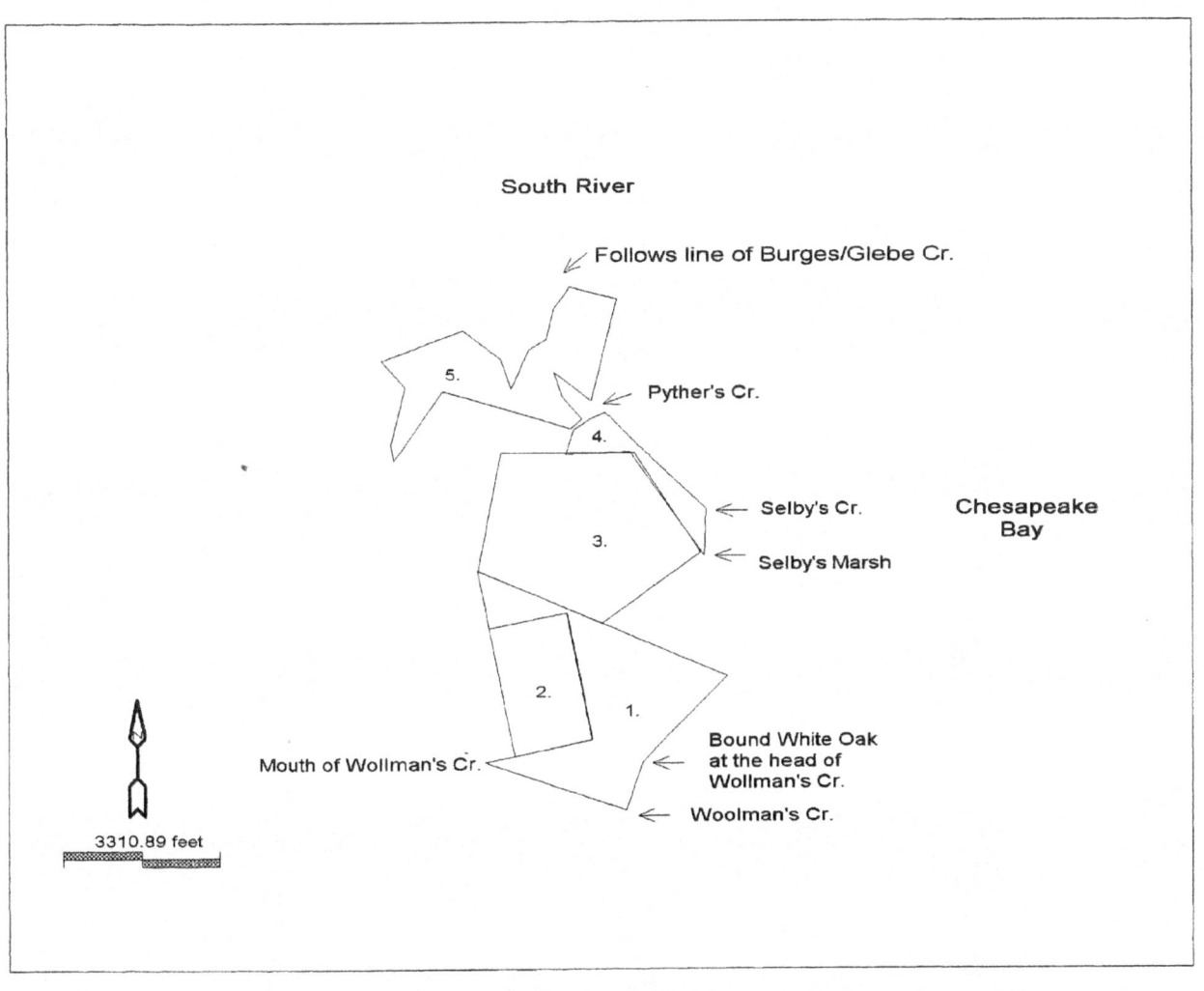

1. Selby's Stopp
2. Poplar Hill
3. Selby
4. Linham's Search
5. Brewer's Chance

Appendix K

Area to the north and west of Rhode River

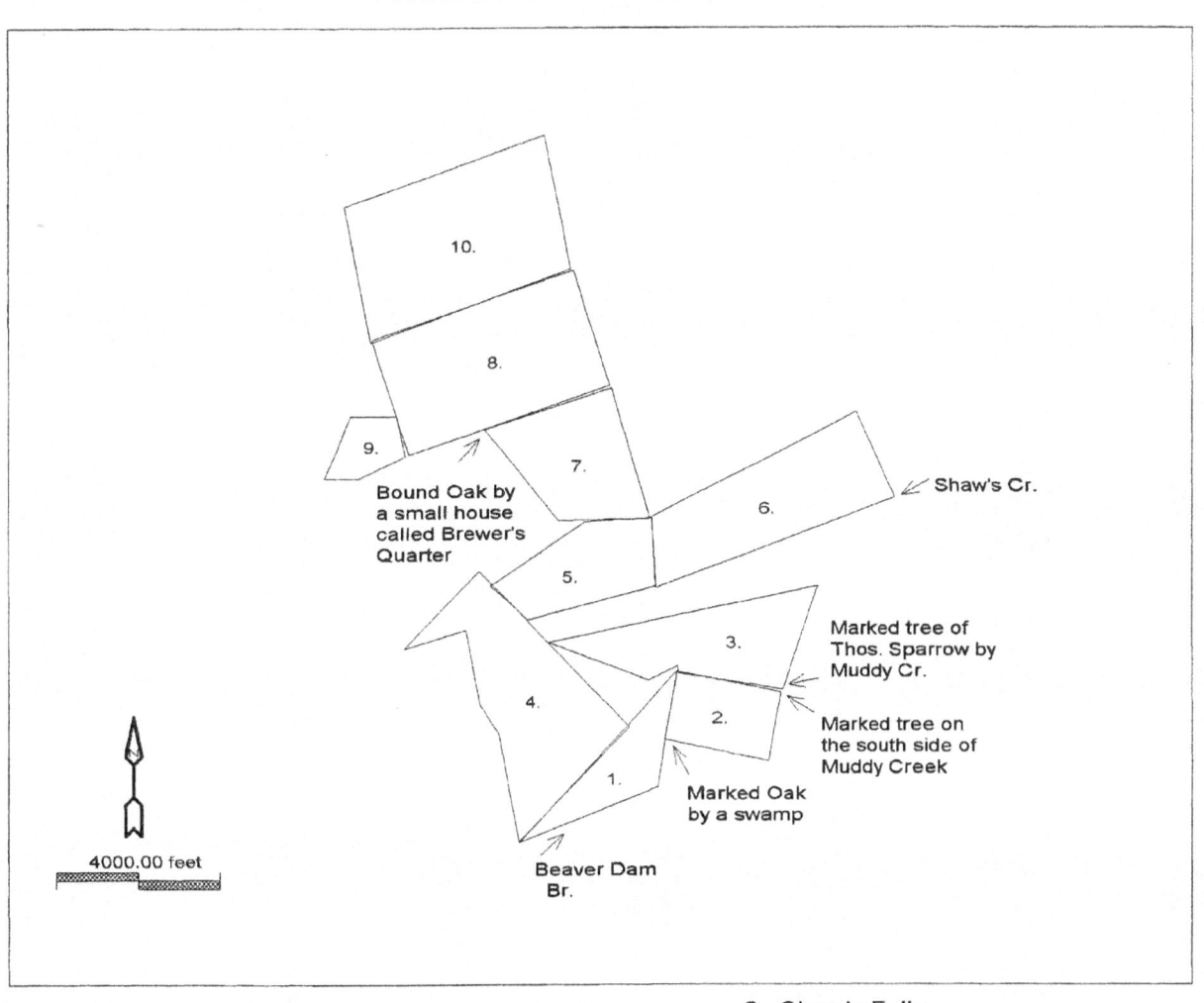

1. Triangle Neck
2. Beaver Dam Neck (Mc)
3. Hasslenutt Ridge
4. Lark's Hill
5. Poplar Ridge
6. Shaw's Folly
7. Hall's Inheritance
8. Bessonton
9. Younger Besson
10. Brewerston

Appendix L does not exist

Bibliography

Anne Arundel County Church Records of the 17th & 18th Centuries, F. Edward Wright, Family Line Publications, Westminster, MD, 1994

Abstracts of Anne Arundel County Land Records, Vols. 1-4, Rosemary Dodd and Patricia Bausell, Anne Arundel Genealogical Society, Pasadena, MD

Chesapeake Bay Country, Swepson Earle, Third Edition, Thomsen-Ellis Co., Baltimore MD, 1929

First Families of Anne Arundel County, MD 1649-1658, Vol. 1, Donna Valley Russell, Catoctin Press, 1999

Foundations of Representative Government in Maryland 1632-1715, David W. Jordan, Cambridge Press, 1987

Map- Original Landgrants on the South Side of the Severn River, Caleb Dorsey, 1958 (held at Maryland State Archives)

Maryland, A History 1632-1974, Walsh and Fox, Maryland Historical Society, 1974, Baltimore, MD

Maryland Rent Rolls Baltimore and Anne Arundel County 1700-1707, 1705-1724, reprinted by Clearfield, 1996

Old Homes and Families of Howard County, Maryland, Celia M. Holland, copyright 1987, by Celia Holland. Privately printed.

Providence Ye Lost Town at Severn in Maryland, James E. Moss, distributed by the Maryland Historical Society, Baltimore, MD, 1976

The Evolution of a Tidewater Settlement System – All Hallows Parish, MD, 1650-1783, Carville V. Earle, University of Chicago Press, 1975

The Founders of Anne Arundel and Howard Counties, J.D. Warfield, Kohn & Pollock, Baltimore, 1905, reprinted by Heritage Books Inc.,1995, Bowie, MD

The Making of England 55BC-1399, 2nd Edition. C. Warren Holliston, D.C. Heath & Co., Lexington, MA, 1971

Index of Tracts

Tract	Page
Abingdon	1
Abingdon Part Of	1
Abingdon Resurveyed	2
Anthony's Purchase	2
Arnold Gray	3
Arnold Gray Resurveyed	3
Ayne	4
Batchellor's Hope	4
Beard's Habitation	5
Beaver Dam Neck (Gray)	5
Beaver Dam Neck	6
Besson's Den	6
Bessonton	7
Breewer's Chance	7
Brewerston	8
Bridge Hill	8
Bright Seate	8
Burges	9
Burges His Right	10
Burges' Choice	9
Champe's Adventure	10
Cheney Hill	11
Cheney's Hazard	11
Cheney's Neck	11
Cheney's Purchase	12
Cheney's Resolution	12
Cheney's Rest	13
Chilcott's Increase	13
Clark of the Councill	14
Clarke's Inheritance	14
Clarken Well	13
Coape's Hill	15
Collierby	15
Covell's Folly	16
Coxby	16

Davis His Rest	17
Dodderidge's Forrest	17
Dodon	18
Duvall's Addition	18
Duvall's Delight	19
Duvall's Pasture	19
Duvall's Range (Marin Duvall)	20
Duvall's Range (John Duvall)	20
Duvall's Range Resurveyed	21
Efford's Delight	21
Elizabeth's Fancy	22
Elk Thickett	22
Elk Thickett Resurveyed	23
Eversail	23
Foldland	24
Fortune	24
Foster & Lewis	25
Foster's Point	25
Francis His Addition	26
Franklin's Enlargement	26
Freemans Fancy	27
Freemanston	27
Gater's Range	28
Godwell Resurveyed	28
Gray's Chance	29
Gray's Land	29
Green's Beginning	30
Green's Town	30
Hall's Inheritance	31
Harrisses' Range	31
Haslenutt Ridge	32
Hasslin	32
Hazlenut Ridge Resurveyed	33
Hedge Park	33
Herring's Purchase	34
Hester's Habitation	34
Hickory Hills	35
Honest Man's Lott	35
Hugging's Advantage	36
Jacob's Point	36
John's Cabbin Ridge	37
Jones His Lott	37
King's Venture	38

Lappston (1)	38
Lappston (2)	39
Larkin's Choice	39
Larkinton	40
Lark's Hill	40
Lavall	41
Lawe's Chance	41
Linham's Search	42
Linnescomb's Lott	42
Linthicum Walks	43
Littleton	43
Love's Neck	44
Lugg Ox	44
Maddox Adventure	45
Margaret's Fields	45
Merriton's Fancy	46
Middle Plantation	46
Middle Plantation Resurveyed	47
Mitchell's Addition	47
Morley's Grove	48
Morley's Lott	48
Nettlefold	48
Obligation	49
Owen Wood Thickett	49
Parrishes Purchase	50
Phelps His Choice	50
Phelps His Luck	51
Pierpoint's Branch	51
Pinkston's Folly	52
Plumpton	52
Poll Cat Hill	53
Poplar Hill	53
Poplar Neck	54
Poplar Ridge	54
Powell's Inheritance	55
Puddington	55
Puddington's Enlargement	56
Puddington's Harbor	56
Rachell's Hope	57
Rich Neck	57
Ridgely's Chance	58
Robin Hood's Forrest	58

Roedown Security	59
Roper Gray	59
Roper's Range	60
Roundabout Hill	60
Rowdown	61
Rutland's Purchase Enlarged	61
Scorton	62
Selby	62
Selby's Stopp	63
Sharp Point	63
Shaw's Folly	64
Shaw's Folly Resurveyed	64
Slatbourne	65
Soldier's Fortune	65
Soloman's Purchase	66
Sparrow's Addition	66
Stinson's Choice	67
Surplus Land Within Cheney's Neck	67
Sutton's Addition	68
Tangerine	68
Taylor's Addition	69
The Addition (Gassaway)	70
The Addition (Gray)	70
The Addition (Chilcott)	69
The Burgh	70
The Conclusion	71
The Diligent Search	71
The Enlargement (Welsh)	72
The Equality	72
The Friends Choice (Jones & Gray)	73
The Happy Choice	73
The Indian Range	74
The Iron Mine	74
The Landing (Proctor)	75
The Plaine (Wilson)	76
The Plaine (Yate)	75
The Security (Brewer)	77
The Tryangle (Taylor)	77
The Schoolhouse	76
Timber Neck	78
Townhill	78
Townhill Choice	79
Triangle Neck	79

Turkey Neck	80
Uggams' Advantage	80
Unnamed Cert (Myles)	80
Unnamed Cert (Pyther)	80
Unnamed Patent (Townhill)	82
Unnamed Patent (Jones)	81
Unnamed Patent (Grosse)	81
Unnamed Patent (Pell)	82
Unnamed Patent (Emmerson)	81
Velmeade	83
Wade's Encrease	83
Walter's His Lott	84
Waterford	84
Wayman's Marsh	85
West Puddington	85
What You Will	86
White's Ford	86
White's Ford Part Of	86
White's Hall	87
White's Plaines	87
Williams His Addition	88
Williams His Angle	88
Wilson's Grove	89
Wrighten	89
Wrighton	90
Wyngate's Rest	90
Younger Besson	91

List of Owners and Their Tracts

Arbuckle, Archer	Elk Thickett	1659
Arnold, Richard & John Gray	Arnold Gray	1670
Beard Hester	Hester's Habitation	1674
Beard, Richard	Beard's Habitation	1663
	John's Cabbin Ridge	1666
	Poplar Neck	1663
Besson, Thomas (Capt.)	Besson's Den	1650
	Bessonton	1650
Besson, Thomas (the younger)	Younger Besson	1659
Brewer, John	Brewer's Chance	1667
	Brewerston	1659
	Larkington	1663
	The Security	1664
Brewer, John Jr.	Collierby	1678
Burges, Edward	Burges His Right	1688
Burges, William (Capt.) (Coll.)	Burges	1651
	Burges' Choice	1666
	The Burgh	1650
Burroughs, William & Ann	Surplus in Cheney Neck	1696
Champe, John	Champe's Adventure	1670
Cheney. Richard	Cheney Hill	1659
	Cheney's Hazard	1663
	Cheney's Neck	1663
	Cheney's Purchase	1663
	Cheney's Resolution	1663
	Cheney's Rest	1663
Chilcott, James	Chilcott's Increase	1672
	The Addition	1670
Clark, John	Clarken Well	1665
Clark, Richard	Clark of the Councill	1701
	Elizabeth's Fancy	1702

Clarke, Neale	Clarke's Inheritance	1670
Coape, George	Coape's Hill	1683
Covell, Ann	Covell's Folly	1663
Cox, Edward	Coxby	1650
Davis, Evan	Davis His Rest	1672
Dearing, John	Velmeade	1667
DeLapp, Adam	Lappston (1)	1659
	Lappston (2)	1664
Dodderidge, John	Dodderidge's Forrest	1696
Duvall, John	Duvall's Delight	1695
	Duvall's Range	1695
	Honest Man's Lott	1704
Duvall, Lewis	Duvall's Pasture	1705
	Eversail	1709
	Middle Plantation Res.	1708
Duvall, Marin	Duvall's Addition	1670
	Duvall's Range	1672
	Lavall	1658
	Middle Plantation	1664
Efford, Will	Efford's Delight	1704
Emmerson, Thomas	Unnamed Patent	1658
Foster, John	Foster's Point	1671
Foster, Richard & Lewis, John	Foster & Lewis	1666
Foster, Richard	The Conclusion	1666
Francis, Thomas	Thomas His Addition	1674
Franklin, Robert	Franklin's Enlargement	1670
	Hickory Hills	1667
Franklin, Robert & Beard, Richard	The Indian Range	1665
Freeman, John	Freeman's Fancy	1663
	Freemanston	1659

Gaither, John	Poll Cat Hill	1687
	Roundabout Hill	1687
Gaither, John, Jr.	Abingdon Part Of	1699
	Abingdon Resurveyed	1701
Gassaway, Nicholas	Poplar Ridge	1654
	The Addition	1688
Gater, John	Gater's Range	1675
Gates, Jane	White's Ford	1693
Gates, Jane *(the elder)*	White's Ford, Part Of	1693
Gossum, Patrick	Townhill Choice	1652
Grammar, John	The Schoolhouse	1700
Grany, John	Beaver Dam Neck	1671
	Gray's Chance	1684
	Gray's Land	1684
	Haslenut Ridge	1665
	The Addition	1672
Green, George	Greene's Town	1673
Green, John	Green's Beginning	1683
Gresham, John	Fortune	1687
Grosse, Roger	Unnamed Patent	1658
Hall, Christopher	Hall's Inheritance	1670
Hanslap, Henry	Ayne	1683
Harness, Isaac	Harness' Range	1670
Hasslin, Jeremy	Hasslin	1658
Hedge, Thomas	Hedge Park	1675
Herring, John	Herring's Purchase	1684
Huggings, Richard	Huggings' Advantage	1664
Jones, Robert	Unnamed Patent	1658
Jones, William	Jones His Lott	1673
	Waterford	1676

Jones, William & Gray, John	The Friend's Choice	1670
King, Joseph	King's Venture	1704
Larkin, John	Larkin's Choice	1670
	Lark's Hill	1663
Law, William	Lawe's Chance	1675
Linham, John	Linham's Search	1688
Linnescomb, Thomas	Linnescomb's Lott	1677
Linthicum, Hezikiah	Duvall's Range Res.	1703
Linthicum, Thomas	Linthicum Walks	1701
Love, Robert	Love's Neck	1664
Loyd, Robert	Triangle Neck	1666
Macconnough, Dennis	Beaver Dam Neck	1662
Maddox, Thomas	Maddox Adventure	1683
	Rachell's Hope	1683
Merriton, John	Merriton's Fancy	1687
Miller, Christopher	Soldier's Fortune	1704
Mitchell, William	Mitchell's Addicion	1704
Morley, Joseph	Morley's Grove	1674
	Morley's Lott	1671
Myles, Thomas	Unnamed Cert.	1652
Nettlefold, George	Foldland	1661
	Nettlefold	1662
Parker, George	Godwell Resurveyed	1679
Parrish, John	Parrishes Purchase	1700
Pell, William	Unnamed Patent	1658
Phelps, Walter	Elk Thickett Res.	1701
	Phelps His Choice	1685
	Phelps His Luck	1687
Pierpoint, Henry	Pierpoint's Branch	1673

Pinkston, Peter	Pinkston's Folly	1700
Powell, James & John	Powell's Inheritance	1685
Price, Edward	Bright Seate	1673
Proctor, Robert & Gaither, John	Abingdon	1664
Proctor, Robert	Slatbourne	1676
	The Landing	1668
Puddington, George	Puddington	1650
	Puddington's Enlargement	1663
	Puddington's Harbor	1663
	West Puddington	1650
Pyther, Will	Unnamed Cert.	1650
Richardson, William	The Diligent Search	1678
Ridgely, William	Ridgely's Chance	1694
Roberts, Andrew	Sharp Pointe	1666
Roper, William	Roper's Range	1670
Roper, William & Gray, John	Roper Gray	1683
Rutland, Thomas	Rutland's Purchase Enlg.	1700
Saughier, George	Margaret's Fields	1670
Saunders, James	Batchellor's Hope	1670
	The Equality	1685
Selby, Edward	Selby	1658
	Selby's Stopp	1688
Selby, Thomas & Edward	Poplar Hill	1655
Shaw, John	Shaw's Folly	1666
	Shaw's Folly Res.	1672
Smith, Anthony	Anthony's Purchase	1699
Smith, James	Jacob's Point	undated
Snowden, Richard	Robin Hood's Forrest	1686
	Turkey Neck	1698
Snowden, Richard, Jr.	Walter's His Lott	1704

Sparrow, Soloman	Soloman's Purchase	1695
Sparrow, Thomas	Sparrow's Addition	1675
Stinson, John	Stinson's Choice	1684
Stocket, Francis	Dodon	1671
Stocket, Henry	Bridge Hill	1671
Stocket, Thomas	Obligation	1676
Sumers, John	Little Town	1704
Sutton, Thomas	Sutton's Additon	1688
Taylor, Thomas	Roedown Security	1675
	Rowdown	1670
	Taylor's Addition	1672
	The Tryangle	1672
	Wrighton	1661
Terrat, Nicholas, Jr.	Wrighten	1697
Townehill, Edward	Unnamed Patent	1658
Tydings, Richard	Hazlenutt Ridge Res.	1680
Uggamms, Rich. & Wheeler, John	Timber Neck	1665
Uggams, Richard	Uggam's Advantage	1664
Wade, Robert	Wade's Encrease	1679
Walker, George	Plumpton	1663
Wayman, Leonard	Owen Wood Thickett	1688
	Tangerine	1695
	Wayman's Marsh	1706
Welch, Silvestre & John	Arnold Gray Res.	1703
Welsh, John	The Enlargement	1704
Westhill, George	Scornton	1659
White, Jerome	The Iron Mine	1668
	White's Hall	1664
	White's Plaines	1669
Williams, Benjamin	Williams His Addition	1687

Williams, Benjamin	Williams His Angle	1688
Wilson, Robert	The Plaine	1671
	Wilson's Grove	1672
Wyngate, Thomas	Wyngate's Rest	1674
Yate, George	The Happy Choice	1671
	The Plaine	1677
Young, Wm. & Duvall, Marin	Rich Neck	1665

South River Hundred Prople Index
(Also includes people mentioned in the tract drawings)

Allamby, Phillip 39
Arbuckle, Archer 16, 22, 24, 30, 36 (2), 51 (2), 80
Arbuckle, Dyna 22
Arnold, Richard 3(3)

Barnett, Ann 67
Bateman, William 75
Beard, Hester 34
Beard, Rachell 54
Beard, Richard 5, 7, 24, 26, 30, 37 (2), 53, 54, 57 (2), 63, 71, 74 (2), 78
Besson, Ann (The Elder) 6
Besson, Ann (The Younger) 6
Besson, John 54
Besson, Thomas (The Elder, Capt.) 6, 7, 8, 54, 62, 68, 70 (2), 91
Besson, Thomas (The Younger) 6, 91
Blomfield, John 83
Blomfield, M. 45
Blunt, James 74
Boetler, Charles 83
Brewer, John 7, 15, 40, 42, 77, 78 (3), 81
Brewer, John (The Elder) 8, 15
Brewer, Mrs. 51 (3)
Brewer, William 30, 31
Brooke, Baker Esq. 30
Brown, Ellis 15, 40,
Brown, Thomas 17
Bufford, John 90 (2)
Burges, Benjamin 9
Burges, Ursala (Madame) 63
Burges, William (Capt, Coll.) 9 (2), 10, 14, 35, 41, 51, 55 (2), 60, 63, 68, 70, 77, 79, 83
Burges. Edward 10. 27 (2), 75, 88, 91
Burns, Elizabeth 24
Burrage, John 56
Burroughs, William 67
Burrought, Ann 67
Butler, Tobias 41
Cadger, Robert 81 (2)

Calvert, Charles Esq. 70, 75
Carroll, James 52, 84, 85
Challinor, Thomas 75
Champe, John 10, 39, 48
Cheney, Charity 11
Cheney, Richard 11 (3), 12 (2), 12, 13, 14 (2), 25 (2), 29, 30 (2), 51 (2), 57, 67, 71 (3), 72, 74 (2), 78, 83 (2), 88

Chilcott(e), James 13, 28
Chilcott(e), John 13
Clark (e), Neal (e) 4.14.19
Clark, John 13. 57
Clarke, Francis 74
Clarke, Richard 14, 22,26
Clarkson, Robert 52
Coape, George 15
Cole, Thomas 35
Collier, John 15,16
Connaway, James (Capt.) 64, 70
Covill (Covell) John (The Elder) 9, 16,41
Covill (Covell), Ann 9, 16, 36, 46 (2), 47, 57, 80
Covill, (Covell) John Jr. 9
Cox, Edward 6, 16, 68
Cox, Joan 16

Darnall, Henry (Coll.) 2 (2), 4, 43
Dartford, Joan *Use Edit Check to find
Davis, Evan 9, 15, 17, 43
Davis, Robert 23
Davis, William 8
Dearing, John 4, 83, 84
Delapp, Adam 33, 34, 38, 39, 42
Dodderidge, John 17
Dorsey, John 29 (2), 34, 51, 88
Dryer, Samuel 17
Duvall, Elizabeth 89
Duvall, John 19, 20, 35, 44, 49, 86 (2), 89
Duvall, Lewis 19, 23, 47
Duvall, Marin (Maryne, Mareen) 4, 8, 9, 18, 20, 28, 41, 46, 47, 48 (3), 49, 52 (2), 57, 59, 71 (3), 78

Efford, Will 21
Eliott, Daniel 68
Emerson, Thomas 38, 81
Ewan, John 40
Ewen, Richard
Finley, James 1
Finley, Jerome 1
Foster, John 25
Foster, Mary 25
Foster, Richard 5, 25, 29, 71
Francis, Thomas 26
Franklin (Franklyn) Robert 4, 9, 26, 35, 37, 74, 83
Freeman, Elizabeth 27 (2)
Freeman, John 27 (2), 41 (2)m 87
Frizzell 28
Frizzell, William 29

Fry, David 59

Gaither (Gater/Gather), John 1 (2), 28, 48, 53, 60, 80 (3), 89
Gaither, John Jr. 2
Galloway, Samuel 86
Games, Thomas 79
Gassaway, Nicholas 31, 32, 33 (2), 54, 70
Gates, Jane (The Elder) 86, 87
Gates, Jane (The Younger) 86, 87
Gates, Joseph 86, 87
Gillum, John 83
Gorsuch, Charles 88
Gossum, Elizabeth 82
Gossum, Patrick 79, 80, 82
Grammar, John 76
Grange, John 55
Gray, John 3(3), 5, 17, 29 (2), 32, 33, 59, 73, 84
Gray, Rachell 3
Gray, Robert 3
Green, George 30, 83
Green, John 30
Gresham, Richard 24
Grosse, Roger 80, 81

Hall, Christopher 31, 51
Hall, Henry 14
Hall, John 63
Hanslap, Henry 4, 15, 30, 59
Harness, Isaac 31, 43
Harper, Stephen 74
Hasslin, Jerome 32
Hatt, Ann 35
Hatten, John 80
Hedge, Thomas 33
Herring, John 34
Hill, Clement 61
Hilliard, Thomas 70
Hippsley, Thomas 56
Hisson, George 62
Holland, Anthony 70
Holland, George 36, 75
Hopkins, Gerald 4
Hopkins, Gerrard 86
Horring, John 67
Howard, Ruth (Mrs.) 35
Howell, Thomas 81
Howerton, John 76 (3)
Huggings, Richard 36, 55 (2), 56
Hutton, John 36

James, Robert 81
Jones, Annis 81
Jones, Robert 81
Jones, William 5, 37, 73, 84 (2)
Joy, Margaret 56
King, Joseph 38, 72
Knighton, Thomas 73
Larkin, John 32, 39, 40 (2), 77 (2), 79
Larkin, Thomas 73
Lawe. William 41
Lewis, John 25
Linham, John 42
Lloyd, Edward 81
Loarson, Edward 42 (2)
Love, Robert 44
Loyd (Lloyd), Robert 42, 44, 54, 79
Lynthicum(Linthicum/Lynecomb/Linescomb), Thomas 33, 34, 42, 43
Lynthicum, Hezikiah 21

Macconnough (McConough), Dennis 6,32,79
Macubbin, John 40
Maddox, Thomas 45,57
Mahalone, Annis 81
Mahalone, Dermott 81
Mansfield, Walter 90
Martin 19
Mascole, Richard 45
Mears, John 1
Merriton, John 46
Miles (Myles) Thomas 80
Miller, Christopher 65
Mills, Thomas 69 (2)
Mitchell, William 47
Morley, Joseph 48 (2)
Nettlefold, George 6, 7, 24, 28, 31, 35, 36, 46 (2), 48, 52, 56 (4), 68 (2), 74, 80, 91
Nettlefold, Ruth 24

Oberton, Sarah 74
Orchard, Richard 5
Parker, George 28
Parker, William 28, 29
Parrish, John 50
Parrott, Gabriel 30
Pawson, John 76
Pell, William 45, 82
Pennington, Elizabeth 82
Pennington, William 38, 45
Phelps, Walter 23, 50, 51, 67

Pierpoint, Henry 51
Pierson, Thomas 46
Pinkston, Peter 52
Poole, David 4, 10, 18, 26, 69, 73
Powell, James 55, 89
Powell, John 55, 89
Preston, Richard 5, 76
Price, Edward (Edwin) 4, 8, 15
Proctor, Robert 1, 2, 27 (2) 48, 60, 65, 75, 89
Puddington, Comfort 85
Puddington, George 5, 9, 18, 27 (2), 36 (2), 46 (2), 52, 53, 56 (2), 57, 75, 78, 85
Puddington, Jane 55
Puddington, Mary 85
Pyther, Will 80

Richardson, Daniel 14
Richardson, Francis 83
Richardson, Thomas 10, 42, 68
Ridgely, Henry Jr. 58
Ridgely, William 52, 58
Roberts, Andrew 33
Robins, Elizabeth 85
Roper, William 8, 59, 60
Rumsay, William 63
Rutland, Thomas 61
Sanders (Saunders), James 4, 72
Saughier, George 45, 54
Selby, Edward 15, 24, 2, 53 (2), 62, 63
Selby, Edward Jr. 63
Selby, Thomas 53
Shaw, John 9, 26, 33, 64 (2)
Simkin, Robert 35
Skinner, Andrew 46
Skinner, Augustine 35
Smith, Anthony 2
Smith, James 36
Smithrick, Thomas 33
Snowden, Richard 28, 29, 41 (2), 58
Snowden, Richard (Jr.) 21, 31, 65, 68, 80, 84
Sparrow, Soloman 2, 50, 66
Sparrow, Thomas 7, 26, 36, 66
Stephenson, William 81
Steward, David 51
Stimson (Stinson), John 33, 46, 53, 67
Stocket(t) Henry 8, 18, 49
Stocket(t), Francis 8, 18, 49
Stocket(t), Thomas 8, 18, 49
Stockets 37, 61
Stone, Edward 40

Sumers, John 43
Sutton, Thomas 68

Talbott, Richard 71
Taylor (Taillor), Thomas (Coll./Esq.) 15, 20, 28, 33, 40, 59 (2), 61, 69, 70, 77, 84
Taylor, William 90
Terrett, Nicholas 89
Terrett, Nicholas Jr. 89
Townhill, Edmond 34, 78, 79, 82
Towning, Ed 34, 36 (2)
Turner 28
Tydings (Tideings), Richard 24, 33
Uggams, Richard 78, 80
Version (Verson), John 80

Wade, Robert 83
Walker, George 30, 46, 52, 75 (2)
Ward, Lawrence 76
Warfield, Richard 35
Wattson, Elizabeth 13
Wayman, Leonard 28, 29, 49, 68, 85
Welsh (Welch), John 3, 29, 72
Welsh (Welch), Silvestre 3
Welsh, John the elder 3
Westhill, George 62, 70
Wheatly, William 30
Wheeler, John 71 (2), 78
White, Jerome (Esq.) 4, 20, 28, 31, 44, 45, 60, 69, 70, 74, 77, 87 (2)
Williams, Benjamin 47, 88 (2)
Wilson, Robert 17, 30, 31, 51, 60, 76, 89
Withers, Samuel 1
Wyneat (Wyngate), Thomas 90
Yate, George 4, 8, 10, 13, 18, 20, 26 (2), 28, 30, 34, 35, 36, 39, 41, 42, 45 (2), 57, 61, 64, 65, 69 (2), 70 (2), 73 (2), 74, 75, 77, 90
Young, William 57, 78

www.ingramcontent.com/pod-product-compliance
Lightning Source LLC
Chambersburg PA
CBHW081133170426
43197CB00017B/2847